Milan Kundera's Fiction

Milan Kundera's Fiction

A Critical Approach to Existential Betrayals

Karen von Kunes

LEXINGTON BOOKS
Lanham • Boulder • New York • London

Published by Lexington Books
An imprint of The Rowman & Littlefield Publishing Group, Inc.
4501 Forbes Boulevard, Suite 200, Lanham, Maryland 20706
www.rowman.com

6 Tinworth Street, London SE11 5AL

British Library Cataloguing in Publication Information Available

Library of Congress Cataloging-in-Publication Data

Names: Kunes, Karen von, author.
Title: Milan Kundera's fiction : a critical approach to existential betrayals
    / Karen von Kunes.
Description: Lanham : Lexington Books, [2019] | Includes bibliographical
    references and index.
Identifiers: LCCN 2019008343 (print) | LCCN 2019010965 (ebook) | ISBN
    9781498510813 (Electronic) | ISBN 9781498510806 (cloth : alk. paper)
    | ISBN 9781498510820 (pbk. : alk. paper)
Subjects: LCSH: Kundera, Milan—Criticism and interpretation.
Classification: LCC PG5039.21.U6 (ebook) | LCC PG5039.21.U6 Z75 2019
    (print) | DDC 891.8/6354—dc23
LC record available at https://lccn.loc.gov/2019008343

For my daughter, Alexis von Kunes Newton,
who loves Milan Kundera's novels.

Contents

Foreword

Daniel W. Pratt

A simple postcard sets off the action of Milan Kundera's first novel, *The Joke*. After feeling jilted by his girlfriend who has decided to spend the college break at a two-week Marxist education course, Ludvik sends her a postcard reading "Optimism is the opium of the people! A healthy atmosphere stinks of stupidity! Long live Trotsky! Ludvik."[1] The authorities read the postcard, and Ludvik is brought before his friend Pavel Zemanek, who expels Ludvik from the Communist Party. Ludvik ends up in prison for several years and Zemanek becomes a well-liked professor. The crux of the plot lies in how we interpret those lines, as merely a joke or as a meaningful act of subversion. Unfortunately for Ludvik, in the Stalinist Czechoslovakia of 1950, there was no such thing as a meaningless joke.

Milan Kundera is undoubtedly the best-known author associated with the Czech language. His 1984 novel, *The Unbearable Lightness of Being*, has been translated into over thirty languages and was made into a major motion picture starring Juliette Binoche, Lena Olin, and Daniel Day-Lewis only four years after its publication. Kundera is regularly compared, both by others and in his own words, to other great authors from Central Europe—Witold Gombrowicz, Robert Musil, and Franz Kafka, to name a few—as well as to the great ironists of Europe—Lawrence Sterne, Denis Diderot, and Gustave Flaubert. Kundera has been a perennial nominee for the Nobel Prize. No other living authors associated with the Czech language can boast of that kind of worldwide renown and popularity.

This awkward description of Kundera as "an author associated with the Czech language" displays one of the problems of working on Kundera: he defies easy identification. Although he was born in 1929 in Brno, Czechoslovakia, he has not lived there since 1975 and insists on being called a French or Franco-Czech writer today. He writes in Czech only marginally, at least partially due to the early difficulties in finding translators from Czech for his works, and he considers his French versions—even of his earlier novels originally in Czech—to be the definitive versions of the texts. As a young man, Kundera was an avid supporter of the new Communist regime, joining the Party in 1948, and, although he was thrown out two years later, he continued to support it in his poetry and rejoined it as a reformist in 1956. He grew increasingly critical of the party hardliners in the 1960s during the Prague Spring, and his work was banned in Czechoslovakia after the Warsaw Pact Invasion of 1968. Heralded as a dissident and a martyr in the West, Kundera became one of the leading Czech expatriates in literary circles after his move to Paris. Although he rejected the term dissident, it was, and is, often applied to him and his novelistic work. After the fall of Communism in Central Europe, Kundera removed himself from politics, focusing more on his novels and essays. Never forthcoming about himself in the first place, Kundera has shied even more away from the spotlight as he has gotten older.

In the past decade, however, Kundera's reputation has lost some of its shine. In 2008, the Czech journal *Respekt* published an article accusing Kundera of denouncing a spy for the *Státní bezpečnost* (the Czech secret police), because of a suitcase left at his dorm. Although Kundera had never denied being a member of the Party, he called the accusation an "assassination." Kundera never held the kind of popularity he has abroad in the Czech lands, partially because his works were banned, but also because he moved away from the Czech language, so this accusation confirmed the negative opinion that many had of him. In addition to this accusation, Kundera's 2014 novel *The Festival of Insignificance* was widely panned. Its rejection inspired a number of critics to return to his older works with less sympathy.

In his ninety years of life, Kundera has been a member of the Communist Party, a reformist, a dissident, a traitor, a musician, a poet, a novelist, a dramatist, an essayist, an exile, a Frenchman, and a Czech, among many other things. However, these labels have been applied by others, not by Kundera, himself. As someone who fiercely guards his own privacy, we will probably never get a direct response from Kundera about who he is. His official biography simply states: "Milan Kundera was born in Czechoslovakia in 1929 and since 1975 has been living in France." This is hardly enough foundation upon which to build a biographical interpretation of Kundera's works, let alone a biography.

In the following pages, Karen von Kunes does something of the sort, although the book is not a traditional biography by any means. Instead, von Kunes begins with a close reading not only of Kundera's artistic works, but also of the other documents of his life, including the police report that came to light in 2008. This is not the traditional biographical interpretation that Barthes rejected in proclaiming the death of the author, but rather reading the author *as a* text, or in Ricoeurian terms, as a narrative. If Kundera is only willing to offer us his texts, then we can only get back to him through those texts. For von Kunes, this road leads back through the recurring motif of a *suitcase*.

Kundera's work revolves around the question of significance and meaning. In *The Joke*, the postcard is either significant or merely a joke, but that reading has broad reverberations. The ambiguity of meaning, and the question of who has the authority to decide what that meaning is, remains at the heart of all of Kundera's work. Once that meaning is established, however, the whole structure of significance shifts. In a similar fashion, Karen von Kunes's reading of the meaning of a *suitcase* in Kundera's life and works shifts our understanding of both Kundera and his oeuvre.

Daniel W. Pratt, PhD
McGill University

NOTE

1. Milan Kundera, *The Joke* (Definitive version fully revised by the author, New York: Harper Perennial, 1993) 34.

Acknowledgments

I would like to thank specialists, scholars, and friends whose generous time and expertise made this book possible. Above all, I am indebted to the Archivist-historian at the Prague *Ústav pro studium totalitních režimů,* Mgr. Adam Hradilek, who has been extremely helpful in providing me with and guiding me through many valuable documents on the "Kauza Kundera." I would also like to kindly thank him for granting me permission to reprint two documents for which he holds the rights. In addition, I appreciate the assistance of Matěj Hradilek who supplied me with specific data for my text.

The Yale Council on European Studies supported my research trips to gather crucial information, and I am indebted to its members for their encouragement to bring this book to its final stage. My very special thanks go to Lora Johns, the Yale Law School Librarian, as well as to Jared Dworken, a Yale graduate in Psychology. Each has spent endless hours carefully reading my manuscript and making valuable comments to significantly improve my first drafts. My deep appreciation also goes to Dr. Jan Čulík of the University of Glasgow, and the editor of *Britské Listy*, who made valuable comments and recommended additional sources after reading my manuscript in its pre-final version. I also would like to thank him for conducting my interview on the "Kauza Kundera" for Czech television and thus allowing its viewers to evaluate yet another interpretation of Milan Kundera's 1950 incident. I also owe a special debt to Professor Daniel Pratt of McGill University who wrote a Foreword and specified my contribution to scholarship.

I owe a debt to James William Piereson, Esq., of Harvard Law School, who came up with the most suitable title for this book after my long struggle of searching for its appropriate name. Likewise, I am grateful to Marie H. Kurfiřtová, an Independent Scholar at the Harvard Davis Center for Russian and Eurasian Studies, for her sharp eye catching the "last-minute" inconsistencies in my text, and for suggesting a suitcase and a book as an evocative image for the front cover. I also wish to recognize the Slavic Department faculty and Yale administration for continually supporting the Yale Czech studies curriculum—language, literature, film, and culture. And above all, I wish to recognize hundreds of students who, in the past two decades, contributed their insights into the reading and interpreting of Kundera's works in my classes and seminars.

I wish to thank my editors, Amy King and especially Kasey Beduhn, for their professional guidance, advice and patience throughout the process of working on this book. And last but not least, I would like to express gratitude to my husband, Robert R. Newton, a Special Assistant to the President of Boston College, who has been patiently waiting to see my book both at the Boston College library and in our home library bookcase.

Stylistic Notes

In a generic context, such as referring to *the reader*, the masculine pronoun *he* implies both genders, masculine and feminine. When denoting a specific person, the distinction between *he* and *she* applies.

Czech words are indicated with their diacritical markings unless they are quoted from (or refer to) texts that ignore their use. Diacritical markers are omitted in names publically known in such forms (i.e., *Milos Forman* rather than *Miloš Forman*).

Any foreign text quoted in English was taken from a published translation acknowledged in the Notes and Bibliography. If a source is acknowledged only in Czech (or any other language) but is quoted in English in the text, it means that its translation has been provided by the author of this book.

The period (a full stop at the end of a sentence) has been removed from all the websites listed in Notes and Bibliography because often the period prevents the opening of the source.

Introduction

This book originated as a manuscript on Milan Kundera's identity. I have drawn on literature and related fields, centering on investigations of a *detective* nature. I have aimed to address the complex issues of Kundera's shifting identity as witnessed through the actions of the characters in his novels and plays.

The core of the critical analysis is a close examination, if not a *dissection*, of a police report of March 14, 1950, that mentioned Milan Kundera's name and came to public attention fifty-eight years later, after it was released in the Prague newsmagazine *Respekt* on March 13, 2008. Immediately translated and reprinted in *The New York Times* and by the media around the world, the police statement was understood by reporters, journalists, and readers in a straightforward manner: twenty-year-old student Milan Kundera denounced Miroslav Dvořáček, a young army deserter and illegal escapee to Germany, who was then arrested by the police.

The premise of this book is to show to what extent this statement is correct, erroneous, or distorted, and, above all, why and how this incident has influenced Kundera's writing career and supplied him with creative nourishment and endless possibilities of imagination, originality, and meaning, while molding his identity as one of the most celebrated post-modernist novelists and thinkers. The police report contains two sentences, seemingly innocent but crucial for revealing the mystery of Kundera's creative endeavors. When studied carefully, the report provides significant insight into his past that impacted the trajectory of his life and work. To various degrees, the meaning and potential applications of the two sentences have been reflected in every single novel authored by Milan Kundera; awareness of these sentences could therefore shed new light on his novels. As versatile and popular as he has become, he has also become a fierce guardian—to the point of absurdity—of his private life. Implicit in the above statements is the discovery outlined in this book that might provide innovative ways to reading and interpreting Kundera's novels and drama plays, and to understanding his life.

In digital science, the process of analytical digging, reconstructing, and reflecting would be termed *hacking*; in literary analysis it falls under *scholarly inquiry*. However, the inquiry in this book deviates from a traditional critical approach based purely on literary theory. It contravenes the approach for interpreting post-modernist and post-structuralist works, as laid out in Roland Barthes's landmark essay, "The Death of the Author." Barthes's theory rejects literary analyses within the biographical context of the author. In his novels and analytical essays, Milan Kundera emphatically warns against using the *hacking* criticism approach, claiming that the two—the author's life and the author's work—are separate entities that have little in common. If I fail to respect Mr. Kundera's wishes, it is not only because Milan Kundera's own writings at times ignore the rule of Barthes's theory but, above all, because the substance of the two confusing, yet crucially meaningful sentences within the 1950 police report.

And while separate, the author's life and the author's work are not necessarily mutually exclusive. At the same time, as Kundera insists that they diverge, he also claims that whatever he wanted to say, and whatever he wanted his readers to know, he did say in his novels. Therefore, implicitly, his novels hold the key to understanding Milan Kundera, the man.

Following Kundera's favorite structure of the novel in seven parts, this book is divided into seven chapters. It begins by analyzing the concepts of immortality and identity, or rather betrayed identity, as espoused in his *Immortality* and *Identity* (with references to his earlier works as well), wrapped under the umbrella of existential perception. The second chapter introduces the so-called "Kauza Kundera," the police report and its unfortunate consequences by examining Kundera's past as a young Communist poet against the background of Czechoslovakia's politics of totalitarianism of the 1950s. This chapter focuses on the dissection of the police report, deposited in the public records of the Prague Security Services Archives. It also attempts to elucidate the circumstances that led to the incident. Kundera himself admitted to a friend that today no one would understand the climate of that period.

The three critical chapters that follow constitute the main body of this book. They are constructed around an *invisibly visible* hook: a *suitcase* found in the police report as well as in all of Kundera's novels and plays. Here the arc is rather argumentative, providing a number of arguments for and against the "Kauza Kundera," and its direct reflection in his works. It is dominated by the themes of betrayal, randomness, guilt, and death. To some extent, every single novel is subjected to analysis; however, in this book, only the sections in each novel that are directly representative of the themes under discussion are examined in depth.

The final two chapters are closely related to the main argument, but partly distanced from its central topic. A great deal of what is perceived to be an incomprehensible deprecation in Kundera's portrayal of female characters is placed here within the political and socioeconomic contexts of Kundera's native country, and comparative links are drawn with Milos Forman's films and works of additional artists, primarily Czech. The closing chapters show how Kundera's works can be interpreted within a variety of fields, not only in literature, politics and history but also philosophy and cognitive science. Selected works by Singaporean and Chinese fiction writers, Goh Poh Seng and Wang Xiaobo, are mentioned for comparison.

It would be a mistake to think that a goal of this book is to diminish the value of Kundera's work; on the contrary, my aim is to reveal his literary genius, his deep insight into human interactions and the human *id*, his marvelous verbalism and challenging ideas that leave almost every single statement to an open possibility. He plays creatively and wittily to confuse his readers on purpose. Likewise, the approach to analysis in this book is partly speculative criticism based on open possibilities of facts, ideas, and interpretations. In addition, I aim to clarify some obscure corners of his early literary achievements and of his latest (if not last) interviews in order to understand his persona in relation to his own creative process and his works. However, this book is a critical work that does not shy away from criticism. Furthermore, it positions Kundera within the crossroads of criticism in his native country (the former Czechoslovakia), his adoptive country (France), and the current Western, if not international, criticism. To sum up, my aim is to clarify what has often puzzled Western critics and provided grounds for bitter criticism on the part of Kundera's compatriots.

In this respect, Kundera understands how cultural barriers can lead to misunderstanding. He once pointed out why Bertolt Brecht's stage adaptation of *The Good Soldier Schweik* had missed the comical dimension of Jaroslav Hašek's novel. Like Brecht, others missed the humor in Bohumil Hrabal's and Josef Škvorecký's works because they failed to understand Czech humor as the humor of the powerless. It was not until 1979 that Václav Havel encapsulated the historical concept of a powerless nation in his political essay *The Power of the Powerless*, which clarified why Czechs laugh when they do. They laugh precisely in the darkest hours of their history when there is nothing to laugh about.

The traditional literary theory presented in this book is split into various sub-theories, such as literary, philosophical, psychological, and historical. Therefore, this work does not attempt to analyze Kundera's novels comprehensively or to critically uncover various levels of literary interpretation. This task has been successfully accomplished by Fred Misurella, Maria Banerjee-Nemcova, Aaron Aji, Eva Le Grand, Jakub Češka, and most recently by Jason M. Wirth. Rather, as pointed out, the analysis seeks to illustrate the wide-ranging impact of the two fateful sentences recorded by the police.

Despite his shortcomings, Milan Kundera continues to be viewed as a great man of letters, an artist of wisdom, feelings, and appreciation for artistic endeavors. He has rightly been deeply concerned about current postmodernist trends, which oust art at the expense of technology. Some forty years ago at a dinner in Paris, he encountered a situation in which Federico Fellini's films were judged as outdated, without merit. It was then that Kundera for the first time realized what a significant role art had played in his native country in the cruelest times of totalitarianism. Like his fellow writer-in-exile, Věra Linhartová, he concluded that henceforth he would remain apart: no longer a Czech writer, he would not become a French writer. He would be an author on his own terms, defending his own position and views.

And because they bridge so many domains, his works will be interpreted, analyzed, and criticized for decades to come. The interpretation from the perspective of cognitive psychology introduced in the closing chapters of this book shows that Kundera's immense popularity has gone beyond the literati, philosophers, historians, or politicians; it has reached as far as scientists. However, most importantly, it has reached ordinary readers who love to be challenged by a novel written with insight and depth of humanity. That is where the power of Milan Kundera's novels, plays, and critical writing lies.

Chapter One

The Author's Identity Unfolding

PRIVATE LIFE MEANS PRIVATE

A number of critics agree that Milan Kundera is one of the most influential contemporary writers, albeit quite controversial. Internationally, he is the best-known Czech novelist, whose fame quickly spread to many corners of the globe, including China, Korea, and India. Discourses on his works and scholarly quotes from his writings appear in a variety of publications on topics ranging from history, literature, and philosophy, to science and law. However, little is known about the author's life and identity.

Kundera has guarded his private life more *privately* than any other writer, vigorously speaking of the significance of inquiry in his novels and obsessively downplaying the relation between an author's life and his created works. In the past two decades, he has subjected his novels to reediting and retranslating (if not readapting), and introduced his own drawings on the front jacket of his newly reprinted books. The critic Brian Ward considers the gradual shrinking of his "official biography" to two sentences—Milan Kundera was born in Czechoslovakia in 1929 and since 1975 has been living in France—to be *the function of his fictional characters in the view of the authorial character*. Its purpose, Ward states, "is to exacerbate the ambiguity of his 'real' identity," which in Ward's view is "an unusual literary phenomenon."[1]

Kundera has his own reasons for keeping his *private life private*—be it on the dust jackets of his books, in press, media, interviews, or personal contacts; however, he does not keep *his reasons* private. In *The Unbearable Lightness of Being*, his commercially successful novel, he reinforces the idea of privacy through his free-spirited character Sabina: "A man who loses his privacy loses everything, Sabina thought. And a man who gives it up of his own free will is a monster."[2]

In his novels and stage plays, Kundera skillfully plays with words, metaphors, mythology, history, and politics, but above all, with his fictional characters, his readers, and himself. In each of his novels, he delves deeper and deeper into the interaction with his own identity, expressed purely on a novelistic platform. Readers thoroughly familiar with his works might be able to reconstruct a carefully deconstructed *life of the author by the author*. But Kundera warns against such an interpretation: "The novel's sole *raison d'être* is to say what only the novel can say."[3]

FAKE FAME: MONSTROUS IMMORTALITY

Immortality, Kundera's opus #7 and the very last novel written in his native Czech, was published in English in 1999. One can only speculate that it was intended to be a transitional link to assure his posthumous *immortality* in the *Pléiade* of great European writers. Except for Mr. Kundera—a fictionally real character in the novel—Czech novelistic characters no longer have a place in this complex and, at times, perplexing novel. The idea of immortality and death walking hand in hand like 'an inseparable pair' is presented in a fanciful passage where Goethe and Hemingway meet in the other world to discuss the impact of fame in the afterlife. "Immortality means eternal trial,"[4] explains the fictional Goethe to Hemingway and goes into detailing the way that readers, scholars, and critics (such as Gertrude Stein and American professors) have descended or would descend in judgment upon the author's life and work. In Kundera's view, these critics may use and misuse valid information as well as unsubstantiated gossip, analyzing and classifying it in order to reach conclusions that are often preconceived and erroneous. In his book of essays, *The Curtain* (2005), Kundera considered artists' immortality through fame to be a form of megalomania—"the most monstrous of all."[5]

In *Immortality*, Kundera depicts Ernest Hemingway—a posthumous character—to be highly dissatisfied because he is judged for his personality and human faults rather than for his works. The fictional Hemingway does not object to examination or criticism of his novels: "I wrote them in such a way that nobody could delete a single word. To resist every kind of adversity."[6] The words of a fictional Hemingway speak for the author of *Immortality* the very same way. He claims: "If a reader skips a single sentence of my novel he won't be able to understand it."[7]

Likewise, Kundera hints that he foresees possible posthumous controversies of his life, and thus attempts to defend his writings only at the *existential level*. The only morality of the novel, he proclaims, is the "exploration of man's existence, a poetic meditation on existence," and its role is to examine "the enigma of existence."[8] Truly enough, his novels abound with "enigma"—puzzling, mysterious occurrences that his characters either resolve or go along with the inexplicable. He goes even further, stating: "The novel is not the author's confession; it is an investigation of human life in the trap the world has become."[9]

PARABASIS OR CONFUSION?

Kundera often digresses from novelistic situations to present his authorial comments and views. Influenced by Denis Diderot, he has adopted the eighteenth-century playwright and novelist's literary approach of playing with fiction and reality, often in the form of games, interacting and arguing with the audience so that it becomes difficult for the audience to untangle the real from the invented. This intrusive fourth-wall-breaking approach, loosely categorized as *parabasis*, has been known for centuries. It was used in ancient Greek comedy and drama: during an intermission a choral ode was addressed to the audience to express the author's views on social, political, and religious events, independent of the play action.

The author's intrusions in Kundera's novels are frequent. As soon as the reader becomes engrossed in a story, the narrator reminds him that what he reads is a rendition of the author's thoughts and vision; he undercuts the reader at every point of his engagement: *the novel is a novel, not real life.* For instance, in *The Unbearable Lightness of Being* the narrator tells that Tomas's birth took place in the author's imagination in a moment of providence when he was staring at the wall opposite his window. Revealed in Part Five, "Lightness and Weight," this information is a progression of his discontinued thought introduced at the start of the novel: he has been thinking about Tomas for many years. The short chapter on Tomas is preceded by a two-page discourse on Nietzsche's ideas on eternal return and Parmenides's perception of two opposites, lightness and weight. This random presentation of facts remains Kundera's preferred literary structure; to him the story itself isn't important. Rather, he aims to engage the reader's mind through essays and sub-essays, philosophical discourses, social commentaries, historical facts, and other similar devices. In showing the creative birth of Tomas, Kundera rejects any linkage to or potential confusion of the author's curriculum vitae with Tomas's life résumé. He says: "The characters in my novels are my own unrealized possibilities. That is why I am equally fond of them all and equally horrified by them."[10]

As a means of justification, these statements have allowed Kundera to move easily within his own fictional text, context, and subtext; his own personality subdued, he alludes that what he writes about does not represent him as a real person. Nonetheless, as challenging and complex as his works can be, some readers and critics regard him as an obsessed writer, an erotically preoccupied flamboyant philosopher. Others attack him brutally, claiming that to some women, "Kundera is a repulsive author who is not particularly worth reading, whereas he has become almost a cult figure for the intellectual audiences of *The New York Times Book Review* and *The New York Review of Books*."[11]

Brian Ward has attempted to explore Kundera's biographical identity as a function of subverting his historical and political identity in the context of "dissident writers."[12] It is common knowledge that after the military invasion of his native Czechoslovakia by the Warsaw Pact at the blossoming of the Prague Spring in August 1968, Kundera was persecuted. Within two years, he lost his membership in the Communist Party and his lectureship position at the Prague Film Academy (FAMU); his books disappeared from the book-stores and libraries, and he was not allowed to publish officially. Brian Ward quotes the critic Adam Thirwell, who like himself, has been puzzled by Kundera's "refuting the exile identity," by his disclaiming sympathy and profit from his dissident status that the readers and critics have attributed to him.[13] Thirwell points out Milan Kundera's incongruence with history as a negative factor for his readership. Ward presents two hypotheses of Kundera's refusal to be identified as a dissident writer:

a. his biographical information could become the source of misinterpretation of his work;
b. he does not wish to share with his readers the deeply ambiguous feelings that he holds for his native country.

To a certain degree, Ward's hypotheses presume that Kundera's conjunctions are already inserted into his novels as a part of authorial intrusions and philosophical digressions. Petr Bílek defines Mr. Kundera, the fictional character who steps into *Slowness* with his wife Véra, as *the public image of the author*. He argues that this image is designed to be easily consumed by the public. It creates a caricature of the real Mr. Kundera and that allows him—the private man who created this persona—to distance his true self from the public.[14] But why would the author want to create a caricature of himself to confuse the public and his readers, for whom he composes his novels and on whom his reputation, trajectory, and destiny as a writer and novelist depends? Would he really distance himself from the public just to insure his privacy?

Ward's hypothesis and Bílek's interpretation remain at a static platform and on the level of speculation. Evidently, their hypotheses lack the power of *discovery*, the same kind of discovery that Kundera considers to be the most important substance of a novel. Their interpretations and views don't reveal *why* Kundera has, over the decades, developed a deeper thirst for wanting to remain *privately private*. Why has he craved to hide his identity so eagerly and gradually? And why, above all, has this thirst persisted after the fall of

Communism, a system that he used as an adversary to create contextual tensions in his writings, and which provided his novels and essays with plentiful "nourishment," helping him establish his literary career and fame?

EXISTENTIAL PERSPECTIVE

If Kundera's readers approach the theme of identity from the *existential inquiry* perspective, they might be able to trace his characters searching for their identity in all his novels. Since the 1967 publication of *The Joke* in Czechoslovakia, Kundera has been strongly opposed to his novels being perceived and analyzed from political, cultural, or territorial angles, claiming that his intention is not to depict the reality of a given society (such as showing the brutality of Communist politics in *The Joke)* but rather, he regards his novels within Martin Heidegger's definition of existence, *in-der-Welt-sein* ("being-in-the-world"). A novel is "a poetic meditation on human existence"[15] that embodies man's life, which is subjected to continual changes as a result of global changes in the world that surrounds him. In this respect, *The Joke* becomes a non-political novel that Kundera calls a *love story.* Taken out of literary context, this definition loses its politicized value by being reduced to the bare essentials of existence—love.

But what is existence? One may define it is as a constant struggle in man's life—life which Kundera calls "a trap"—to justify his own self-worth and purpose, his own being, via his identity within the boundaries of ever-lasting, universal existence. But isn't the notion of man's existence akin to the existence of the novel by the author's own definition?

"The novel's spirit is the spirit of complexity," reveals Kundera in his *The Art of the Novel,* and instructs the reader: "Things are not as simple as you think."[16] The spirit of complexity within a context of simplicity—that is, an illusory simplicity—has been revealed long before Kundera. One could re-call, for instance, the opening lines in Lev Tolstoy's *Anna Karenina* about happy families who are "all alike" but the unhappy ones being unhappy each in "their own way." Likewise, Franz Kafka reveals the complexity of man's identity in the opening lines of his novella within a simple surreal context: Gregor Samsa wakes up one morning from "unsettling dreams" to find out that he has been transformed into "a monstrous vermin."[17]

It is the singleness of the complexity of human nature (a topic that Kundera often points out) that *identifies* man's identity at many levels, including the novelistic, artistic, and authorial. It is a unique particularity of an unhappy family in Tolstoy, or the awkward realization of Kafka's Gregor becoming an insect while retaining human characteristics, experience and ways of thinking. At every stage of his works, Kundera implies that man's identity is lost in crowds of happy families, naked bodies on nude beaches, in the polyphony of modern mass media that he terms "megalomania," and in conformity to political and humanistic ideologies, or in the kitschy aspects of romance and love stories.

Such is, for instance, Tomas's theory of the "one-millionth part dissimilarity" that makes a woman's body attractive, and distinguishes her from another woman. This "one-millionth part dissimilarity"—this tiny imperfection—*identifies her identity*. It is Jean-Marc who reiterates Tomas's view in *Identity*, a novel Kundera wrote in French in 1998. Getting closer on the beach to a woman that he had thought to be his beloved Chantal, Jean-Marc sees her turning into "old, ugly, pathetically other," questioning where the difference between the two women, the real and the imagined one lies. Kundera's *literary* idea of identity runs parallel to the *philosophical* idea of eternal return, based on Friedrich Nietzsche's eternal recurrence *ad infinitum:* "Everything recurs as we once experienced it." And he equivocally asks: "What does this mad myth signify?"[18]

It means that the loss of identity occurs when the same event repeats itself, he explains, pointing to Robespierre's identity as an example, which is tied to the French Revolution, unique for having happened in history only once. A frequent recurrence of the same kind of revolution would transform Robespierre into a public *monstrum of a kitsch*, a kind of degrading medium of mass culture. "The spirit of identity" acquires a variety of shapes in Kundera's works. Immortality itself is nothing but a disguised yearning for *post-mortem identity*.

Bettina Brentano, a fictional character in *Immortality,* desires to reach immortality through the assumed immortal fame of Goethe. In her letters, she assures Goethe that she will love him for eternity. In her longing for finding her own distinct identity in the predominantly male-dominated world of the eighteenth to nineteenth centuries, Bettina finds a refuge in establishing love affairs with a kaleidoscope of famous men—musicians, artists, writers, and politicians. Her desired identity is not being a wife, mother, or a person on her own; she acts as the extended ego of renowned men, hoping that after their death and her own death she will be recognized and celebrated as a part of their world and accolades.

However, some sources have reached the conclusion that the real Bettina Brentano published her correspondence with Goethe not as historical documents but "in the light of her own highly poetic imagination."[19] One may interpret her *poetic imagination*—a craving for her own identity—in the view of David Hume, the eighteenth-century Scottish philosopher. Hume believed that memory is the foundation of personal identity; in his opinion, we exist so long as we have a distinct recollection of ourselves as such. But what are these recollections of Bettina? Needless to say, human memory fades, and whatever remains will have remained preserved in some sort of tangible forms of recollections, such as personal letters in Bettina's case. In Kundera's novel, preparing her correspondence with Goethe for publication, Bettina realized that neither in her letters to him, nor in his letters to her would she be identified as the person she wanted to be; her platonic love affair with Goethe seemed "a mere sketch for a masterpiece." Thus she rewrote Goethe's letters and her own, embellishing and dramatizing their content. She did it, as Kundera describes it poetically, "in order to be tossed upward to the heights where the God incarnate in history dwells."[20]

One might admire Kundera's ability to connect the idea of the identity of various characters through the means of a motif, such as gesture as presented in Bettina, a historically novelistic character, and Laura, a purely fictional character. In his novel, Kundera attributes the idea of gesture to Edmund Husserl, a German phenomenologist born in Moravia like Kundera himself. Husserl perceived gesture as a part of human consciousness, being deeply connected to, rather than separated from, the physical world. When humiliated in her love affair, Laura throws her hands forward; and while her gesture didn't mean anything concrete, it meant a lot, something vaguely descript in the sense of wanting to sacrifice herself, "to give oneself to the world, to send one's soul soaring toward the blue horizon like a white dove."[21] Her gesture of contributing to charitable organizations is leveled with Bettina's acts of sacrificing herself to help others; it suffices to remember Bettina's plea to the Prussian King to spare the leader of the Polish revolution, Ludwig Mieroslawski, from execution.

Kundera sees Bettina and Laura's gestures as identical, and one can trace similar or "identical" gestures of other characters, from Lucie in *The Joke* to Chantal in *Identity* to Madame La Franck in his latest French novel, *The Festival of Insignificance*. However, looking beyond the fictional characters and their gestures, it could become an indisputably fascinating inquiry into the authorial identity. Kundera uses each novel as a platform for shifting his own identities novelistically: from a young Communist poet to an unsuccessful painter, and even to an unemployed and disregarded actor who pretends to speak in a non-existent language to gain attention. The author says about his characters: "I am equally fond of them all and equally horrified by them. Each one has crossed a border that I myself have circumvented. It is that crossed border (the border beyond which my own 'I' ends) which attracts me most. For beyond that border begins the secret the novel asks about."[22]

In his article, "The Incredible Lightness" in *The New Republic*, the late Harvard Professor Stanisław Barańczak predicted Kundera's path of taking one step at a time: after *Slowness* with only one Czech fictional character involved, naively ridiculous and laughable, he saw Kundera's next step in erasing all the traces of his Central European origins.[23] Professor Barańczak didn't have to wait long; two years after *Slowness*, Kundera published *Identity*, the second novel written in French of a similar length (fifty-one chapters condensed into 168 pages) and similar spirit. But the previous flirtatious novella with only a few traces of Czech culture, history, or consciousness has now turned into a blurred present-age mediocre French reading. Was it another Kunderian joke? A fine line, which Kundera has attempted to draw between himself and his characters, blending with them but reminding his readers that *the novel is not the author's confession?*

THE POWER OF THE WORD

The Czech language per se has always been the key to Kundera's poetics. In her article "Totožnost člověka ve světě znaků" ("Man's Identity in the World of Signs"), Sylvie Richterová presents a thesis of identity within a symbolic system of signs, in which man himself becomes a sign.[24] Kundera's novelistic characters function as a part of the whole system, in which the word determines their destiny. It is a combination of several words on a postcard that creates a value system and eventually leads Ludvik in *The Joke* to destruction; that is, a verbal message gives birth to a novel. Kundera's frequent use of letters (Tamina's lost letters or Mirek's old love letters that he is unable to retrieve in *The Book of Laughter and Forgetting,* Bettina's forged letters, or Jean-Marc's anonymous letters to Chantal) provides a semiotic code, which becomes the driving force in the characters' behavior. This structural intersection is where gestures and language may become mutually exclusive, giving way to unpredictability in characters' behavior and in identifying their identity. Chantal's sentence: "Men don't turn to look at me anymore,"[25] is one of these semiotic codes that springs from a separated system of gesture. Chantal does not mean to say anything of this sort to Jean-Marc; she has just experienced an unpleasant encounter in a café with a young man. His muscular arm tattooed with a snake around the body of a naked woman detracts from her intended message: to let this young man know how much his loud music is disturbing her. Nothing unusual happened at the moment of interchange; however, the communication between the young man and Chantal was reduced to words and sentences that had no relation to the meaning of Chantal's thoughts. Moreover, this communication of the non-communicated message leaves her frustrated, and when Jean-Marc meets her, he finds Chantal's face old, and "her glance strangely harsh," thinking that from now on the image of the woman he had been waving to at the beach would replace the image of the one he had loved. The sentence she says to Jean-Marc in her defense of a sudden change in her mood, "Men don't turn to look at me anymore" exists independently of reality. Its meaning is as invalid as famous Ludvik's slogan: "Optimism is the opium of the people! A healthy atmosphere stinks of stupidity! Long live Trotsky!"[26] Yet, both statements are fully valid as gestures on which the *fabula* and the *sjužet* are constructed in *Identity* and *The Joke* respectively.

Not only language as a whole, but individual words and their meanings have always mattered to Czech writers, Kundera in particular. One can recall, "Words misunderstood," a fictional chapter in *The Unbearable Lightness of Being,* in which the author explores the essence of relationships based on miscommunication premised upon differing semantic and cultural interpretations of words. The chapter "Sixty-three Words" in *The Art of the Novel* has a similar function. In his acceptance speech for the 1989 Peace Prize of the German Booksellers, Václav Havel, the playwright and former President of Czechoslovakia, said: "Words are a mysterious, ambiguous, ambivalent, and perfidious phenomenon. They can be 'rays of light in the realms of darkness,' or 'lethal arrows.' . . . Worst of all, at times they can be the one and the other. And even both at once!"[27]

Marketa Goetz-Stankiewicz termed Havel's exploration of the word: *the word's double nature.* This "double nature of the word" when reduced to signs is subsequently utilized in ideological and "hilariously banal tautologies," such as Communists propaganda. A number of theorists, including Mikhail Bakhtin, have studied the interdependency of a word and its meanings within the context of changes in identity. Sylvie Richterová believes that the problem of identity of man is interconnected with the problem of identifying signs.

For Milan Kundera, the meaning of the word and the meaning of the novel remain primarily existential. His literary technique of ellipsis is constructed on Leoš Janáček's aesthetic approach to musical composition: "only the note that says something essential has the right to exist."[28] Like Franz Kafka, Kundera dislikes what he calls "the lyricization of prose in novels." Defending Kafka's stylistic purposefulness, he defends his own. Kafka's creative imagination is "no less rich than Verlaine's or Rilke's," he claims in his *Testaments Betrayed*, giving various examples of how translators have betrayed Kafka's aesthetics by enriching the most elementary words, yet existentially justified, by replacing them with *visual images*, such as "never ceased to experience" for the verb "to have." One can easily understand why Kundera agonizes over his own words translated into a foreign language. Concerning *zášť* rendered as *aversion* in *The Joke,* the author explains: It is not because "rancor" conveys a different nuance of *zášť* but because its meaning places the reader "on a different level of aesthetic perception."[29]

Kundera has an intimate relationship with his own words, warning his readers not to skip sentences in order to understand his novels. However, he acknowledges that he himself is "the greatest skipper" not only of words and lines but of pages. As he claims, novelistic characters are his own "unrealized possibilities;" the so-called *mirror stages*—using the expression of Jacques Lacan, the French psychoanalyst who reinterpreted the Freudian theory on *self* in relationship to post-structuralism and language. This literary *self* can be compared to an imaginary child, and as a mirror situation suggests, the relationship between this artistically created child and the author is essentially narcissistic.[30] Thus, Kundera's identity is not only related to each of his characters, each sentence, and even each word, but also to any outside criticism his works receive. In fact, he has been very sensitive to negative criticism—his old friends say that it influences him badly.

A forcible turning point in his writing career occurred when he transplanted himself from Prague to Paris. It was nostalgia and feelings of homesickness that led him to create of *The Book of Laughter and Forgetting.* This was also the time when he realized that he needed to create a new, exciting form, an original structure, something unusual that would attract non-Czech readership, since his books were hardly read by Czechs due to their unavailability in the 1970s. As Kundera ponders, he consciously created a historic shift within the poetics of the novel, following the traditions of the Central European approach by responding to four *appeals* and combining them into one thematic unity through a series of motifs: the appeal of *play, dream, thought,* and *time.*[31] Each of these *appeals* has been explored as a specific theme in the works of the literary giants/predecessors: Cervantes, Rabelais, Sterne, Proust, and Diderot. Kundera believes that he has contributed to the *sequence of discoveries* of the novel with his style—a bright mosaic of fiction, comedy, dreams, history, real experience, etc., blending these elements into one whole, a smooth and artful unity, only to be disrupted by his unending battle with his translators, fighting literally over every single word in his original texts.

BETRAYED IDENTITY

"The Velvet Revolution came too late for me,"[32] confesses Kundera in his "Author's Note" in *Nesmrtelnost,* the Czech edition of *Immortality.* After obtaining the *nationalité française* in 1981, he became obsessed with French language and culture. The same year, he translated his Czech play *Jakub a jeho pán: Pocta Denisu Diderotovi* into French, *Jacques and his maître, Homage to Denis Diderot,* that he based on Diderot's novel of 1778, *Jacques le fataliste et son maître.* Simultaneously, Kundera was writing his first nonfiction work in French, *The Art of the Novel.* In 1984, his mother died in Brno, and he felt that his last thread leading to his native country was broken. He had reached a stage in his life when his own identity was at stake. The borders to Czechoslovakia were closed and Kundera was convinced that they were to remain so forever.[33]

The novel *Immortality* is evidence of Kundera's first *testament of his betrayed* identity. Written in Czech, it bears no traces of Czech and Moravian culture except for passing references. His major concern is the everlasting judgment of his works after his death, the "eternal trial," as his fictional

Goethe calls it. Just like his fictional Hemingway, Kundera hopes that after his death he will be able to rest in peace, his works remaining untouched. With his prominently specific novelistic essay style that includes numerous critical notes and interpretations of his own works, Kundera leaves little space for critics to judge his works posthumously. He walks in lockstep with the conviction of Roland Barthes, the French literary critic, who argued against interpreting an author's work in the context of his autobiography, claiming in his 1967 essay "The Death of the Author" that the author's identity is a separate entity from his creation. [34]

Two years later at the French Society of Philosophers, Michel Foucault presented an essay "What is an author?" in which he further analyzed the role of an author and questioned what constitutes his body of work. He alluded to the literary theoreticians who evaluate writing like a game, and which goes beyond its rules and limits, "creating a space into which the writing subject constantly disappears." [35] Foucault refers to previous attitudes of writing when it was acknowledged as "the sacrifice of life" and authors were standing *with* their works; however, since Flaubert, Proust, and Kafka, "the right to kill, to be its author's murderer" has been a prevalent concept. The writer has become absent—"the dead man in the game of writing." [36] Yet inasmuch as Kundera desires it, he concurrently ignores the structuralists' sardonic enunciation of "the death of the author," and blatantly enters *Immortality* as the fictional companion of the already obscure character of Professor Avenarius. The emergence of the fictional Mr. Kundera interacting with Professor Avenarius confuses the reader with the inconsistency of his appearance and Avenarius's actions.

Is *Slowness* the second testament of Kundera's betrayed identity? Readers can see the author farcically laughing and dancing along with the "laughable characters" of his own *Commedia dell'arte*. It is Mr. Čechořipský that Kundera puts in the center of this short piece, a novella with an allusion to a stage drama, presented in French. But Mr. Čechořipský is a Czech. He is a very awkward Czech, raising the suspicion that the cumbersome figure of Mr. Čechořipský alludes to Kundera himself. Better yet, Mr. Kundera is laughing at himself, in the guise of the comic, pitiful face of this Czech entomologist who forgets to read his paper at a Paris convention while overwhelmed by his own emotions of a longtime Sisyphean sufferer under the Communist regime.

What would be the third stage of Kundera's betrayed identity, in the face of the laughable man Čechořipský, after being stripped of his own unique style and expression of writing in his native Czech? Some critics question whether his novel *Identity* should be evaluated as less challenging or even a kitschy progression of Kundera's new identity. Less erotic and humorous than his previous novels, with no political message, *Identity* is a linear narration, uncovering the rapid progression of feelings of a man and a woman who attempt to hide "their true faces." Long before Chantal, the reader is able to figure out that the forged letters she receives come from her lover, Jean-Marc. However, by no means is she a naive heroine of a cheap romance novella! Kundera has achieved complexity even in this slim and seemingly simple volume. Like his other novels, this one is concerned with a heavy theme but a light structure, and it might serve as an allusion to the return of the French novel to its homeland.

Would Kundera truly attempt to return to the novel's origins, to Rabelais and Cervantes? In fact, the open-ended episodic structure of *Identity* is reminiscent of Voltaire's *Candide* of the French Enlightenment period, both resembling a picaresque novel. One could assign it to the category of the eighteenth-century *conte philosophique*, which was based on a variety of subgenres, such as erotic tales in the tradition of Boccaccio, travel episodes, didactic and parodistic tales. Voltaire's *Candide* was no exception. The purpose of the picaresque novel was to satirize, self-parodize, and amuse. This might exactly be what Kundera intended to achieve with *Identity*, if not with most of his novels; but certainly with his *Identity* and, possibly, with his own personal identity.

In his article "Milan Kundera," the Czech literature lecturer at the University of Glasgow, Jan Čulík, partially reports Kundera's interview with a British writer, Ian McEwan, in which Kundera said: "We constantly rewrite our own biographies and continually give matters new meanings. To rewrite history in this sense—indeed, in an Orwellian sense—is not at all inhuman. On the contrary, it is very human."[37] By this statement, Kundera attempted to free himself from the pressure and responsibility to produce an objective autobiography and to uncover his genuine identity. He was unable to produce one, just as man is unable to produce an objective "history of politics." Recognizing that man's identity is in constant flux, Mr. Kundera was free to create an identity suitable "for all seasons," however, only until the fateful date of October 13, 2008. Past this date, his brief statement in *Immortality* might illuminate his works: "Only a reason deprived of reason can lead to such an unreasonable horror."[38]

NOTES

1. Brian Ward, "A Big Piece of Nonsense for His Own Pleasure: The Identity of Milan Kundera," in *Limina*, vol. 8 (2002): 144. http://www.archive.limina.arts.uwa.edu.au/__data/page/186574/8Ward2.pdf

2. Milan Kundera, *The Unbearable Lightness of Being*, trans. Michael Henry Heim (New York: Harper Perennial, 1985), 113.

3. Milan Kundera, *The Art of the Novel*, trans. Linda Asher (New York: Harper and Row Publishers, 1988), 36.

4. Milan Kundera, *Immortality*, trans. Peter Kussi (New York: Harper Perennial, 1992), 36.

5. Milan Kundera, *The Curtain*, trans. Linda Asher (New York: HarperCollins Publishers), 93.

6. Kundera, *Immortality*, 36.

7. Kundera, *Art of the Novel*, 26.

8. Kundera, *Art of the Novel*, 26.

9. Kundera, *Art of the Novel*, 26.

10. Kundera, *Unbearable Lightness*, 221.

11. Bronislava Volková, "The Unbearable Heaviness of Being, Or Is It Lightness? Kundera's Values," *Kosmas, Czechoslovak and Central European Journal* 12, no. 2 (1997): 17.

12. Ward, "A Big Piece of Nonsense," 144–47.

13. Ward, "A Big Piece of Nonsense," 144–47.

14. Ward, "A Big Piece of Nonsense," 144–47.

15. Kundera, *Art of the Novel*, 35.

16. Kundera, *Art of the Novel*, 18.

17. Franz Kafka, *The Metamorphosis*, trans. Stanley Corngold (New York: Bantam Classic, 1972), 1.

18. Kundera, *Unbearable Lightness*, 3.

19. *The Columbia Electronic Encyclopedia*, 6th edition, on Achim von Armin. http://www.infoplease.com/encyclopedia/people/arnim-achim-von.html

20. Kundera, *Immortality*, 164.

21. Kundera, *Immortality*, 163.

22. Kundera, *Unbearable Lightness*, 221.

23. Stanislaw Barańczak, "The Incredible Lightness," *The New Republic* (September 8, 1996): 43.

24. Sylvie Richterová, "Totožnost člověka ve světě znaků," in *Slova a ticho* (Praha: Arkýř Československý spisovatel, 1991), 66–70.

25. Milan Kundera, *Identity*, trans. Linda Asher (New York: Harper Flamingo, 1998), 21.

26. Milan Kundera, *The Joke*, definitive version fully revised by the author (New York: Harper Perennial, 1993), 37.

27. Václav Havel, "Words on Words," trans. A.G. Brain, *The New York Review of Books*, January 18, 1990 , 6.

28. Kundera, *Art of the Novel*, 72–73.

29. Kundera discusses the difficulty of translation in the part "Sentence" in his *Testament Betrayed* on pp. 101–9.

30. Terry Eagleton, *Literary Theory* (London: Blackwell Publishers, 1996), 143.

31. Kundera, *Art of the Novel*, 15–16.

32. Milan Kundera, *Nesmrtelnost* (Brno: Atlantis, 1990), 343–44.

33. Kundera, *Nesmrtelnost*, 343–44.

34. Roland Barthes, "The Death of the Author," 1967 trans. Richard Howard, *UbuWeb Paper*, 2–6.

35. Michel Foucault, "What is an Author?" Originally presented at the Société française de philosphie, February 22, 1969. The quotes are from the English modified trans. Josué V. Harari.

36. Foucault, "What is an Author?"

37. Jan Čulík, *Britské listy*, 2000, http://blisty.cz/video/Slavonic/Kundera.htm

38. Kundera, *Immortality*, 237.

Chapter Two

If You See Something,
Say Something

IDEOLOGICAL LYRICISM

In the Preface of the 1986 edition of *Life Is Elsewhere*, published by Penguin Books, Milan Kundera addresses the issue of "the lyric age" of his non-heroic hero, the young poet Jaromil. He describes Jaromil as a talented poet, a sensitive man "with great imagination and feeling" and calls on readers to refrain from judging him as a bad poet. However, after introducing positive features of his somewhat erratic, if not controversial, fictional character, the author exclaims: "Of course, he is also a monster." As justification for Jaromil's behavior, Kundera reveals: "But his monstrosity is potentially contained in us all. It is in me. It is in you. It is in Rimbaud. It is in Shelley, in Hugo. In all young men, of all periods and regimes."[1]

The Preface evolves into clarifying human existence via an aesthetic treatment of existential novels—novels without reference to any given historic, cultural, ethnic, or political periods, or geographic locations. The author terms the aesthetic treatment of existential issues in the novel *an anthropologic laboratory*, for it explores the basic premises of human existence ever since the awakening of man's intellectual consciousness. In the anthropologic sense, *Life Is Elsewhere* is an examination of the nature of a man who searches for his identity during the turbulent years of his life in a political situation, into which he has been thrown by the "satanic irony of history." In the last paragraph of the Preface, Kundera reveals to his readers that he obtained the idea for *Life Is Elsewhere* in the mid-1950s and completed the manuscript in 1969, only to see its first publication four years later in translation in France. The following year, the English version came out in Peter Kussi's translation, followed by additional editions. However, the Preface by the author seems to be only in the Penguin edition of 1986; in subsequent editions it was deleted.

THE YOUNG COMMUNIST POET

That the idea of writing *Life Is Elsewhere* came to Kundera in the 1950s is not an insignificant detail. It is known that Milan Kundera entered the Communist Party circa 1948, as was customary for his intellectual avant-garde peers, a consequence of their disillusionment with the previous political system inflicted by the atrocities of WWII. The Communist leadership assumed its power immediately after the February 25, 1948 putsch. By then, Milan Kundera was a Party member and a student of literature and aesthetics at Charles University. In the same year, he took oral entrance exams to study directing at the recently established Prague Film Academy (FAMU). The academic committee agreed that Milan Kundera was an exceptional and rare candidate: a young man of vast and superior knowledge and culture, of critical reflection and analytical thinking. [2]

During his course of study in 1949, he exchanged letters with his friend Jaroslav Dewetter, in which they criticized a highly placed Party functionary, allegedly Stalin himself. Initiated by Dewetter, the letters were accessed and read by the secret police (StB), and both students were consequently stripped of their Party membership in 1950, along with their friend, Jan Trefulka, who defended Dewetter (not Kundera) at a meeting. But only Dewetter and Trefulka were expelled from the University; Kundera was allowed to continue his studies at FAMU. After the completion of his study program in 1952, he became a FAMU lecturer in world literature and screenwriting. This rough sketch of his earlier biography differs slightly in the details, depending on the sources consulted.

However, one fact remains consistent. In 1953, Kundera asked to be reinstated into the Party. By this time he had published the first volume of poems, *Člověk, zahrada širá* (Man, a Wide Garden) and the second in 1955 *Poslední Máj* (The Last May), both collections celebrating the spirit of Communist teachings. Some of his verses about the country's everlasting friendship with the Soviet Union became popular song lyrics: "Sovětský Svaz a naše země navždycky navždy spolu jsou" (The Soviet Union and our country ever and forever remain together). [3]

Poslední Máj became a handy propaganda tool; a series of poems written in a proscribed form of socialist realism, the volume was widely distributed in schools and other educational establishments. Some critics (Jiří Holý specifically) believe that a young Kundera was commissioned to write this piece. It depicts the WWII-era interrogation of prisoner Julius Fučík, a Communist journalist and a resistance fighter, by Böhm, a German interrogator.

Böhm took Fučík to Petřín Hill, hoping that touched by the beauty and splendor of Prague panorama sprawling below Petřín, Fučík would denounce the enemies of the Nazi regime in order to free himself. In Czech culture, Julius Fučík was known as a martyr for his *Notes from the Gallows,* a series of reports that he allegedly wrote on cigarette paper and gradually smuggled out of his cell. After his death, Fučík's notes were edited and published by his wife Gusta; however, several years later the authenticity of the *Notes from the Gallows* was questioned. In the 1990s, it was proved that the work was somewhat altered by Communist censorship to highlight its propaganda message of Fučík's bravery. Prior to this discovery, Kundera had referred to Fučík's cultural contribution in his own works.

There is no doubt that Kundera's was formerly a zealous and dedicated Communist: his earlier work, his statements, his friends, critics, and historians, all attest to this fact. For the most part, his living contemporaries and friends, including the writers Arnošt Lustig, Pavel Kohout, Ivan Klíma, and Milan Uhde, agreed that he was an introvert, a reserved man with a fragile soul who was more critical than destructive and more positive than negative—a positive builder of socialism,[4] as Uhde described him. But he was not a fanatic, many would attest; for instance, when Kundera returned from a trip to the Soviet Union in 1954, he confidentially communicated to Uhde that the October Revolution might have been the most horrible crime of the twentieth century.[5]

In 1956, his membership in the Party was reinstated as a result of the political Thaw that Nikita Khrushchev initiated with his "Secret Speech" at the 20th Congress of the Communist Party of the Soviet Union on February 25, 1956. In his speech, the Soviet leader unveiled a range of atrocities committed by Stalin during his dictatorship and called for the eradication of the Cult of Personality, citing the false accusations made by many citizens, as well as a grim distortion of Marxist-Leninist teaching. The Czech leadership of Antonín Zápotocký followed the Soviet suit and entered the period of de-Stalinization.

THE PERSONAL THAW

In this period, Milan Kundera's trajectory was influenced by his own personal thaw. He contributed his ideas on art to Prague magazines and journals and gave public lectures, gaining a considerable circle of readers and followers. In his article "O sporech dědických" (On Disputes of Inheritance), he raised his voice against censorship that condemned avant-garde poetry as decadent. In reference to his *Poslední Máj,* he pointed out the influence of the European avant-garde on his work, attempting to prove that the avant-garde conformed to the framework of socialist realism. In 1957, he published his third and last collection of poems, *Monology* (Monologues). This highly success-

ful poetry volume on the topic of unrequited love included motifs of antinomy and themes that he would later develop in his novels. At the time of their
appearance, the poems in *Monology* made a strong and continuous impact on
readers until the 1960s. Between 1964 and 1969, Kundera edited and republished them three times with 66,000 copies sold.[6] Even today, these poems
are highly popular among young Czech readers, some praising them as highly as *The Unbearable Lightness of Being*, and due to their sporadic accessibility desiring to see additional reprints. However, the gradual metamorphosis of nearly two decades from Communist poet to worldwide novelist forced
Kundera to critically review his earlier works, both poetry and plays. He
began to regard them as immature, imperfect, or incomplete, especially his
poems. His feelings of discomfort came not only from his initial (most likely,
at that time, honest) beliefs in the greatness and justice of a society built on
teachings of Marxism-Leninism, but also from the simplistic clichés and
propaganda that suffused his poems.

In his *Britské listy,* Jan Čulík disputes that Kundera's "Stalinist verses"
are naïve at first glance; rather, upon further examination, they reveal complex textual structures and motivations. For that reason, Čulík claims, it
remains difficult to explain the author's reasoning behind them. In his view,
Kundera's simplicity serves as a form of accessibility of his verses to the
masses and manual workers with basic education. He calls the Kundera of
this period "a Party functionary of mild progress within the boundaries of the
laws." Čulík explains that Kundera opposed the Stalinist Orthodox regime,
but only moderately—within the laws and only up to a point where his life
and recognition would remain intact. He attributes Kundera's fame during
this period to his becoming an innovator of moderate criticism. In Čulík's
view, there could have been other "innovators" of modern poetry, such as
Catholic poets who composed genuine poetry, but these poets were persecuted and jailed, as their art opposed the aesthetics of socialist realism. Ultimately, Čulík concludes that Kundera's personal involvement with the Communist Party and its doctrine became his life trauma. His life and artistic
trajectory have been "justifying and repairing mistakes of his youth."[7]

While Čulík's statement could be disputed, it holds some facts. Kundera
has continually refused to give rights for reprinting, translating, or otherwise
touching his artistic creations of this period. On the one hand, his works
should not bear the label *autobiographical*; on the other hand, his life struggles as a man, musicologist, poet, playwright, screenwriter, novelist, literary
critic, or painter—in one word, an artist—are interwoven in each of his
works and reflect his ever-changing identity accompanying his personal and
artistic growth. He admits this fact in the words of Ludvik in *The Joke*: "But
which was the real me? Let me be perfectly honest: I was a man of many
faces."[8]

THE KAUZA KUNDERA: A MAN OF MANY FACES

The reality of *"a man of many faces"* struck on October 13, 2008. This was the day when the cultural Prague newsweekly *Respekt* published a piece with a headline "Udání Milana Kundery" (Milan Kundera's Denunciation). Adam Hradilek, the archivist of the Institute for the Study of Totalitarian Regimes, and Petr Třešňák, an editor of newsmagazine *Respekt*, coauthored the piece. They accused Milan Kundera of denouncing Miroslav Dvořáček, a young man who, after fleeing from Czechoslovakia to Germany, was hired by the American Intelligence Service. On March 14, 1950, Dvořáček returned to Prague to complete his secret assignment and while taking a tram he saw his school friend, Iva Militká, walking down the street by the Prague Bridge. He quickly got off to greet her. Walking her to the university dorm, he asked Militká to stow his suitcase there, which he intended to pick up late in the afternoon. But when he returned to fetch his suitcase, two policemen were waiting in his friend's room to arrest him. The storyline itself, on which the argument of denunciation is based, has been quite familiar: its absurdity reminiscent of Josef K.'s situation in Franz Kafka's novel, and its various aspects told and retold in Kundera's novels.

The authors of the *Respekt* article underestimated Kundera's fame in the international arena. Their piece caused uproar in all corners of the world where his works had been read, discussed, studied, analyzed, appreciated, and loved. Foreign newspapers rushed to disseminate the stunning news, focusing on the catchy word *denouncer.* The weekly *Respekt* provided reflections by the authors of the article and interviewed contributors, each of which offered perspectives of varying credibility, trying to prove whether or not Milan Kundera was, in fact, guilty of denouncing the young deserter and spy. On the whole, the article is a one-sided interpretation of the document that Hradilek allegedly stumbled upon while researching to provide facts to his distant relative, Iva Militká, for her intended memoirs on the case.

The magazine cover drawing depicted the threatening, anger-filled, and worried face of Milan Kundera, a pencil with the inscription *District Police Headquarters, Prague 6* stuck behind his ear, an immediate visual representation of the tone of the story inside. The subtitle placed at the bottom of the cover page blared: "A story of a man whom a famous writer in 1950 put into prison for 14 years." Its blatant visual aspect has been criticized in the manner of French structuralism and the persuasive power of labeling by Jakub Češka, a professor of semiotics at Charles University, who departed his critique from Roland Barthes's, *Mythologies* (2004). Nine months after the "Kauza Kundera" (as Czechs named the affair), a journalist of Czech origin and Senior Editor at *The New York Review of Books,* Jana Prikryl, provided a comprehensive outlook on the situation in *The Nation* online. She interviewed Mr. Hradilek, who had just returned home from a Fulbright semester at Columbia University, where the storm that his revelation caused in Prague had not struck him with full force. He defended his piece by stating that "the Czech Republic needs to confront the hard facts of what happened under Communism, one fragment of the ugly mosaic being the police report . . . whose sixty-year-old ink indelibly named Kundera."[9] Hradilek explained to Ms. Prikryl that he was under pressure to publish the article because the story had already leaked. He confided in her that Kundera's name had long been associated with this case, a fact known by Hradilek's relatives and several journalists. But he was taken aback by the "hysteria" his article caused. He attributed its textual misinterpretation to French media, which announced that "Kundera had collaborated with the secret police."[10] Hradilek said that it was not true; this wasn't what his article said. He insisted on the authenticity of the police report, and also stated that the Institute was open to the public to verify the information. "No one would be trying to dig up something on Kundera, because then it would be really like an inquisition institute,"[11] he concluded.

To prove the truthfulness of Hradilek and Třešňák's article, *Respekt* published a copy of the original police report. It is a clearly legible, typewritten document with a number of typos with the corrections retyped over most errors, and other spelling errors remaining. The report was written and signed by the policeman, Jar. Rosický (Jar. being a common abbreviation for Jaroslav). The time frame of 4:00 p.m. and 8:00 p.m. indicates that the report was written after the arrest took place. It is clear that Milan Kundera was not present at the time of the arrest and of the writing of the report. As to the originality of the document, it appears indisputably authentic to the naked eye, and apparently it was examined and confirmed by historians and specialists, Hradilek stated. The one-sheet document has been bound within the arrest report and other documents compiled on Miroslav Dvořáček under the archival code: V 2052 MV. It has been accessible to the public since October 3, 2006 when its "Secret" designation was lifted. Rosický's name appears to be signed with a ballpoint pen rather than an ink pen (the signature does not show typical ink irregularities and color fading, visible with passing years). The report might therefore predate its signature because ballpoint pens were not in common use in Czechoslovakia in 1950. However, the volume of documents on Dvořáček's case contains several other signatures by Rosický and other StB members also signed with ballpoint pen. The text remains faithful to the original as printed in *Respekt*. A number of reports compiled in Dvořáček's dossier remain unsigned, as was customary.

As for the morphology of the text itself, the report contains verbal infinitives ending in -*ti*, a typical spelling of that time, as well as some abbreviations and forms considered archaic or obsolete today (such as, *vstrž., strž., fy, ku, týž, orgánové)*. The words that catch the reader's eye, obviously, are the name of *Milan Kundera,* his date and place of birth—*April 1, 1929 in Brno*—

and his Prague dormitory address, *Tř. Krále Jiřího VI*, all of which information is independently verifiable.

However, one word prominently attracts the reader's attention: the memorable verb *udat*. It was this verb that made Czechs jump out of their skin. Placed right after Kundera's address, it could be utterly misleading at first glance. *Udat* has two meanings, which are distant, and yet somewhat interrelated: a) "to state, say, report;" b) "to denounce." In the text at hand, the past tense form *udal* indicates the meaning of *stating, saying, reporting* (and not *denouncing*) because the subordinate conjunction *že (that)* is attached to the verb: *udal, že (he stated that)*. The meaning of *denouncing* is conferred only if *udat* is followed by a direct object in the accusative case and the grammatical object is a living person (alive or dead), such as *udal muže (he denounced a man)*, which is not the case here. This divergence of meanings roughly corresponds to other forms of verb derivation such as prefixation, as in the English *announce-denounce*.

In summary, the document states that Milan Kundera came to the police station at 4:00 p.m. to say (state or report) that, "in his dorm resides a student, Iva Militká, who told a student, Dlask, from the same dorm, that she had met with a certain acquaintance, Miroslav Dvořáček, the same day in Klárov in Prague. Allegedly, he left one suitcase in her place with an intention of getting it during the afternoon on March 14, 1950."[12] The report does not claim anything else. It does not state or imply anything about Milan Kundera's involvement that would compromise him. He was twenty years old; two weeks shy of his 21st birthday.

Based on this information, the policemen Rosický and Hanton went to Militká's dorm room and searched the suitcase; it contained no sensitive materials: only two hats, two pairs of gloves, two pairs of sunglasses and a small jar with "cream" (which, in fact, was shoe polish). In their narration of the events, the authors of the *Respekt* article deleted the central and crucial part of the official report, in which the reader learns that it was Iva Militká (and *not* Milan Kundera) who told the police that Dvořáček had allegedly deserted the Army and escaped illegally to Germany, where he had allegedly lived since the previous year (1949). Once the list of political defectors was verified and Dvořáček's name found among the blacklisted escapees, the officers Rosický and Hanton remained in Militká's room, waiting for Dvořáček. He was arrested upon entering around 8:00 p.m. (the specific time of 7:30 p.m. is listed in the prison report). During his personal search, the police found an ID bearing his alias name, Miroslav Petr. The twenty-two-year-old Dvořáček stated that a German firm issued his ID card to send him to Czechoslovakia to establish a commercial contact with the Ministry of Technology. Allegedly, he was supposed to contact an engineer named Solman, who was employed by the Ministry.[13]

Kundera, who had been silent for the past twenty-five years, ignoring journalists and anyone who attempted to interview him, finally spoke on the phone from his Paris domicile when the affair erupted. Visibly upset and defensive, his voice agitated and rising, he denied remembering or knowing any actors of the affairs, calling the article—which was published on the day of the Frankfurt Book Fair opening—an "assassination of an author," and imperatively asking and stating that he couldn't have denounced someone whom he didn't know and against whom he had no motives to act. He denied the whole episode, saying, "according to me it is not true." He only wondered how his name got into the sixty-year-old report. "It's the only mystery that I don't know how to explain,"[14] he persisted. Reporters and critics were surprised by his evasive reaction, which was void of solid analytical interpretation and typical Kunderian detachment, as well as a sense of irony and paradox.

By 2008, most people directly involved in the affair, unfortunately, had passed away or appeared to be seriously ill and refused to answer any questions. Only Zdeněk Pešat, a literary historian who resided in the same university dormitory, and knew both Kundera and Dlask, released this statement, referring to March 1950: "Dlask mi řekl, že to oznámil bezpečnosti"[15] (Dlask told me that he announced it to the security). But even Pešat, in poor health and bedridden in 2008, refused to provide further comments to the media. His statement could not be verified because Dlask, the key person, had passed away a decade before the "Kauza Kundera" broke. As imprecise and ambiguous as Pešat's statement is, it could still imply that Dlask had informed security through someone else (here, obviously, Kundera), or that by "security" he meant the Student Head of the dorm, which at that time was Kundera. To question Pešat's statement about Dlask, Militká said that Dlask revealed to her in 1992 that he had told Kundera about Dvořáček on March 14, 1950, after he and Militká had finished lunch that fateful day.

Once the news came out on October 13, 2008, Kundera threatened to sue *Respekt*. However, he later retracted his threat. Apparently he has been warning his friends for years not to release any information about him while he is alive. He doesn't answer the phone, has an assumed name on his doorbell, and refuses to be recognized as Milan Kundera if someone approaches him. He visits his hometown Brno only incognito, registering in hotels under assumed names, and his old Moravian friends say that he loves to wander on his own, starring at the faraway hills of his native Moravia with a misty gaze.

In her article, Jana Prikryl expresses her concern about Kundera's perpetual silence: "As specious as it is to place the civic health of the Czech Republic on Kundera's shoulders, it's also undeniable that he owes the truth, as best as he remembers it, to Miroslav Dvorácek and Iva Militká. Sometimes his antipathy toward the media seems as curdled as the Czechs' allergy to his success."[16]

Does Kundera owe the truth to Dvořáček and Militká?

It is striking that all the blame falls on Kundera alone, especially since it was Militká who provided the essential information on Dvořáček to the police that led to his arrest, as the report *seems* to undeniably state. But here is the catch. The problem is actually a morphological nuance, almost turning the report into a "detective case." The fourth sentence of the report, referring to Militká, is written in the passive voice, which gives *two possible interpretations*, not necessarily noticeable to native speakers even after the first several readings. Due to its flexible word order and the frequent use of nonessential (superfluous) words, especially in spoken language, Czech often can be confusing, in particular to non-native learners of Czech (more details in Chapter Four, Note 13). The fourth sentence can be interpreted as meaning that: a) either the statement was directly produced by Militká, assuming the two police officers came to her room and questioned her, and she gave them the statement about Dvořáček; or b) the statement was made on behalf of Militká by Kundera at the police station. Clearly, Mr. Hradilek and Mr. Třešňák took into consideration the b) possibility and so did Militká. In several interviews conducted in 2008, she insisted on the fact that she never encountered the police. In her recollections she stated that when she returned to the dorm, immediately ("some") two people (meaning two *men* as evident from grammatical ending -*i* in the past tense) took her to the next room (literally, a room opposite from her own) and told her not to do anything foolish. That the person who was supposed to visit her would be arrested and she should not try to (and couldn't) warn him, because it would be pointless, and they locked the door. ("Když jsem pak přišla na kolej, tak mě hned nějaký dva lidi vzali do protějšího pokoje a řekli, ať nedělám hlouposti. Že ten, kdo má ke mně přijít, bude zatčen a že ho nemůžu varovat, protože je to zbytečné, a zamkli dveře."). When she was asked who these two men were, she replied that she didn't know, but that she *did not think* that they were secret police (StB). She thought they were students who were trying to protect her from being involved in the case. They were dressed in casual civilian clothes, and didn't show her any identification or say where they came from (in the original text, Militká claims: "Nevím. Nemyslím si, že estébáci. Myslím si, že to byli studenti, kteří nechtěli, abych se do toho případu zapletla, kteří mě chtěli chránit. Byli oblečeni do domácího. Neukazovali legitimaci, neříkali, odkud jsou"). While she repeated her side of the story with various, slightly different details (in another interview, Militká claimed that the two men were students because they were young), importantly, she made no statement that she was asked or interrogated directly by the two police officers about Dvořáček. Therefore, from her and Hradilek's points of view, she was entirely uninvolved in any direct reporting. For that reason, the authors of the *Respekt* article felt free to delete her name as a culprit when publishing the police report. Inevitably, they assumed that readers would interpret the copy of the actual report (which they pasted in their article) the very same way.

THE LINGUISTIC MYSTERY OF THE POLICE REPORT

However, their interpretation is questionable, if not incorrect, for the obvious following reasons (the original report is free from parentheses as seen in the picture below—here, they are used to indicate the word-for-word translation into English for a better understanding):

1. The first sentence describes who Milan Kundera was, and what he reported: "Iva M i l i t k á, who resides in the dorm, said to a student Dlask of the same dorm that she met today (the same day of the report) a certain acquaintance, Miroslav Dvořáček in Prague at Klárov." (Kundera's and Militká's last names are emphasized by spaces between each letter).
2. The second word in the next sentence is *prý*, and it is *the little secret word* of indirect reporting. It is translated as "apparently, allegedly, the information comes from a second hand—not directly from the speaker," and the speaker or the receiver of the information could question the truthfulness of the information. *Prý* is the key word, communicating that Kundera was told by someone else (we assume by Dlask) that Dvořáček stowed his suitcase in Militká's place (dorm room) with the intention to fetch it in the afternoon.
3. The sequence of the described events follows in chronological order. The third sentence reveals that based on this statement (Kundera's statement), the two police officers, Rosický and Hanton, went to the place (dorm room), where they examined the suitcase. Evidently, this statement implies that Milan Kundera was not with them, nor was he present at the inspection of the suitcase.
4. The *fourth sentence is the key* to properly understanding the report. This is the sentence that gave the Militká and the Hradilek team an opportunity to profit from and distort the interpretation of the report. It states: "According to Militká's declaration (statement), Dvořáček had supposedly deserted the Army (service) and, apparently, since the spring of last year was supposed to be in Germany, to where he illegally departed (left illegally)." The expression *according to Militká* makes the statement clear in English: it was Militká who provided the police with the information on Dvořáček. However, the Czech original is ambiguous and could be interpreted as if Kundera provided this information rather than Militká because Militká is not a grammatical subject in this sentence, or an active grammatical agent, since it is

8—6/4

OVNB 6 odd.II Praha 6.

V Praze dne 14.3.1950.

Z á z n a m :

Dnešního dne o 16 hodině dostavil se ku zdejšímu oddělení studující
Milan K u n d e r a nar.dne 1.4.1929 v Brně,bytem v Praze VII,Student-
ská kolej,Tř.Krále Jiřího VI a udal,že v této koleji bydlí studentka
Iva M i l i t k á,která sdělila studujícímu Dlaskovi a téže koleje,
že téhož dne se sešla na Klárově v Praze s jistým známým Miroslavem
Dvořáčkem.Tento prý si k ní dal do úschovy 1 kufr s tím,že si pro něj
přijde během odpoledne dne 14.3.1950.Na základě tohoto hlášení bděšel
na místo vstřm.Rosický společně se strm.Hantonem,kde provedli prohlídku kufru,ve kterém byly 2 klobouky,2 páry rukavic 2 brýle proti
slunci a krabička krému.Podle prohlášení Militké Dvořáček měl událi-
vě sběhnouti z vojny a snad měl býti od jara minulého roku v Německu
kam ilegálně odešel.Nahlédnutím do knihy pátrání bylo zjištěno,že týž
jest hledán KVNB odd.IV v Plzni pod.č.E 2434/49-IV k zatčení.Na základě tohoto zjištění zůstali výše uvedení orgánové ve studentské koleji střežit v pokoji uvedené Militké.Kolem 20 hodiny se jmenovaný Dvořáček skutečně do tohoto pokoje dostavil a byl zatčen.Při osobní pro-
hlídce u něho byl nalezen občanský průkaz na jméno Miroslav Petr o
kterém Dvořáček prohlásil,že jej dostal v Německu od jisté fy která
jej poslala do československa za účelem navázání obchodních styku této fy s ministerstvem techniky.Týž měl vejíti ve styk s jistým ing.
Solmanem z Vršovic Tolstého ulice č.4 který jest na tomto ministerstvu
zaměstnán.

Jar. Rosický [signature]

[stamp: OBVODNÍ VELITELSTVÍ SC 5]
624/1950-II

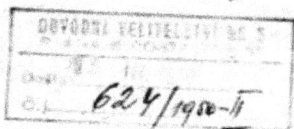

Figure 2.1. Published with Adam Hradilek's permission

written in the passive voice. Nonetheless, it should be clear that this
information was given by Militká (and not Kundera) because the sentence lacks *the little secret word prý,* which—as a marker of indirect
reporting—would indicate that it wasn't Militká who gave this information directly to the police, but someone else, possibly Kundera. It

could imply anyone else, since some time elapsed between Kundera's reporting at the police station and the arrival of the two policemen at the dorm, and Kundera's name no longer figures in the report. However, only if the statement in the fourth sentence of the report were placed immediately after Kundera's report in the first sentence, and only if it would contained *the little secret word prý,* would it be clear and undisputable that it was Kundera who made the statement on Dvořáček's Army desertion and illegal escape to Germany, on the basis of which (as the report states) Dvořáček was arrested.

5. These two possible interpretations entirely imbalanced the whole story and caused tremendous harm to Kundera and his future legacy. For instance, Jana Prikryl grasped the meaning of the report correctly, but on the basis of her deduction, incorrectly states: "two officers went to the dorm, inspected the suitcase and questioned Militká." As shown above, nowhere does the report state that the two officers questioned Militká, and clearly, Militká vehemently denies being questioned. From reading about the general reaction of the public, it is unquestionable that most Czechs interpreted the fourth sentence of the report as in the b) statement; (i.e., the version provided by the Militká-Hradilek team). Subsequently this version was fed to foreign reporters who, without further examination of the original police report, only repeated what Hradilek wrote, often with additional distortions. But more objective and perceptive in the interpretation of the police report has been Harvard professor of Czech literature, Jonathan Bolton, who in his interview with Karel Hvížďala on September 19, 2009 in *iDnes.cz,* noticed the significance of the *suitcase* from the police's viewpoint, and who also criticized Hradilek's approach of the "Kauza Kundera" reporting. However, if there is any doubt about the above-given interpretation in this manuscript, the additional evidence resides in a report by the Deputy Minister for Czechoslovak National Security report, published in a booklet in 1951 (see the last two paragraphs in *The Suitcase, the Bearer of All Evil*).

WHERE IS THE TRUTH?

Of course, any suggestion that Kundera owes them the truth "as best as he remembers it," as Jana Prikryl demands, presumes that he is withholding the truth and must be guilty. He already expressed "his own truth," or *his subjective truth,* over the phone, claiming that the denunciation was a lie *according to him*. He might have been implying that the denunciation was a lie *in his current perception* of himself as the twenty-year-old student. In his novel *Ignorance* (published in 2000), one recalls Josef's perception of himself after he discovered his own *former* identity in his old diaries which he had completely forgotten about, to the degree that he was unable to recall the described events or even recognize his own handwriting. "Josef tries to understand the virgin boy, to put himself in his skin, but he is not capable of it,"[17] the author, Milan Kundera, writes.

A post-modernist, Kundera would not declare the absolute truth about an event that took place six decades ago, because his identities of the past and of the present have diverged entirely. His own truth may not necessarily coincide with reality, but it may be an equally valid reality in his own eyes: a perception of reality as a writer and his commitment to writing. His perspective and his interpretation could be in contrast to a purely objective view of the reality of the distant past. Jana Prikryl might be mistaken in claiming: "He may be damaging his legacy more by refusing to discuss that chapter of his and Dvorácek's lives . . . "[18] For the lack of definitiveness alone, Kundera's works should be read and interpreted by generations to come because they contain mystery and no conclusions.

Needless to say, a number of questions remain unanswered and a one-hundred-percent true conclusion may never be reached. Now *only* Milan Kundera holds the truth, because all others involved have passed away, including Iva Militká in 2015 (as her grandson Matěj Hradilek confirmed in his e-mail to the author of this book). In fact, the episode itself is so Kafkaesque in its account of story reconstruction that it resembles a novelistic outline of its own. There is little to conclude because there is only one *expected* conclusion: Kundera's straightforward *yes*: Yes, I went to the police to report. But careful investigators could have arrived at this conclusion even without Mr. Kundera.

THE THREE ACTORS

Clearly, there are three key actors in the whole episode—Militká, Dvořáček, and Dlask. Quoted in the *Respekt* article, Militká said that she and her family were helping Dvořáček and his friend Juppa—both Czech Military's Air Force Academy students prior to deserting the Army—with their illegal escape to Germany in January 1949. In doing so, Iva Militká's interest was personal, not political. She had known Dvořáček since her childhood and dated his best friend, Juppa, her high school sweetheart. She planned to escape herself (via a fake marriage to a Western citizen) to join her boyfriend, whom she still loved. Encouraging her, Militká's parents were looking to find a fake "husband" for her. But Militká's feelings for her boyfriend turned out to be short-lived. At Charles University she became involved with a student of aesthetics, Miroslav Dlask, a devoted young Communist bursting with enthusiasm, who had lost most of his relatives in concentration camps under Hitler. With no great sorrow, she traded her loyalty to her beloved Juppa for her new boyfriend. Later, she found out that Dlask was assigned to her by the Youth Committee as a "buddy friend" to watch over her during the students' brigade and direct her toward the progressive ideology of the Communist regime. This fact, however, did not change her feelings for Dlask and her dream of a promising bright future.

Paradoxically, she recalls this period as the most beautiful in her life. One day, for instance, she and a friend took a stroll on the Petřín Hill, talking and dreaming. Her friend dreamt about the Soviet Union, and Czechoslovakia becoming one of its Soviet republics. Militká and Dlask sang Czech and Russian folk songs, in happy agreement with everything around them. They loved *Katyusha,* a Russian war song about a soldier who protects the border against the enemy while Katyusha, standing on a steep riverbank, pines for him, singing. "It was truly a wonderful time," Militká said in her interview on October 18, 2008 for *Aktuálně.cz.*[19]

Militká's personality represents a naïve character that is not unknown in Kundera's works. In *The Joke,* readers would recognize a blind devotion to Communist ideals in the strikingly naïve Marketa whose feelings for the Party and her prospective love object, Ludvik, are ridiculously confused. As a couple, Dlask and Militká are partial reminders of the characters Pavel and Helena in their pro-Soviet popular propagandist enthusiasm. Just like Helena in the novel, the real-life young Militká lacked a sense of commitment and clear judgment. In fact, in her interview for *Aktuálně,* she presents herself as bluntly ignorant during that period of Communist enthusiasm. In the political climate of terror, fear, and persecutions, people were proclaimed enemies of the new regime and persecuted. A number of professors and students at Charles University where Militká studied were thrown out, ending up as innocent victims in prison. But she had a wonderful feeling of freedom, she says. She didn't have a radio, didn't read newspapers, never saw a copy of the notorious Communist daily *Rudé právo* (Red Law), and was entirely unaware of political processes. She had a feeling that she could say and do whatever she pleased. It is not surprising that later, when she read Kundera's novel *The Joke,* she resented it. One wonders to what extent she was able to find allusions (intentional or not) to herself and her husband in its fictional characters.[20]

As she admits, Militká had no idea how dangerous it was to escape to the West and return as a spy. Enamored with everything around her, however, she was still thinking of joining Juppa in Germany. In one interview, she claims it was so until the day Dlask assured her of his love for her and convinced her to stay; in another, she reveals it was not until she found out she was pregnant with his child that she changed her mind. Being confused and influenced by the blurred vision of her ideological red glasses, it is no surprise that she brought Dvořáček into her dorm without realizing serious consequences.

In his prison declaration, Dvořáček stated that he warned Militká that it might not be wise to keep his suitcase in her dorm. She didn't see any problems with it and even offered to let him stay overnight. Given his experience in the Czech Military's Air Force, his escape to the West and, having received a thorough training by the secret service in Germany, it was equally childish on his part to keep his suitcase in a university building, a place that was vigilantly watched by Communist apparatchiks. As a spy for the American Intelligence Service, Dvořáček had come to Prague once before but was unable to complete his assignment. At that time, he had an eerie feeling of being watched and followed by the police, so he frenetically changed the course of his destination, succeeding in returning to Munich.

On March 14, 1950, he was dispatched to complete his unfinished assignment; thus, he should have been well aware of the potentially dire consequences of associating with Militká. If nothing else, he should have at least warned Militká to keep his visit to herself and suggest to her that, in the worst-case scenario, she give out his name as Miroslav Petr, as indicated on his fake ID, the only identification he carried to prove his identity (albeit fake).

Naturally, the subjunctive "should have" can't change the course of the history. The reality of the past tense "had" and "have had" has been executed and completed, and each member has paid a high price for performing "had done" instead of "should have done." All her life, Militká felt guilty for the harm she caused, she said in her interviews for *Respekt*, and *Aktuálně.cz*.

Fortunately, Dvořáček's death sentence was reduced to twenty-two years of hard labor, including notorious uranium mines, and luckily he was released after fourteen years of service, thanks to the relaxing of the political climate in the mid-1960s. The farm workers, the Touš family, who twice helped Dvořáček cross the border in the darkness of thick woods, suffered severely once their illegal activity was discovered. One of the farmers was executed, and a number of others spent years as political prisoners in forced labor. Dvořáček's prison report states that the police already knew about the activity of the Touš family, who helped many Czechs crossing the border to Germany. The Touš family members' involvement with Dvořáček only reinforced the reasons for the police to arrest them—it did not seem to have initiated it.

Dlask seems to be the only conspicuous winner in the "Kauza Kundera." Apparently he avoided talking about the incident his entire life, taking the details with him to the grave. The weekly *Respekt* reports that Militká and Dlask married under difficult circumstances: her parents were bitterly opposed to their marriage; nonetheless, the wedding took place because of her pregnancy. It was Dvořáček, the most injured, who actually showed the strength of his character. Even when tortured by prison interrogators, he never released the names of Militká, her parents, or relatives who assisted him and Juppa in their illegal escape in 1949. He knew that his arrest was initiated by Militká, but selflessly spared her whole family persecution. In retrospect, the alleged chain of the denouncement had passed via three stages of the key players, and each could have easily blocked the information before it had reached Kundera and the police: Dvořáček > Militká > Dlask ‖ to > Kundera > Police.

The March 14, 1950 episode, as depicted in *Respekt,* remains full of gaps, holes, and unclear situations, which, like scattered pieces of an intricate puzzle, don't fit quite together. It has been evaluated and reevaluated by many experts, Czech and foreign scholars, ordinary citizens, and Kundera's friends and enemies, with no conclusion reached. Kundera, a solitary soldier, stands alone with his vision of crossing that border, beyond which the existential inquiry begins. The most intriguing elements of this real-life drama seem to grow from little sprouts into sprawling motifs that govern the bulk of Milan Kundera's work: the randomness of events, impulse, love and betrayal, deception, political plight, irrational behavior, secret police, prison—all veiled in confusion and paradoxes, suffering, different levels of various perceptions, and fused into an existential inquiry of *laughter and forgetting.* There is no escaping from this real-life mess and confusion, as there is no escape in Kundera's novels. There are no happy endings. Each character is *trapped by his or her own conscience* and in the history of the time.

THE SUITCASE, THE BEARER OF ALL EVIL

In the Prague Hall of Marxism-Leninism in 1951, Jaroslav Jerman, the Deputy Minister for Czechoslovak National Security, delivered a public lecture titled, "O obraně země proti vnitřním a vnějším nepřátelům" (On Defending Our Country against Internal and External Enemies), which was then printed under the same title in a twenty-page booklet in 22,000 copies by the Svoboda Publishers. In his speech, Jerman encouraged the cooperation of the public with the police to uncover anti-regime activities. He emphasized the responsibility of each honest citizen who loved his country and family to help the police just as Soviet people did.

> "We have to deal with the fact," he continued, "that some of our people still look upon cooperation with security organizations as denunciation. He who collaborated with police during capitalism and [Nazi] occupation was a denouncer. But today, when it is the people who are in power, reporting any kind of suspicion or case of criminal activity is not denouncing. We have to convince our people that it is a civic duty; and that such an action protects our country, every single person, his or her family and children."[21]

Jerman's words about each citizen's *civic duty* to report anything suspicious sounds quite familiar. In our current age of global terrorism, the governments of progressive countries, including the United States, distribute a similar message: *If you see something, say something.* And often, when people do report "something," their acts save innocent lives.

Jerman's speech took place one year after the Dvořáček episode. But the buzzing motto of encouraging people to report unusual situations had been circulating since the Communist government took power in 1948. As a propaganda slogan, it had been used by prior regimes as well, particularly during the German occupation and WWII. In these situations the human instinct is *fear within fear*. People are *afraid to report* and, by the same token, they are *afraid not to report* because not reporting could be harmful as well. After all, they could be accused of being guilty of hiding crucial evidence, and the punishment for that is equally severe: imprisonment or death.

Several days after the "Kauza Kundera" came into its existence, a journalist, researcher, and editor, Adam Drda, published a short opinion-plus piece in the newspaper *Hospodářské noviny* (Economic News),[22] in which he addressed the issue of denouncing as a daily occurrence in a totalitarian system. After analyzing a number of police reports from the past, Drda arrived at the conclusion that *voluntary reporters* played a critical role in enhancing the country's stability. They enjoyed a privileged position and certain advantages: at times, only their partial names or initials were recorded, their names did not appear on official roasters, they were not pressured to sign their declarations, and they were not subject to additional questioning. In the new democracy of the post-1989 Velvet Revolution, *voluntary reporters* were free of the lustration process, a law that was introduced in Czechoslovakia under President Václav Havel to uncover the actors of atrocities committed by the Communist regime. They are called here *silent helpers*. They were valuable for their deeds, not for their names; occasionally, their names were purposely omitted. In many cases, *silent helpers* had no reason to denounce except for their civic duty; in other cases, driven by envy or jealousy, they intended to harm acquaintances or neighbors whom they disliked for one reason or another (the occurrence of getting neighbors arrested in Soviet Russia to get their apartment has been described in Alexander Solzhenitsyn's *Cancer Ward* with all its consequences affecting both sides, the denouncers and the injured). If their denouncement was uncovered later, it usually occurred in connection with unrelated cases, not by conducting a systematic search.

In his article, Mr. Drda gives an example of the horrific simplicity of *silent helpers* from a report dated 1949. A resident of the village Nebesa (Heavens), in western Czechoslovakia near Germany, told the police that a short while before a young man had asked him how far and in what direction the border was located. The police patrol reached the young man and, because he refused to stop after their instructions, they started shooting. He collapsed, his intestines bulging out of his body. He died in the local hospital shortly after the patrol brought him in. His name, Josef Polek, was released, but the name of the villager, *the silent helper*, has remained unknown.

Drda gives yet another example of reporting, this time a laughable one, from the so-called normalization period. An independent good-cause "Czech Children" foundation that was formed in the late 1980s distributed promotional pamphlets in neighbors' mailboxes. A significant percentage of citizens went to the police to report the "suspicious" documents found in their mail.[23] This harmless but simplistic episode proves to what degree an oppressive regime would brainwash people and how—out of fear and a sense of self-preservation—it drove them to commit deeds that undermined rationality and decent logic.

Milan Kundera's reason for the alleged reporting at the police station in Prague 6 can be summarized as follows: he had no reason and yet every reason to do it. As the Student Head of the university dormitory, he had an obligation to maintain order and report anything suspicious. In the tense political climate, one *suitcase* brought in by an unknown outsider could certainly qualify for further investigation by authorities. If he hadn't pointed it out, he might have been punished for not reporting it.

However, if Kundera intended to bring anything to the attention of the police, it was the object, *the suitcase*, and not the people named in the report, just like the police report indicates. The stylistic approach of the report is evidence of this fact: *one suitcase* (along with the indication of time specifications) becomes the key information in the sentence and is placed last, in a position of emphasis, to reveal the purpose of the message. The names of the three actors, Militká and Dlask (insiders) and a *certain* Dvořáček (an outsider) function only to verify the truthfulness of the statement and to identify the location of the action. The three names stand on the same structural level of the sentence; they all play a similar role in acknowledging the existence of *the suitcase* in the dorm: Dvořáček—in his possession of it, Militká—allowing it in and leaving it in, and Dlask, the passive witness, actively acknowledging its reality and tangibility by unequivocally trusting his girlfriend's message. If, indeed, Kundera had gone to the police station, he might have revealed the names of the three actors as proof of credibility, and possibly on the insistence of the officer Rosický. The report does not include this information.

The following sentence of the report supports the thesis of *reporting an object* (the *suitcase*) and *not denouncing a person* (Militká, Dlask, and a *certain* Dvořáček): "Based on this report [of Milan Kundera], the officer Rosický, together with the officer Hanton, left for the location where they searched the *suitcase*, in which were 2 hats, 2 pairs of gloves, 2 pairs of sunglasses and a small jar of cream."[24] This English sentence is a word-for-word translation of the Czech original. As indicated before, until the point when Kundera's name became involved and after the police arrived in the dorm and searched the contents of the *suitcase*, there had been no mention of an agent of Western intelligence, army deserter or illegal escapee. Dvořáček was perceived as an ordinary citizen, albeit suspicious because of his *suitcase* stored in a dorm he didn't belong to.

It is unclear why Dlask would have had the urge to share the March 14 morning episode with Kundera. Some sources suggest it might have been because of his jealousy; after all, Militká told Dlask that Dvořáček might stay overnight. Others say that he intended to protect his girlfriend from potential consequences. In his report of April 2009 on the "Kauza Kundera," Jan Kalous from the Institute for the Study of Totalitarian Regimes enters a footnote in which he quotes from the so-called reminiscent novel *Oblouk* (An Arc) by Jiří Stránský, a former political prisoner. It was published by Nakladatelství Hejkal, Havlíčkův Brod, one year after the events took place. In his book, Stránský supports the "jealousy" thesis. Jan Kalous quotes a brief conversation with Mirda (a domestic form of Miroslav and an allusion to Dvořáček) who told him that he knew that he who had denounced him was a writer. The writer was a friend of a young man (allusion to Dlask) who dated a girl (allusion to Militká) whom he, Mirda, knew well because he had dated her previously. Driven by jealousy, the young man (allusion to Dlask) complained to his friend-writer about Mirda's presence in his girlfriend's room, and his friend-writer replied that he would take care of it ("že to zařídí"). Then the narrator of the novel says: "I'm sure that Milan Kundera didn't do it to harm but understandably because he worried about his writing, which made him famous around the world."[25] This refers to the denouncement that took place in 1950 (and not to Kundera's reaction to the 2008 episode), and clearly lacks logical sense (at least the way it is presented in Kalous's note). In 1950, Kundera was a student, not a well-known writer (his first book of poetry only came out in 1953).

Dvořáček apparently suffered a stroke after being contacted in 2008 by Hradilek concerning his article in the *Respekt* magazine. Like others involved in the case, he refused to speak to the press. In the summer of 1968, after the Soviet invasion of the country, he successfully exited Czechoslovakia, and lived in Sweden until his death in 2012. He remained convinced that it was Militká who had denounced him and said that it did not make any difference to him whether it had been she, Kundera, or anyone else. Unlike Kundera's novelistic character Ludvik in *The Joke*, Dvořáček did not blame anyone but himself for his arrest and his long years of hard labor.

As evidenced from the above examples, reports on the case have been contradictory and inconsistent, and statements and quotes have often been taken out of context. They contradict not only one another but at times the contradiction occurs within the single authorship in one article. Reports published in languages other than Czech often carry additional textual nuances and misinterpretations, linguistic and cultural, disseminated by foreign sources. Milan Kundera has been painfully aware of the *phenomenon of truth distortion*, calling it *journalistic reduction* of complexity to simplicity, and exposing it to critical examination, particularly in his *Immortality*.

As fascinating as it might be, it is also painful to read the original reports of Dvořáček's arrest and imprisonment, released by the Institute for the Study of Totalitarian Regimes, and available in their original form in the archives and online. Kundera's name no longer figures in these documents; it was customary to release selected information to the accused, and ultimately, it was the accused who was forced to speak, not the interrogators. However, Kundera's initials reappear once again in the official police documents in connection with the case, in the lecture given by Jaromír Jerman in 1951.

In his speech, the Deputy Minister for National Security praises the student M.K., extolling him as an example of a good citizen. He summarizes the March 14, 1950 episode, giving initials M.K., and M.E. only. Militká's initials M.E. (as in Militká Eva) were misrecorded either on purpose or in error. The name of Dlask is omitted, but the name of Miroslav Dvořáček is spelled out fully. Like in the original report, Jerman claims that two National Security (SNB) members (police officers) went to the female student's room and searched the *suitcase*, which they found "bez závad" (free of defects), that is, free of sensitive documents. This search was initiated by the information M.K. had brought to the attention of the police. Jerman continues: "However, during the search the female student reported that Dvořáček deserted the army and escaped to Germany." Only after *her report*, the two officers remained in her room, waiting for Dvořáček in order to arrest him, emphasizes Jerman.[26]

What are the conclusions of the Kauza Kundera?

In all likelihood, Milan Kundera was involved in the case, at least to some extent. The two documents mentioning his name—one using his full name and the other his initials—serve as written historical evidence. Unless both were forged in later years—which is highly unlikely—these two reports reveal the truth.[27]

IN THE MIDDLE OF THE STORM

In his defense, Kundera gave an interview to ČTK, the Czech Press Agency, on March 13, 2008, the audio of which is available online on *Novinky.cz*.[28] In defending himself and referring to Dvořáček, he said: "I never saw that person, I didn't know him at all, that's the only thing I remember."

Clearly, Kundera admits remembering something: a situation in which he *never saw that person*, and *didn't know him at all*, a correct statement, according to the police report (the adjective *jistý, "a certain"* in reference to

Dvořáček implies that he didn't know him). Saying *the only thing I remember* evokes itself a specific situation. Had he not known and never heard of this situation, his reaction would have been a pure detachment and honest and stunning surprise, not an agitated and angry response. In reference to Militká, Kundera stumbled on the verb *to recall*, "a já tu paní Militkou si neumím předst . . ." (and that Mrs. Militká, I cannot reca . . . her), correcting the unfinished verb *představit si* (recall, imagine) immediately into *taky neznám* (neither I do know [her]). Yet, in his handwritten note he dedicated his first volume of poetry to her and her husband (see the illustration in Chapter Five).

As for his name showing up in the report, Kundera acknowledges it, saying that "it is a mystery to me how it got in there," and he doesn't know how to explain it. He repeats it several times, using *záhada* (mystery), and partially swallowing the word *tajemství* (secret). A great master of words, Kundera had no intention of using the noun *secret*; it looks as if he realized in the process of thinking that *tajemství* could be a damaging word, and he swallowed its ending so listeners could easily miss it.[29] He also suggested that someone else might have used his name to pretend to be he, Milan Kundera. However, he did not elaborate on this idea, nor did he mention any name, including Dlask's.

All this "evidence" supports the idea that, if Kundera went to the police station, his decision was based on the impulse *if you see something, say something*. Furthermore, it supports the conclusion that Kundera went to report only a *suitcase* that was brought into the section of the university dormitory that he was in charge of supervising.

And finally, arguments supporting Kundera's involvement are the literary devices in his novels. The motif of a *suitcase* repeats frequently, and motifs of hats and sunglasses to a certain degree too.[30] Often they drive the plot and become subjects of analytical interference or philosophical conclusions. *The suitcase* functions as a premonition of something sinister to happen; in many novels, it is *the bearer of all evil*, a heavy dose of the expectation of alarming revelations.

Despite all the arguments for and against, Milan Kundera should be exonerated of the *denouncer* label *attributed to him* by the *Respekt* magazine and by the media. By spreading falsely interpreted information about him, they have depreciated his character, his works, and his role as a writer. They have deprived him of the possibility of being nominated for and possibly receiving the Nobel Prize for literature that he rightly deserves.

NOTES

1. Milan Kundera, *Life Is Elsewhere*, trans. Peter Kussi (New York: Penguin Books, 1986), vi.

2. Adam Hradilek, "Udání Milana Kundery," *Respekt*, no. 42 (December 10, 2008): 40–41.
3. Hradilek, "Udání Milana Kundery," 40. My translation of the text is as close as possible to the Czech original. Occasionally, the wording is adapted to idiomatic English for better comprehension. In this quote, for instance, the word-for-word translation is: "The Soviet Union and our country ever and forever together are."
4. Hradilek, "Udání Milana Kundery," 40–43.
5. Hradilek, "Udání Milana Kundery," 40–43.
6. Milan Blahynka, "Čekání Milana Kundery," *Světová literature živě* (April 3, 2009): www.literarni.cz
7. Jan Čulík, "Byla éra stalinismu dobou 'naivní bezstarostnosti'?" *Britské listy* (October 25, 2002): http://blisty.cz/art/11931.html
8. Kundera, *The Joke*, 33.
9. Jana Prikryl, "The Kundera Conundrum: Kundera, Respekt and Contempt: How Did Milan Kundera Antipathy toward the Media Become as Curdled as the Czechs' Allergy to His Success?" in *The Nation* (May 20, 2009): https://www.thenation.com/article/kundera-conundrum-kundera-respekt-and-contempt/
10. Prikryl, "The Kundera Conundrum."
11. Prikryl, "The Kundera Conundrum."
12. Hradilek, "Udání Milana Kundery," 40–41.
13. Hradilek, "Udání Milana Kundery," 40–41. This close translation of mine attempts to preserve the style of the report. In prison reports, the small jar with cream was itemized as a shoe polish container.
14. Zdeněk Pešat, "V Kunderově kauze udával student Dlask, tvrdí pamětník," in *Novinky.cz* (October 15, 2008): https://www.novinky.cz/domaci/152041-v-kunderove-kauze-udaval-student-dlask-tvrdi-pametnik.html
15. Zdeněk Pešat, "V Kunderově kauze udával student."
16. Prikryl, "The Kundera Conundrum."
17. Milan Kundera, *Ignorance*, trans. Linda Asher (New York: HarperCollins Publishers, 2002), 81.
18. Prikryl, "The Kundera Conundrum."
19. "Kauza Kundera: Přes 50 let žiji s pocitem viny." An interview with Iva Militká by Eliška Bártová and Ludvík Hradilek for *Aktuálně* (October 18, 2008): www.aktualne.cz
20. "Kauza Kundera."
21. Jan Kalous, "K obsahu jedné přednášky. Jaroslav Jerman o Dvořáčkově případu, Studie a články," *Paměť a dějiny*, Praha: Ústav pro studium totalitních režimů, no. 4 (2009): 48. http://www.ustrcr.cz/data/pdf/pamet-dejiny/pad0904/048-051.pdf
22. Adam Drda, "Problém udavače aneb Komu je Kundera podobný?" in *Hospodářské Noviny* (October 16, 2008): 11.
23. Drda, "Problém udavače aneb."
24. Kalous, "K obsahu jedné přednášky," 48.
25. Kalous, "K obsahu jedné přednášky," 48. In the novel *Oblouk*, this episode is depicted on pp. 138–39.
26. Here is the original printed in *Paměť a dějiny*, Studie a články: „K obsahu jedné přednášky. Jaroslav Jerman o Dvořáčkově případu" by Jan Kalous on p. 50: „Dne 14. III. 1950 dostavil se na okresní oddělení VB v Praze 6 studující M. K. a oznámil, že studentka M. E. sdělila jeho kolegovi, že se sešla na Klárově se svým známým Miroslavem Dvořáčkem a tento prý ji požádal o uschování kufru, pro který si prý přijde během odpoledne. Na základě tohoto hlášení odešli dva příslušníci SNB do bytu studentky a udělali prohlídku kufru, jehož obsah byl však bez závad. Během prohlídky však jmenovaná prohlásila, že Dvořáček zběhl z vojny a uprchl do Německa. Po této výpovědi orgánové čekali v uvedeném bytě na Dvořáčka a po jeho příchodu tohoto zatkli."
27. The author of this book carefully examined the original document and the whole Dvořáček's file in the Archiv bezpečnostních služeb, Na Struze 3, Praha 1. There is no doubt that the report is the original. Curiously enough, Milan Kundera questioned the mystery of how his name got into the document but did not question the authenticity of the report.

28. Video included in Zdeněk Pešat's article in *Novinky.cz* (October 15, 2008): https://www.novinky.cz/domaci/152041-v-kunderove-kauze-udaval-student-dlask-tvrdi-pamet-nik.html

29. Video included in Zdeněk Pešat's article.

30. The motif of a hat figures in *The Book of Laughter and Forgetting*, as well as in *The Unbearable Lightness of Being*, and of sunglasses in *Immortality*. Using these two items by Kundera might be a random choice; though he might have known via rumors they were inside of Dvořáček's suitcase.

Chapter Three

The Suitcase, the Bearer of All Evil

THE BRIEFCASE

To grasp Milan Kundera's identity, it is necessary to observe him, the creator, in relation to his fictional characters who have crossed that *border that attracts him the most*, as he puts it, and *where his I ends*. It is where the secret of the novel lies, he tells his readers. And inevitably, it is where the secret of the author's mind and concerns lie as well. It is where his identity is veiled in mystery.

Kundera calls a writer "an explorer" who seeks to uncover the unknown part of existence through his thoughts, expressed by his voice and presented in a form suitable to a literary work. Citing Herman Broch, Vladimir Nabokov, and William Faulkner, he summarizes the approach to revealing the author's biography through a common metaphor: it is like destroying "the house of his life" and rebuilding "the house of his novels" from the same material—stones. His metaphor is of note—one structure (author's life) is rendered into another (author's novel). It also implies that the "stones of an author's life" remain to form a new structure, "a novel built from the author's life stones." One might add two more items, the substances of rebuilding: the foundation and mortar. After the building is completed, then comes the biographer to undo the novelist's house and redo it with his own foundation and mortar. "All their labor cannot illuminate either the value or the meaning of a novel, can scarcely even identify a few of the bricks,"[1] argues Kundera and compares Kafka to Josef K. What will happen the moment the author attracts more attention than his novelistic character? "Kafka's posthumous death begins,"[2] he replies.

The reverse order of deconstruction and reconstruction is far from a scientific method of learning about an author's identity; however, it should

43

illuminate, at least to a certain degree, the path on which he has been walking and what has taken him onto such a particular road.

In the case of Kundera's path, it is encumbered with a *suitcase*. The *suitcase* is the foundation of his "house of the novel," and it has been actively present throughout his novels. The imagery of a *suitcase* seems to correspond to a real-life valise that caught young Kundera's attention on March 14, 1950 when he, as a freshly devoted Communist, most likely on an impulse, allegedly informed the police about its appearance in a dorm room of a female student.

"Something unavoidable hung in the air,"[3] tells the narrator in *Life Is Elsewhere*, in a scene where Jaromil, desperate to distance himself from his controlling mother and obsessed with losing his virginity, finally puts his hand around a girl and squeezes her arm. The girl, a university student, had approached him at a proletarian poetry meeting, admiring his eloquence during the discussion. Speaking in the self-assured voice of his mentor—a surrealist painter—Jaromil overcame the feeling of his youthful insecurity and joined the debate by defending André Breton's surreal art of poetic expression and hidden meanings of the subconscious in a manner of his mentor-painter. Jaromil repeated the painter's ideas, contrasting them with the celebratory proletarian verses of Jiří Wolker, the founder of Czech working-class poetry. Excited by his success in the debate, the girl's close proximity, and her admiration for his intellectual poet's mind, he touched her in the park where they took a stroll, still ecstatically discussing poetry; he being unaware of the girl's *briefcase*. When she drops it by his feet, it alerts him: "The briefcase thus dropped on the scene like a message from heaven,"[4] reveals the narrator, and the thump of the briefcase initiated the couple's prolonged intimacy of passionate kissing. After this brief prelude to lyric love, the girl picks up her briefcase and only now Jaromil notices that it is "heavy and impressive looking, full of books." The idea of the briefcase containing "material of higher learning" intoxicates him. The couple makes another, seventh round in the park and pauses to kiss again. When their kiss is over, a bright light illuminates their silhouettes and *two policemen* approach them, demanding their identification cards. The narrator reveals that with their trembling fingers, they handed their ID cards over to the policemen. And when Jaromil got home, his anxious mother reproached him, and "a sense of some dark guilt began to spread over him."[5]

XAVIER'S BRIEFCASE

However, the most evocative scene where the foundation is the *briefcase*—an allusion to the real life *suitcase*—is in Part 2: "Xavier," in *Life Is Elsewhere*. It is written in a highly surreal mode, one image overlapping another in the form of dreams. Like mortar, the images and symbols are supporting details that hold together the structure of rebuilding "the house of this novel, of this tale." Xavier enters onto the scene as a student in the springtime, few years after the war, during the 1948 revolution period. He carries a *briefcase*, which connects his life as a student with his life in the real world. He walks on Prague's Charles Bridge, and leaps over the windowsill of a yellow house located near the bridge; he used to pass by the house, but its window was always closed. Now it is open, a rococo cage with a bird visible on the wall. Xavier throws his brown *briefcase* into the room, then he leaps again to follow his briefcase, leaving the ledge and a moat paved with stones below him.

Kundera creates Xavier as a surrealistic alter-ego persona of Jaromil. His name is derived from the Basque place name *Etxa berri*, meaning "a new house," (*Xaberri* > *Xabier* in Basque, and *Xavier* in Old Spanish), and birthplace of Saint Francis Xavier, one of the founders of the Jesuit Society. Xavier appears in Jaromil's fantasies and seems to reach whatever Jaromil wishes but is unable to accomplish. He gains admiration from women, seduces them and betrays them, crosses permitted boundaries, causes the death of an authority figure/policeman, and carries secrets that have an impact on society. But Xavier really isn't a man of action; he is an eternal dreamer who does not "live one single life" but several lives at one time, stepping from one "life" into another, from one dream into another, and into yet another, piling up dream after dream like one box inserted into another, a bigger one, and into the next even bigger, continuing endlessly from box to box or dream to another dream.

Once inside the room, the focus remains on Xavier's *briefcase* under his feet. As soon as he tries to reach for it, a woman appears in the door. Both surprised, they stare at one another; then Xavier points at the *briefcase*, explaining that it is "full of important things." The narrator arouses the readers' curiosity, attunes them to expect the unexpected but immediately disappoints them with the *briefcase*'s content: a math notebook, a science class textbook, and a composition workbook. The Czech composition titled *How Spring Arrived This Year* gains the primary importance. Xavier explains to the woman that it wasn't easy for him to write it and he would hate to have to rewrite it, and how annoying it would have been to lose the *briefcase*, stressing the significance of his composition homework. If he lost it, he would fail the course and would have to repeat the class. Could this be an allusion to Kundera's fear of possibly being excluded from the university (not only from the Party as he was), as some of his friends from students' years have suggested? Their reasoning was that he could have regarded "a strange *suitcase*" as a set trap to see how he, the student-in-charge of the dorm, would react to it.

The conversation exchange about the *briefcase* takes almost two pages in this part of the novel. Xavier and the woman are reassuring one another how good it is that the *briefcase* is there. She listens to him while he speaks; he observes her gestures, her "nebulous face" of "softness, melancholy and fright" over something that "happened to her long ago." He squeezes her shoulder, but she tells him he needs to leave because her husband is coming. Xavier, sensing the upcoming danger, decides to stay to protect her. He throws himself under a bed, trying to catch a glimpse of the husband, but sees only his boots. During the woman's intercourse with her husband, the bed "sways rhythmically" above Xavier, but he remains powerless until he sneezes. The sneeze alerts the husband. He notices the *briefcase* and walks to the wardrobe, rummaging in it to find an intruder. Xavier gets out from under the bed and grabs the husband by the collar; now he sees that the husband is dressed in the dark blue uniform of a policeman. From this point on, the scene becomes more surreal. Xavier shoves the policeman inside, locks the wardrobe and keeps the key, laughing about the woman's prospect of finding her husband's skeleton dressed in a police uniform and boots a year later.

After the brief intimate interlude, encouraged by the yellow glow of the setting sun that entered the room, Xavier invites the woman to follow him on his journey to "a new home." This new home is where a wardrobe and birdcage don't matter; only the presence of a loved one is of the essence. He is set to go, the woman—now his beloved—becomes an "aquatic being"; he lies down, the Prague river murmurs, everything becomes quiet and blue (a symbol of death in poetry, exemplified by the German Romantic movement and represented by the poet, Novalis). The policeman is condemned to death in the wardrobe and Xavier is condemned to his dream that will lead to another dream and yet another one.

By now, the reader understands that Xavier has his own rules of living: his dream is his life, and real life is his dream. His next dream is a journey with his classmates to a mountain cottage. Here, the narrator reveals crucial information about Xavier (and possibly about Milan Kundera). He gets onto the train in the last moment, "in the nick of time, at the eleventh hour," proud and dragging his *briefcase*. His "quite unexpected" last-minute arrival happened "thanks to a sudden impulse," reveals the narrator. Once on the train, Xavier wonders what "possessed him to take part" in this journey with his classmates. He finds them boring: their lives void of surprise and adventure, they follow their schedules punctually and to the minutest detail, obeying "blindly, automatically," and "without a single mistake," what they have been taught. Xavier is singled out in many other respects; for instance, for being the only one without skis on this trip. Once off the train, he interacts with an older woman in a red sweater; however, his mind is on one of his female classmates, a little "snowmaiden" with big blue eyes that he noticed on the platform of the train. She watches Xavier out in the freezing weather through a window of a house into which the woman in a red sweater took him. Xavier's two overlapping dreams are framed by a third one: he is back on Prague streets, hearing gunfire at a distance; he is alone, stalking through winding streets and looking around to make sure that no one sees him.

Chapter 10 is a reminder of Josef K.'s journey to the court, a walk through a series of unusual rooms, a path full of treacherous deviations and odd encounters with people who seem to know more than he about his case and his guilt. Similarly, Xavier is led through rooms with odd surroundings to the basement; there sit three men around a table, and he is asked to provide the list with people's names. The list is a part of his composition *How Spring Arrived This Year*, so he needs to retrieve it but can't find his *briefcase*. The man in the cap asks twice where the *briefcase* is. In a short paragraph, the author gives a poetic account of Xavier's thoughts; he is trying to remember where the *briefcase* could be. Once he admits he doesn't have it, the man in the cap reproaches him—if the list falls into the hands of the enemy, "all their hopes would be ruined." Xavier feels guilty not having the list and to "wipe out his guilt," he proposes to lead the men so they would not risk their lives.

The next three short chapters of the Xavier part are filled with a dream-like sequence of hallucinations. In the darkness of a courtyard, Xavier hears gunfire, searchlights illuminate the roof of a five-story building where Xavier climbs over small iron ladders, hiding behind chimneys, and the men he leads are waiting in the courtyard for his directions. He seems to be hearing Frédérique Chopin's *Marche Funèbre* played at a country funeral. The funeral march evokes in him a fusion of his own life with death; he is drowning in a confusion of his own senses—the melancholy of funeral music overshadows hearing the enemy that lay "treacherous snares."

Xavier wakes up into another dream, now lying on the bed in the room with the wardrobe (with the policeman inside). He looks out of the window and sees a funeral procession; mourners dressed in black against the background of white patches of snow, a coffin laid next to a grave, a hole freshly dug up. As the coffin descends, Xavier joins the mourners; his attention centered on an old couple sobbing (the parents of the deceased). Xavier, standing last in the procession line, throws a handful of soil mixed with snow onto the casket. Thus far, the reader doesn't know who is being buried or why, but the narrator tells us that Xavier, a total stranger to the mourners, is "the only one who knew everything that had occurred."[6] In fact, it is the "snowmaiden," a blond girl with big blue eyes in a white dress that Xavier met in the mountains that is being buried. She longed for him in the freezing cold, watching him sadly through the window. The mountain landscape of the funeral is blurred by Xavier's reflection on the knowledge that only he knows—this is repeated twice and dominates his thoughts—the visual of the funeral details (gravediggers' shovels, mourners, dead body) blending with the vastness of the landscape (meadows, hills), which provokes a feeling of sorrow in him. Now he sees his own body as a mask, his body cloaked in a mask, and a hand strokes his face, which he recognizes as "the hand of forgiveness." In the final lines of the Chapter 12, the narrator sets this funeral scene by a motif of Romanticism in poetry: love stronger than death, it will "live beyond the grave."

Chapter 13 depicts Xavier's overlapping vivid dreams; one begins before the previous is gone; each dream brings hands caressing him, each belonging to a different woman as they appear in the scenes of his series of dreams. The hands (of forgiveness) are detached from their bodies and heads, entirely free, floating in space and Xavier wishes they would caress him eternally. In the concluding Chapter 14, Xavier wakes to the initial dream of the house by the Charles Bridge. The woman, the policeman's wife, is waking him up because she is scared of the firing squad that is moving from the bridge into each household, "dragging people out and executing them." Again, the thought of arrest and execution is attached to the list of names of enemies (of the revolution); the list that is only in Xavier's possession. He wants to get out to join his comrades, with whom he planned the events (the arrests and executions), but which he slept entirely through in his dreams.

In the last paragraphs, drawn with intensity, the reader senses the urgency Xavier feels. Without his list, no one knows whom to arrest and whom to execute: "the revolution is blind and ignorant." Despite his strong desire to deliver the list, Xavier realizes that he doesn't know the passcode to unlock it. In people's eyes he is a traitor; therefore, no one would believe him if he releases the names without the list. In his mind, he reaches a compromise: he was in a different life (dream) when all this occurred, and since there is no way for him to save that previous life (people), he could, at least, elevate ("ennoble") the life that he is currently living. And when the woman tells him to take her along as he had promised, he replies that it was long ago, and that he must betray her by departing into real life, the world outside, behind the window of her room.

THE AUTHOR'S PASSCODE: INTERPRETATION OF XAVIER'S PRESENCE IN THE NOVEL

Reading carefully the Xavier part, one wonders to what extent it contains the hidden, "secret code" to the "Kauza Kundera." There have not been many critical articles produced on Xavier, and no one seems to be inclined to "crack the code." Within the periphery of scholarly analysis, Xavier is interpreted as a surreal persona of Jaromil, a bizarre character of bold accomplishments and desire for women. Novelistically speaking, there are no real accomplishments; Xavier has produced more negative destruction than positive deeds. Of course, one should challenge the "reality of the text" not only because it is written in the form of dreams but also because the text is a part of a novel and the novel is not a representation of real life. That's where the author has an upper hand over the reader; he plays with him to complete exhaustion. However, a close examination of Xavier's tale indicates that it was written with a specific intent, not just a textual representation of surrealism and poetry.

Within the lines of psychoanalytic criticism, one could apply Sigmund Freud's theory of symbols and dreams to Xavier's actions to determine what is beneath the surface of his unlikely personality and possibly of the author's *id*. A question surfaces: to what extent did the author's "subconscious" influence the creation and behavior of Xavier?

The most obvious symbol in Xavier's tale is the *briefcase*, inside which is the crucial evidence in the form of a *list of people,* hidden on the last page of the composition about the spring arrival that particular year. The title *How Spring Arrived This Year* is peculiar as well. The official date of spring's arrival in Prague is March 21, and the "Kauza Kundera" event took place just one week before, on March 14. The reader doesn't learn what event is described in the composition, except for two facts: it is extremely important for the continuation of Xavier's studies and above all, for the information on the list, which is cleverly hidden in the composition text. One assumes that its title refers to Xavier's events as described in the novel.

Additional symbols are the *woman* in the room near the Charles Bridge and her husband, the policeman. The woman, whose name we don't learn, is the key person to Xavier's journey—all the events that follow result from this intersection. Initially, Xavier stays to protect her against the danger that the policeman poses to her, despite being her husband. For instance, he could arrest her, among many of the other harms he could impose on her. Symbolically, he did harm her by forcing himself upon her, if not raping her. Hidden under the bed, Xavier heard the woman repeatedly shouting no, no, no, no to the policeman's advances. Once Xavier has locked him in the wardrobe, the woman is safe, but remains "a prisoner" in the room. This scene, inevitably, evokes the image of the real situation described in Militká's interview. After she had released the information to the police about Dvořáček's deserting the Army and his illegal escape to Germany, she was locked in a dorm room across from hers by two men (though she did not confirm they were police officers), who told her that Dvořáček would be arrested, and ordered her to cooperate and be silent.

Xavier betrays the woman by departing into his life of dreams, without taking her along as he promised. At the end of the tale, after his awaking into the "reality" of his first dream, he betrays her once more, saying openly: "Yes, I'll betray you."[7] He does it because the world beyond her existence and beyond the "window of her room" is more enticing and beautiful. In view of the "Kauza Kundera," Xavier's journey could be interpreted as fol-

lows: the student, Milan Kundera, betrayed the woman, Iva Militká, by
spreading the message (to the police) about the presence of a *suitcase* in her
room. As he predicted in his novel, he would betray her by publicly denying
knowing her, as occurred in his interview with *ČTK* on March 13, 2008.

Betrayal is one of the most prominent, if not governing, themes in Kundera's works. It appears in a variety of social, political, and religious situations
as well as personal interactions in almost every work, including his first play,
Owners of the Keys. For instance, in *The Unbearable Lightness of Being*,
Sabina betrays her lover Franz after he asks his wife for a divorce, and
suggests to Sabina that they move in together. She disappears without a trace
by moving to Paris, remaining for him "an invisible goddess" of spiritual
admiration. Sabina is the epitome of betrayals. The narrator says: "One could
betray one's parents, husband, country, love, but when parents, husband,
country, and love were gone—what was left to betray?"[8] The idea of betrayals forms a chain that connects one character with another, one of Kundera's
works with the next one. Franz betrays his wife Marie-Claude because of his
mistress Sabina, and Sabina betrays Franz because of the lightness (freedom), which she has been pursuing as a goal of her life destination. The
literary function of betrayals is further explored in Chapter Five: "The Betrayal" of this book.

The reader understands that *the list* plays the ultimate significance in
Xavier's pursuit. It is in Xavier's possession only and contains secret information that is revealed later in the chapter: the *names of enemies* of the
Communist revolution. "In the nick of time," he arrives to the (train) station
"thanks to a sudden impulse," with his *briefcase* (not skis like his classmates), wondering what "possessed him to take part" in this undertaking.
This information seems to be gradually assembling the pieces of the "Kauza
Kundera" puzzle: the student Kundera has "the list" (knows the names) of
the three players in the Dvořáček affair, and its presumable evidence—the
suitcase. As revealed through Xavier, "his arrival was quite unexpected," he
was "wondering why he undertook it," but "something possessed him, a
sudden impulse, a refusal to obey blindly, automatically, without a single
mistake," and so he reached the police station at 4:00 p.m., or "in the eleventh hour," because Dvořáček was due to return in the afternoon to pick up
his *suitcase*. With "trembling fingers" (of Jaromil, in Part 3: "The Poet Masturbates") he hands his ID to the *two policemen* at the station; however, he
does not release "the names of the enemies," that is, Kundera did not (could
not) reveal that Dvořáček was a deserter, illegal escapee, or a spy because he
didn't have that information (i.e., *the passcode of the day*). At this point,
Jaromil's (Kundera's) mission is completed. Alone, he is walking ("stalking") through side streets, making sure that no one sees him.

As Militká confirmed in one of her interviews, Dlask and Kundera had no
knowledge of Dvořáček being a spy because she, herself, had no knowledge

of it either. This information additionally supports the idea of Kundera's reporting *the presence of a suitcase* in Militká's room rather than the presence of the man, Dvořáček, whom Kundera, according to the police report, described as "an acquaintance" of Militká.

One has to bear in mind that this brief one-time communication was the beginning and the end of Kundera's dealing with the police in Dvořáček's case. It was a passing episode in his life that arose suddenly and ended as quickly and unexpectedly as it came. The whole episode took about one hour, perhaps even less, but no more than two hours. Additional information of the aftereffects, if any, came to Kundera either in random bits of whispering and gossip at the university dormitory or through his own intuition, educated guesses and predictions based on his outside knowledge about arrests, prison, and death sentences as reported about enemies of the regime to the public by the media of the time (press, radio, and street loudspeakers).

It is important to realize that Kundera *did not* have the information that we have today. He did not see the police report with his name on it, and had no knowledge or proof whether or not any report with his name (or without) was produced and kept permanently on the police file. This *unknown* is precisely what has attracted Milan Kundera—the writer—the most: the *unknown of the future with all its possibilities and randomness* that he has extensively explored in his writing. For instance, *The Unbearable Lightness of Being*'s narrator says: "A girl who longs for marriage longs for something she knows nothing about." This "knowing nothing about" is the mystery of life and of the Kundera novel. Therefore, it is not surprising but rather expected that he persists in using the *mystery* aspect to defend himself in the "Kauza Kundera."

Once Kundera left the police station, he returned to his daily routine without experiencing any real conclusion to the episode, while aware of a range of possible consequences. But his *not knowing* was his blessing. The truth of the present reality and future possibility was beyond him, and he knew *that he, and others, might never learn it*. To a degree, the unknown and undiscovered must have been soothing, giving him hope that it would remain a secret, a mystery. It was only Militká who apparently witnessed Dvořáček's arrest. The window of the room she was locked in faced the exit, and she saw *two police officers* taking the handcuffed Dvořáček out of the building. Immediately after her release, she left Prague for her hometown, Kostelec nad Orlicí, to tell her parents that she had caused Dvořáček's arrest. By now, Kundera was entirely out of the picture, back to his student's life. However, as the narrator says about Xavier, he was "the only one who knew everything that had occurred."[9]

Xavier is aware of the religious imagery that appeared "in a long procession" of pointed ends of skis (of his classmates) facing up, "like sacred symbols, like pairs of fingers swearing a holy vow."[10] Eventually, the religious symbols merge with a sense of guilt and forgiveness, and with the countryside funeral set against the landscape of meadows and hills. As Xavier admitted, he was *the only one who knew*, and that the others at the funeral were either an "uncomprehending public" or "uncomprehending victims." The most poignant conclusion of Xavier's chapter—perhaps reflecting Kundera's subconscious (or unconscious) motivations—is his decision to erase his guilt by writing. Xavier realizes that if he cannot save the lost life (of his dreams), he can "ennoble" the one he is currently living. Thus, Xavier's "ennobling" could represent Kundera's creative streak. Producing novels, theater plays, critical essays, and articles might be his way to live in peace with his subconscious for his one-time rash decision to report *the mysterious suitcase* to the police, which unfortunately, as we know today, led to human destruction on a larger scale, despite his knowing or not knowing and despite him. Most, if not all, real life events were not revealed to him until the "Kauza Kundera" came out in October 2008. He had not searched for it in the past, and with time might have forgotten Dvořáček's name. But this life mystery allowed him to play with the ideas that sprung from it, taking them to extremes through literary devices, reaching far beyond the border of reality, which has attracted Kundera the most.

THE CONSCIOUS, THE SUBCONSCIOUS AND THE FORTUITOUS

One could apply the theory of the subconscious that Freud (interestingly enough, born in Moravia like Kundera) viewed as a *negative force*, a center of repression, where all "immoral" impulses are located. However, in Kundera's situation of life-long extensive creative production, Karl Jung's opinion might be equally valid, if not more convincing. Unlike Freud, Jung regarded the subconscious as a *positive force* designed to disseminate wisdom where dreams play the role of a connector between the subconscious and the unconscious. The unconscious, determining what is beneath the surface of one's personality, brings out "the forgotten layer" of conflicts, repressed sexuality, desires, shades of human character (including the *monstrosity* that Kundera mentions in the Preface of *Life Is Elsewhere*), dreams and their sequences, etc., all resurging, one way or another to the surface in symbols and metaphors, whether or not the author intended them to be included.

In order to understand Kundera's personality, one must read between the lines. Czechs have been doing this for decades, if not centuries, because their small nation was overpowered by larger nations and often, they were not able to express their opinions. Kundera interprets it this way: What's hidden in human individualism (identity) is exactly what one wouldn't expect to find.

The "I" of a person is "what cannot be guessed at or calculated, what must be unveiled, uncovered, conquered."[11]

Naturally, Jacques Derrida's philosophy of text deconstruction comes into play as well. In order to understand a literary text, Derrida urges the reader not to "listen to the source itself" but rather to turn to its language and other figures of speech—symbols, metaphors, allegories, etc. This so-called "difference" (French *différence*), as Derrida coined it, requires understanding and grasping of the textual and sub-textual meanings within their relations to other things—other contexts and ways that can be elusive, temporary, and hard to be predicted, seen, or comprehended. One could review the Xavier chapter to find additional relations between the author, narrator, and Xavier (Jaromil's double, and clearly, Milan Kundera's double as well), and reevaluate the meaning of the text in relation to reality and Kundera's identity. In one paragraph for instance, the narrator describes Xavier watching "groups of men in blue denim" on the bridge through the window, and feeling that he should be a part of them, that he belonged to the scene from which he was excluded by "some error." One might speculate about this "error" of exclusion. Is it an error of being excluded from the armed forces of the revolution as described in the novel? Is it an error that Xavier is isolated from his classmates on the ski trip, and does not interact with them? Or is it an error that was supposed to impart a meaning in relation to the author's episode of March 14, 1950?

Another support of Kundera's productivity at the level of the subconscious might be seen in a metaphor of folk wisdom. His creativity has become a *willow*, a mythical symbol of a tree set apart in the meadows near water, into which the author whispers secrets that cannot be released to anyone. This fairytale motif has been introduced and largely spread in Czech culture by means of a satirical poem, "Král Lávra" (The King Lavra) by Karel Havlíček Borovský, a prominent Czech poet of the nineteenth-century National Revival. The story of a king with a donkey's ears is a variation of the legendary story of the Greek King Midas whose ears the God Apollo made long, resembling a donkey's or horse's. In European cultures, the story is about a barber who whispers the secret of the king's long ears into a willow tree to get rid of the burden of holding the secret. This way, he avoids spreading the knowledge among people, and is spared from the death that each barber was met with prior to him. Is it possible that Milan Kundera's novels are weighed down by "thousands of secrets," just like the old willow in the folktale? Is his authorial identity with its *secret codes* embodied in his work, buried in the secrecy of his sentences and paragraphs? Paraphrasing his statement on the lightness and weight dichotomy, one might conclude, that "the only certainty is that this question is the most mysterious, most ambiguous of all."[12] In his interview with Jordan Elgrably, Kundera clearly enunciates that writing is a refuge: "Writing is a form of therapy, yes. One writes to liberate something in oneself. However, this has nothing to do with an aesthetic value. If we confuse this sort of writing—which is entirely sympathetic and legitimate, and has its mnemonic and therapeutic functions—with writing which requires a certain aesthetic, what we consider literature, we fall into graphomania."[13]

In Part Two, "Soul and Body," of *The Unbearable Lightness of Being*, the author includes his subtle comments on fortuities in human life. He describes these coincidences as accidental, coincidental meetings and events that are happening simultaneously despite people's influence and often their knowledge. Tomas and Tereza meet coincidentally: he comes to perform a surgery on a patient in a provincial town, replacing his medical colleague who got sick. She is waitressing in a hotel restaurant and when he enters, Beethoven's music is playing. That "fortuitous occurrence" becomes Tereza's motif for the life of beauty that she longs for. Tomas, a womanizer, is instantly attracted to her; however, he fears if he invites her to Prague, "she would offer him up her life." As much as he fears it, he soon has to deal with her appearing at his threshold, her *heavy suitcase* stored at the Prague train station. Tomas realizes that Tereza's *suitcase* contains her life, which she is offering to him. And because of his erotic Don Juan lifestyle, he rents a room for her so she can move in with her *heavy suitcase*. Only later does he let her move into his place. In this passage, the *suitcase* is a symbol of a *heavy life*, a fateful accessory to the characters' existence, repeated by the narrator throughout the text. As harmless as it looks at first, the *suitcase* bears a *warning sign*. It foresees dramatic changes in the characters' life, culminating either in their own death or in the death of innocent, oblivious characters around them.

In Chapter Eight of Part Three, "Words Misunderstood," Sabina learns through Tomas's son (from his first marriage) about Tereza and Tomas's accidental death. Prior to their death, it was Tereza, "the weak partner" in their relationship, who dictated the course of their life together. She altered his destiny the moment he picked up her *heavy suitcase*. For instance, when returning to Prague from Zurich, ending her unhappy attempt to immigrate, she is "crushed into a corner of the train compartment with her heavy suitcase above her head."[14] Five days later Tomas follows her, realizing he misses her dreadfully. And when she wants to move out to the countryside, he agrees. Their death indirectly results from their choice to live in a rural paradise, a place of serenity away from politics, as Tereza insisted. The truck they were driving from a local dance had poor brakes and it crashed on a steep hill, crushing their bodies to an instant death. And it all started with the *heavy suitcase* that she brought with her to Prague, and prior to the *suitcase* with their coincidental meeting one late afternoon.

We know that during his second mission in Prague, Dvořáček had no intention to meet with Militká. But riding a streetcar and looking out of the window, he recognized Militká walking by the Mánes Bridge. He immediately got off with his *suitcase*, at that moment entirely unaware of how his *suitcase* would change the course of his life and the lives of others forever, leading to arrests, imprisonments, and the execution of one man indirectly involved in his case.[15] The randomness of Dvořáček's fortuitous meeting with Militká that particular morning at that particular time (where, perhaps, mere seconds decided his fate) is noteworthy.

Such a thought can lead to madness. It also leads to questioning Kundera's *chef-d'ouvres* or the major works that he produced during the Communist period in Czechoslovakia, and writing about that period once living in France. Would they be as convincing, intense, and self-absorbed—their foundation supported with the very same elements—if on March 14, 1950, for instance, Dvořáček looked out the other side of the streetcar window at the very moment when Militká was walking on the Mánes Bridge? The idea that a random meeting of two people unrelated to the author could have caused such a *heavy impact* on his work is simply stunning. In his book, *Understanding Milan Kundera*, Fred Misurella points out *Farewell Waltz* and its ill-fated coincidental randomness: "Increasingly Kundera resorts to accidental or incidental ties that become a part of a character's ultimate fate."[16] Fred Misurella gives an example of Jakub, "the bearer of the poisonous pill" that kills the young nurse Ruzena.

In the novel, Jakub has no relation to Ruzena, though he instinctively dislikes her and she dislikes him when they run into one another in a spa town. He hardly knows her name and has no intention of causing her death. However, fate dictates that he, out of curiosity and fortuitous opportunity, slips his lethal blue-colored pill into the vial of tranquilizers that Ruzena forgot on a table in a restaurant. Her medications have the same color and shape as his pills. Jakub carried the lethal pill as a means of ending his life in case it became unbearable in the prison where he was serving time as a political inmate. Released from the prison, he is on his way to leave the country, stopping by the spa where his ward, Olga, is receiving medical treatment. A daughter of his friend, who was executed when Olga was a child, ignores the fact that her father was among those who were responsible for Jakub's arrest. Like Jakub, Olga—intellectual and plain looking—resents the pretty and frivolous spa nurse, Ruzena. The nurse's life is troubled by her unwanted pregnancy: she is unsure whether she was impregnated by a famous jazz musician with whom she enjoyed a night of erotic adventure when he came to town to give a concert, or by her local blue-collar boyfriend, who represents the boredom of a small town and her monotonous future life there.

Fred Misurella remarks that both Jakub and Ruzena "seek an escape from the prison of their existence, the hell of the lives they lead."[17] When Ruzena returns to retrieve her vial, it is an instant of fortuitous clash between the two. Jakub doesn't manage to retrieve his poisonous pill from the capped vial because at the same instant, Olga joins him for dinner, interrupting his intended task. But he manages to grab the vial before Ruzena reaches it, asking her if he could have one pill because he uses the same medication. Their mutual animosity explodes, aggravated by the clash between them that took place shortly before. It was a chase of a stray dog in the park, Jakub holding the dog by the collar and Ruzena imitating her father in attempting to catch the animal with a noose attached on a pole. In this symbolic scene of capturing the unwanted, undesirable element, Jakub is a "winner," leaving with a dog and humiliating Ruzena. In the scene of fighting over the pill, it is Ruzena who *wins her death* by grabbing the vial. As Jakub is about to retrieve the "fateful" pill, she shouts at him that she isn't a mobile pharmacy. Her arrogant attitude, as Misurella defines it, and her "lack of charity, along with the accidental, and superficial, mutual hatred with Jakub, leads to her death."[18]

When arriving at the spa, the backseat of Jakub's car is loaded with more than one *suitcase*. And toward the end of the novel, the reader learns that Jakub unintentionally caused the death of both Ruzena and her fetus. When approaching the border on leaving his native land, Ruzena is already dead, and Jakub, her killer, will remain *unknown even to himself* and to everyone else, except for Olga and Dr. Skreta. While driving, Jakub plays with the idea of his pill causing Ruzena's death, but not having evidence, he ponders her death from philosophical to farcical perspectives. Ultimately, he convinces himself that the supposedly lethal pill, given to him years ago by his friend in the spa town, Dr. Skreta, was a fake. After the border of his country closes behind him, Jakub's own past shuts behind him like a completed chapter in his *book of life*, to which there would be no return. His conscience remains clear, and so do Olga's and Dr. Skreta's. Olga will not reveal the name of the killer and, moreover, she feels a secret pleasure *in knowing the unknown*. Misurella states: "In contrast with the serious, ultimately false moments of Jakub's introspection, Kundera turns the reality of Ruzena's death into farcical melodrama."[19]

In order to reduce her stress after having an argument with her boyfriend, Ruzena consumes Jakub's pill and collapses by the spa pool, her corpse surrounded by curious women-patients, water dripping from their wet bodies amidst Ruzena's boyfriend's outcry. On his knees by her body, he confesses to causing her death with his pushy insistence to marry him, calling for the police and demanding his own arrest.

IN THE NAME OF COLLECTIVE GUILT

The fast-paced plot of *Farewell Waltz* is condensed into five consecutive days, an allusion to a five-act theatrical play: "a provocative game of misunderstandings, strange encounters, and accidents."[20] In this sense, Maria Němcová Banerjee's definition of the novel is perfectly fitting within its frame of fortuitousness. However, she sees the novel's action as "a crucible of absurdity for testing major ideas, in the manner of philosophical fools of the Renaissance,"[21] comparing the philosophical and religious debates of Kundera's characters with François Rabelais's humorous humanistic discourses of Panurge and Thaumaste. Kundera admired and drew from Rabelais, the French Renaissance humanist of fantasy, and writer of great grotesque and picaresque satire. Inasmuch as he might have been influenced by Rabelais, Kundera seems to be influenced by the dilemma of his own life. In an emotional discussion with Olga about political crimes, Jakub's justification that *everyone* was guilty implies *every single person*, including the author.

This idea resonates with Alexander Solzhenitsyn's characters in *Cancer Ward*. The former camp guard, Shulubin compares the ordeal of Oleg Kostoglotov, the political prisoner who had spent a decade in Stalinist labor camps, with living in freedom: "You haven't had to do much lying, do you understand? At least you haven't had to stoop so low—you should appreciate that. You people were arrested, but we were herded into meetings to "expose" you. They executed people like you, but they made us stand up and applaud the verdicts as they were announced."[22] In his exchange with Kostoglotov, Shulubin criticized the Soviet government for forcing each individual to act and think as one man, to be *one man*. Justification in the name of *the collective* rather than *the individual* runs parallel with an ideology of any Communist society (its name being derived from *commune*), a society that has deprived a human being of individualism and essentially propagated the collective *good*, from which it would benefit as "one whole." It equally propagated the idea that *everyone* was responsible for a *collective injury* and, as a consequence, collectively suffered. Therefore, this notion suggests that the act of imprisonment and execution of millions of innocent citizens under Stalin and his subsequent leadership in the former Soviet Union should be regarded as devoid of individual responsibility and, above all, of *moral responsibility*. This, inevitably, applies to Klement Gottwald's Czechoslovakia, a satellite country that was under the strong spell of Soviet leadership, particularly once its Communist Party gained the upper hand in political leadership. In *Ignorance*, Kundera returns to the idea of collective guilt through the internal voice of Josef who understood that every person was *hunting down the guilty*, just like every person was *being hunted down* according to the side from which the political wind was blowing.

As a writer, Kundera embraces this concept with slight modifications; often the political is pushed away by the metaphysical. For instance, the narrator in "Nobody Will Laugh," the first of seven stories of Kundera's first novel *Laughable Loves*, realizes that it is only an illusion that people are able to control events of their lives. He concludes that "the truth is that they aren't our stories at all, that they are foisted upon us from somewhere *outside*; that in no way do they represent us; that we are not to blame for the queer path that they follow; they carry us away, since they are controlled by some *alien* forces."[23]

THE METAPHYSICAL FORCES

Examined from the metaphysical viewpoint, it is easy to excuse an individual from accountability for his own actions in much the same way as in a case of political intrusion. This allows Kundera to explore *the unknown*, a "blind alley" that he calls the place for his best inspirations.[24] The real-life episode of March 14, 1950 is not unlike the *blind alley for best inspirations*. In "Nobody Will Laugh," Wednesday the 14th is the date pinpointed by a local committee during an interrogation of the narrator Klima, an art history lecturer by profession. He vaguely promises but doesn't intend to write a review of Mr. Zaturecky's study on Czech paintings that clearly lacks scholarly value, being a pastiche of published ideas. Mr. Zaturecky's persistence leads into a series of laughable situations on the surface which are serious underneath, interfering with the lecturer's professional and personal life and, in the end, leading to the discovery of the lecturer's girlfriend Klara, who resides unregistered in his attic flat. To mislead the local committee during the interrogation, the narrator portrays himself as a Don Juan, suggesting that he has had so many women that he cannot remember which one of them was in his bachelor's apartment and when. He maintains the charade until a committee member reminds him it was on Wednesday, the 14th. According to Militká, the March 14th arrest happened on Wednesday and so did the narrator's false accusation of Mr. Zaturecky's seduction of his girlfriend, Klara in the story "Nobody Will Laugh." Is this error purely coincidental, or did a Wednesday in relation to the date the 14th stick in the mind of both Kundera and Militká for a specific reason?[25]

The irony of this story is unsurprisingly wrapped up in the lecturer's frivolously playful behavior and justifications for his deceptive intentions, all turning it into a life-changing drama. The narrator has been playing with fate and ultimately, fate played with him. He lost not only Klara but also his lectureship at the university. The story, however, ends on a humorous note; the narrator claims that because his story "was not of the tragic sort, but rather of the comic variety,"[26] it gave him "some comfort."

One can project this *some comfort* as a leading factor in Kundera's approach to the life event of March 14. The following quote, used in the text in reference to Zaturecky and his wife, seems to speak directly of Kundera's feelings about the encounter with Militká in Dvořáček's case: "The connection between her and the incident, in which we'd both played a sad role, suddenly seemed vague, arbitrary, accidental, and not our fault."[27] Yes, every detail seems "vague, arbitrary, accidental, and not *their* fault" in Dvořáček's morning arrival in the Smíchov Railway Station in Prague on the 14th up to his arrest at 7:30 p.m. in Militká's room in the Kolonka dormitory. As he revealed during the prison interrogations, Dvořáček walked from the Smíchov train station to the Prague center in Wenceslaus Square, purchasing two pairs of gloves (one men's, and the other for a female friend other than Militká) on his way, and in the next shop three hats, one which he put on his head. He also bought a *suitcase* for his newly purchased items (in 1950 customers had to supply their own bags for purchased goods), including a shoe polisher, and finally a pair of shoes, which he must have put on because the police did not find them when searching his *suitcase*. He stopped in a public phone booth to look for the number of *Chemapol* to contact Dr. Václavík, an upper management engineer employed by the firm. He was supposed to obtain sensitive information from him about the production of gas equipment (most likely intended for military purposes). In addition, his task was to convince Mr. Václavík to collaborate with Western agents in establishing a secret network for transmitting information between the East and West.

Dvořáček was instructed and intended to stay overnight in Dr. Václavík's flat. After several unsuccessful calls to locate him, he decided to wait in front of *Chemapol* on Panská Street at the closing hour of the firm, hoping to be able to recognize him in person, according to the description he had received in Germany. After failing to identify him, Dvořáček headed by tram No. 22 to Militká's dorm to pick up his suitcase and to stay there overnight.

In reconstructing Dvořáček's journey in view of accidental details that led to the episode of reporting to the police, it is the *suitcase* that personifies the *alien* force that brought about Dvořáček's downfall by involving Militká, Dlask, and Kundera. Had he not purchased it, his timeframe would have been slightly shifted and he would have not run into Militká. And even if he had come across her that day, not having the *suitcase* on him, he probably would not have walked with her up to her room. He certainly must have had alternative possibilities for his overnight accommodations in Prague in case he was unable to reach Dr. Václavík. Dvořáček had attempted to locate the engineer's flat the very same afternoon, searching for his nameplate on several houses on Stalinova třída in Praha 2-Vinohrady, but his search led to nothing.

It was the reporting of a *strange suitcase* in Militká's room that initiated Kundera's *blind alley for best inspirations*. His fantasy, along with his literary and creative vision, has been expansive and alluring. The focal point, which was the ending point for him in real life and the beginning point in his literary career, fascinated and provoked him. He became obsessed with it, and from it he was developing additional literary and philosophical themes, applying them to his novels creatively. He had nothing to fear: he knew that he didn't sign any report at the police station, and if questioned, he could always justify his action in the name of *collective good*. After all, what if the *suitcase* contained a dangerous material that would damage the university dorm or harm students? He must have felt that he did the right thing.

In a similar fashion of developing novel themes, Kundera plays with the musical motif *Muss es sein? Es muss sein!* that accompanies Tomas through *The Unbearable Lightness of Being.* Kundera, blending with the narrator, steps into the text explaining Beethoven's words and melody because, as he tells us, Tomas—whose knowledge of music wasn't particularly good—most likely didn't know the story. Of course, Kundera playfully implies the readers, rather than Tomas. Here Kundera gives a great example of how an artist can turn one little incident (albeit negative) into a work of art. A man owed some money to the composer and when Beethoven requested it from him, the man "mournfully sighed": *Muss es sein?* (Must it be?) to which the composer replied with a laugh, yes, it must be, *Es muss sein.* Using this motif, the composer created his Opus 135, a quartet in which three voices sing *Es muss sein, Es muss sein, ja, ja, ja, ja,* and the fourth chimes in asking for a purse with money.[28] The narrator comments on the solemnity of this simple motif and its metaphysical meaning as if coming from the heavens. He wants his readers to acknowledge how the *trivial* can become the *eternal*. A writer has powers of creation equal to God's, his characters and situations living for eternity and seeming as real as life itself. The musical quartet also serves as a base for the two pairs of lovers: Tomas/Tereza and Sabina/Franz. It is then no surprise that the real-life reported *suitcase* would become a sublime item in Kundera's novels.

The question whether a man *should or should not feel guilty because he didn't know* is carried by Tomas's conscience. He asks: "Is a fool on the throne relieved of all responsibility merely because he is a fool?"[29] The narrator gives an example of a Czech prosecutor, who being deceived by his government in the early 1950s, called for the death sentence of an innocent man. Later it was revealed that these political accusations had no grounds, were unjust and absurd. Can now the same prosecutor say that his conscience is clear, that he is innocent because he believed in the political system that deceived him? Tomas makes a comparison with Oedipus from Greek mythology. Oedipus was unknowingly sleeping with his mother and unknowingly killed his father, but once he learned the truth, he felt guilty and "took his eyes out" to avoid seeing the atrocities he caused. Blind, he left Thebes.

Reading this parable in *The Unbearable Lightness of Being* and knowing the Dvořáček case, one becomes eerily attuned to it by noticing obvious parallels. Early in September 1950, the prosecutor called for the death penalty, but luckily on September 6, Dvořáček's sentence was reduced to twenty-two years of imprisonment (for desertion, espionage, and treason), confiscation of all property and a fine of 10,000 crowns. He was also stripped of his rights as a citizen for ten years. After serving fourteen years, including in the notorious Vojna and Bytíz uranium labor camps near Příbram, he was given a conditional discharge until 1970. Who should then bear responsibility for his sentencing—the prosecutor, the jury, Militká, Dlask, Kundera, or all of society? Or the Communist system that had made its citizens believe it was their duty to blindly follow proscribed dictatorial rules and regulations? This is a question that Kundera perhaps struggles most with, repeatedly inserting the *motifs of betrayal* and *police* into his works. Or possibly on the contrary, he intends to mislead his readers, saying: this topic is so mundane, how can you accuse me of having done anything wrong?

It is questionable how much Kundera knew about Dvořáček's death sentence and/or that it was reduced to imprisonment. We know that Militká learned about the outcome of the trial through her parents (it was well-known in her hometown), continuing her everyday life as if nothing had happened. She and Dlask, two lovebirds, remained absorbed in themselves, producing a family and forgetting about Dvořáček. Unless the rumor was spread into the Kolonka dormitory, or Kundera came across it in the media, the actual facts were unknown to him. Although he could have easily figured out what might have happened to "the bearer of the *suitcase*" if he was found guilty on charges of regime wrongdoings: either death or a Stalinist-type labor camp.

As an imaginary possibility, Kundera depicted imprisonment and life in the army service camp of Ludvik, a young man expelled from the Party and the university for daring verbalism on a postcard he sent to his girlfriend: "Optimism is the opium of the people! A healthy atmosphere stinks of stupidity! Long live Trotsky!"[30] After *The Joke* was published in 1967, many critics claimed that the novel bore the author's autobiographical elements; however, none of them were able to explain their close ties to Kundera's life (except for his Moravian origin, and his expulsion from the Party due to political remarks exchanged in a letter with his friend). Refusing to provide details, Kundera insisted that his novel was of an existential nature, claiming the action had little to do with the regime (it could have been set against a political background anywhere). His outcry, "Spare me of your Stalinism, *The Joke* is a love story!" was quoted in the major international newspapers and periodicals of the time.

Like Oedipus, blinded by his own guilt, Milan Kundera left Prague in 1975 to lecture in Rennes, and eventually settled in France for good. In the early 1980s, he started working on *The Unbearable Lightness of Being* with great compassion, sifting his feelings and opinions by inserting them into his fictional characters. Tomas accuses the Communists of destroying his country and depriving it of its freedom for decades, if not centuries. But now the Communists defended their actions by "their inner purity" and guiltless feelings. "How can you stand the sight of what you've done? How is it you aren't horrified? Have you no eyes to see? If you had eyes, you would have

to put them out and wander away from Thebes!"[31] Tomas claims provoca-
tively; however, calling guilt that results from the *not knowing* attitude "ir-
reparable guilt" sounds a bit *à la* Kundera.

This was a perfectly fitting context for Kundera. He was peacefully living
far from the iron grip of Communist politics; Soviet tanks were stationed in
his country, and Czechs embarked in the despair of a phlegmatic attitude. As
he says through Tomas, Kundera believed there would be no end to Communist dominance, at least not in his lifetime. He expressed a similar stance in
his "Author's Note" of *Nesmrtelnost,* the Czech edition of *Immortality.* He
said that after he was stripped of his Czech citizenship in 1978, he was
convinced that the border to his home country was closed forever.[32]

In his 1989 *New York Times* review (republished ten year later in *Critical
Essays on Milan Kundera*), the author E.L. Doctorow labeled *The Unbearable Lightness of Being* a "disclaimed fiction in which the author deliberately
broke the mimetic spell of his text" to convince his readers that they should
not believe in the existence of his characters; and thus, he, the author "by his
candor became the only character the reader could believe in." This approach
has been practiced for several decades, explains E.L. Doctorow, and gives
the example of Virginia Woolf, who "was bored by narrative," giving a
preference to breaking novelistic conventions. In Czech literature, Kundera is
not alone. Bohumil Hrabal used to revise his novels by dismantling and
reassembling them as a collage, or writing a one hundred-page novel in one
sentence. Along with his "heroine," Hrabal became the protagonist of his
novel, titled *Dubenka* (an American student, April, who he names after the
month of *duben*, April), in which he describes his admiration for Dubenka,
who came to Prague to research his work. As critical as Doctorow is about
Kundera's composition, he praises his "first-rate mind," comparing his ability to reasonably "argue both sides of a question" with Bernard Shaw. He
also admires Kundera's capacity to "get ahead of his story and circle back to
it and run it through again with a different emphasis." In this respect, he is
like Garbriel García Márquez, with the exception that in Kundera's writings,
"García Márquez's levitations are not events now, but ideas."[33]

At the same time, Kundera unwittingly supports E.L. Doctorow's theory
in his Czech version of *Immortality* by saying that *everything that I wanted to
say, I had said in my novels, and if I didn't say something, it is because I
didn't want to say it.*[34] In fact, this statement would have been by far his
absolute best answer when he was interviewed in the "Kauza Kundera." It
would, of course, augment the curiosity of his readers but also increase their
confusion, since his characters carry diverse, often oppositional opinions,
and not necessarily moralistic (inasmuch as their creator does or, at least,
alludes to that fact). For instance, once she finds herself "in the safety of
emigration,"[35] Sabina is placed by the narrator into the category of self-
complacent Czechs. At a meeting in Geneva, her compatriots agree that

Czechs should have fought against the Soviets who invaded their country. When Sabina retorts, "Then why don't you go back and fight?"[36] she is verbally attacked by the speaker of the meeting who accuses her of doing nothing to oppose the Communist regime, just painting her pictures. At other times, Sabina admits that the invasion of her country worked in her favor because of her growing success in immigration as a painter. "Thanks to the Russians, I'm a rich woman,"[37] she says to Tomas over the phone. Sabina, the painter, has as much right to claim this *advantage* as Milan Kundera, the novelist. Why then, shouldn't Kundera resent being labeled a dissident or *émigré* as Western critics expected him to be?

In her 1985 interview "A Talk with Milan Kundera," Olga Carlisle quotes Kundera: "My stay in France is final, and, therefore, I am not an *émigré*. France is my only real homeland now."[38] She importantly assigned Kundera his place in the literary world, saying that Kundera brought Czechoslovakia to the attention of Western readership in the 1980s, similar to what Solzhenitsyn did for Russia in the 1970s, and García Márquez for Latin America in the 1960s. With an approach to existentialism and universalism, "Kundera has succeeded in turning the Czechoslovakia of his youth into a vivid, mythical, erotic land."[39] Referring to Philip Roth's interview with Kundera, Carlisle quotes his childhood dream of becoming invisible using an ointment, and later of becoming famous as an adult, and now, at the pinnacle of his fame in the 1980s, Kundera wishes that the ointment dream of his childhood would once again make him invisible.

Kundera's refusal to be treated as an *émigré* or dissident is nothing new. He explicitly states this in his novels. In *The Unbearable Lightness of Being*, Tomas refuses to sign a petition "Two Thousand Words" (a literary allusion to the historic Charter 77) to free political prisoners. When demoted from a medical surgeon to a window washer, Tomas was approached by two men in a flat where he was assigned to wash the windows that day. He recognized his son, Simon, whom he hadn't seen for many years, as well as the editor who requested changes in Tomas's article on Oedipus. These complex circumstances indicate that the narrator would not take a short cut to say that Tomas refused to sign the document. The narrator extends the situation over ten pages, exposing and justifying Tomas's thoughts from many angles. Physical similarities and facial gestures that Tomas recognizes in his son as his own ultimately play a negative role in his decision. The image of Simon competes with an image of Tereza: Tomas realizes that he "could not save political prisoners, but he could make Tereza happy."[40] Not getting involved in signing political declarations meant being freed from the microscopic eye of undercover agents. It allowed Tomas to make a free decision, regardless of whether his decision was morally right or wrong. In addition, being caught by surprise in an apartment other than his own made him wonder whether the place was bugged. He felt intense aversion toward a possibility of being caught and recorded, and his words being publicly broadcasted: "He was simply afraid of being quoted by the police."[41] He felt menaced by a poster on the wall of a soldier calling to join the Red Army inasmuch as he felt threatened by the imagery of political prisoners, or by his son telling him it was his duty to sign the petition, and by any force being imposed on him in the name of helping others. The paradox and final justification, of course, are that he, a medical professional, was trained to help others but had been stripped of that possibility.

When the man from the Ministry (a secret police agent, StB) gave Tomas the option to sign a declaration in which he would retract his article on Oedipus, he refused. The article could be misinterpreted that Tomas, the doctor, urged Communists to gouge out their eyes for the political and human crimes they committed. Before he understood that he was being interrogated, Tomas accepted a drink in a public place with the Ministry agent. But later he became horrified, asking, what if someone had seen him, someone who knew the Ministry man and concluded that "Tomas was working with the police"?[42] Fatefully, in October 2008 this interpretation was the feared offense that the French press of his "only real homeland now" accused Kundera of committing in 1950 in the homeland he had rejected. Without dutiful research or substantial evidence, French journalists rushed to accuse him of collaborating with *the secret police* in the Dvořáček case. In the novel, however, the author's voice is strong enough in attempting to protect Tomas. A proper upbringing does not teach people how to lie, and so they fall prey to the secret police by becoming their ally, the narrator explains. The reader cannot help but think that Kundera either consciously or subconsciously was referencing his own "proper upbringing," and "falling a prey to the secret police" in 1950. Did he envision the type of upbringing Communists tried to teach their citizens, as spelled out in Jaromír Jerman's speech of 1951 with the M.K. initials? Was this the type of upbringing united by one common idea of solidarity and happiness that falls under the umbrella of *collective guilt* in Kundera's novels?

From reading *The Book of Laughter and Forgetting,* Kundera's faithful admirers know that he, the author, wanted to be a part of "a magical circle" that unites people "like a ring."[43] In Part Three, "The Angels," he is preoccupied with a happy collectivism. He opposes young people united by the angel's laughter of innocence, conformity, and goodness to devil's laughter of individualism, doubt, and cynicism—a laughter denoting "the absurdity of things,"[44] rather than accepting them as meaningful. The fictional characters in this farcical part of the novel are a trio: two American students, Michelle and Gabrielle, and their teacher, Madame Raphael, together representing the laughter of pedantic angels of conformity. Unsure of the role rhinoceros assume in Ionesco's absurdist play, Michelle and Gabrielle conclude that, "the symbol of the rhinoceros is meant to create a comic effect." They demonstrate their presentation by using horns attached to cardboard masks and mimicking the beasts. The whole class feels "a kind of embarrassed compassion"[45] until Sarah, their classmate, kicks them from the back and the class bursts into spontaneous laughter. Madame Raphael takes Michelle and Gabrielle (her favorite students) by their hands and the three of them form a circle, dancing a step to the front and a step to the back and to the sides in happy unison to the "mute horror" of the class. The women's trio absorbed in themselves and unaware of others begins to rise up until they vanish.

Milan Kundera compares the fictional rise of the trio to his own, saying, "I too once danced in a ring."[46] He refers to this dance as celebratory because young Communists with "the smile of happiness" on their faces had many reasons to celebrate: individual ownership was dismantled, private property was confiscated, factories were nationalized, medical care became free, and thousands of people were sent to prison. Expelled from the Party in 1950, Kundera describes his exclusion from the circle and his rise followed by the fall like "a meteorite broken off from a planet."[47] He openly admits that he has been among those who "always retain a kind of faint yearning for that lost ring dance,"[48] justifying it by an evidence of planetary universe, its planets floating in circles. In a chilling section of this novel, he describes the celebrations of young Communists the day after a woman-politician, Milada Horáková, was brutally hanged on false charges of treason and conspiracy. Wandering among these young people, Kundera felt bitter for being "forbidden to enter any of their rings."[49]

In as much as Kundera's authorial voice attempts to convince us that his "dancing in a ring" and his desire to "dance" sprang from *collective pressure*, one needs to acknowledge that Milan Kundera belonged to the privileged class, and his writing about this period is seen from his privileged, highly sophisticated and intellectual stance, especially in parabatic parts where he enters the novel as the real Milan Kundera. The majority of Czechs, the working class—the supposed leading class in Communist Czechoslovakia—did not participate in the "dancing with happy smiles on their faces" because they lived in the harsh everyday conditions of the 1950s, lacking basic staples and housing, and did not have the leisure or energy for "dancing" and celebrating crimes and victories of the Communist Party. They spent endless hours, to the point of exhaustion, waiting in long lines for food to provide for their families and children, especially in big cities.

Of course, *The Book of Laughter and Forgetting* is a novel, a work of imagination and ideas rather than of reality. However, when the author enters his novels, as Kundera increasingly does beginning with *The Book of Laughter and Forgetting*, the readers take his authorial digressions, reflecting his life experiences, for the real facts, as E.L. Doctorow implies. His purposeful breaking up of the composition helps the readers assemble Kundera's identity. His authorial voice allows him to reflect on himself within the history of his country and its dramatic upheavals, to evaluate opportunities for his characters, and to fuse them with real-life personalities into one coherent aesthetic expression. Its compositional frame stands on Kundera's traditional seven parts of the architectonic structure, united by themes rather than characters, and often endowing individual polyphonic voices to each character to create a literary harmony in the musical sense. Since Kundera worked on this novel after immigrating to France, his writing angle is presented from a distance, in a nest of physical and emotional safety, away from the harsh neo-Stalinist normalization period in Czechoslovakia and, thus, some distortion and simplicity of the facts and historical background are inevitable. No longer writing for the Czech audience, he somewhat forcibly explains certain historical and cultural facts to non-Czech readers. Behind his comments and descriptions about himself as a young man—a reject from the Party and from "the leading youth circle"—one feels his anger, muted but present, and his forced defending of his attitude of this period. Inevitably, the reader gets a sense of his unusually complex identity.

THE PAINFUL PAST

In Part One, "Lost Letter" of this novel, his character Mirek (a domestic form of "Miroslav"—like in *Miroslav Dvořáček*) looks back at his youthful affair with Zdena, an unattractive woman and a devoted Party member. He feels ashamed of the love letters he used to send her twenty years ago. Now he wants to erase his past, demanding the letters back so she cannot use them in the future to reopen his past. Kundera opens "Lost Letters" with the political metaphor of a photograph of the first Communist President, Klement Gottwald, standing on the balcony of the famed Old Town Square in Prague in February 1948, the day of the Communist Party's victory. Vlado Clementis, who is seen standing behind him in the original picture, passed him his fur hat so Gottwald wouldn't get cold on that wintry day. In 1952, Clementis was hanged for his "bourgeois ideas" as a part of the Slansky processes, which were show-trials to get rid of inconvenient high Communist government officials, mostly Jewish in origin. The figures of Clementis and two other men (one a photographer) were erased from the original photograph, Gottwald forever standing alone on the balcony, surrounded by empty walls. Kundera comments: "Nothing remains of Clementis but the fur hat on Gottwald's head."[50] His past erased, Clementis has fallen into the history of forgetting.

Contrary to Mirek, Tamina, who remains in immigration after her husband had passed away, has a burning desire to recreate the lost past of her husband through the letters she wrote him when they lived in Prague. Her memories of their life together are fading and the forgetting is becoming unbearable. In *The Book of Laughter and Forgetting*, Tamina represents a character that connects the memory and forgetting in a painful despair of the empty future of an isolated immigrant. Kundera calls this book, written "in the form of variations," a novel for Tamina and about Tamina.[51] The author links the idea of political imprisonment to an emigration forced by political circumstances.

Mirek, an intellectual who opposed the Soviet invasion of his country in August 1968, has been demoted to a construction worker. When driving to see his former mistress to retrieve his love letters, he is followed by a secret police car. He knows he could be arrested any time; yet, "he had been drawn irresistibly to the idea of prison." Kundera makes a literary allusion, saying: "It was probably the way Flaubert was drawn to Madame Bovary's suicide."[52] And Kundera, the writer, is evidently drawn himself to a prison that he describes as "a splendidly illuminated scene of history," in spite of its impenetrable walls. In the end, Mirek is arrested; his books, writings, and papers are confiscated in his apartment upon his unsuccessful return from his former lover: she refused to return his letters. He receives a prison sentence of six years; his friends and his son's sentences were within the same range or less. However, Tamina's sentence is the longest—she meets death, eternity. Isolated and unhappy in immigration, she undertakes a voyage to an imaginary island occupied by children of rigid and sexually appalling discipline. When attempting to escape, she decides to drown herself so her body would be exposed only to the fauna of open sea, away from human evilness. One could predict her death early in the story when a *suitcase* was mentioned in connection to her letters.

Mirek's story is another proof of Kundera's fascination with the secret police, denouncing, and imprisonment. On his way to visiting Zdena, Mirek passes by a barrier guarded by a woman, a denouncer. Surprised to see him, she asks: "Didn't they arrest you yet?"[53] She denounces people gladly, taking pleasure in the power that comes from denouncing them; people were losing their jobs "on the slightest allegation," their lives shattered due to her vicious will.

Czech readers are fully aware that Mr. Kundera wants to erase his past, just like Mirek. He might have more to hide than his Communist past and propagandist poetry of double-edged quality. He has guarded his creative career of this period (1950s till mid-1960s) under a common denominator—*immature creations*—and he had referred to himself as a "relatively unknown Czech intellectual." The reality, however, has been far from the truth. He was a leading force in the liberalization of the official Czech literary scene and one of the major intellectual initiators of the Prague Spring, after giving his speech at the Fourth Congress of the Czechoslovak Writers in June 1967. Along with Václav Havel, Bohumil Hrabal, Arnošt Lustig, and Josef Škvorecký, Milan Kundera was a prominent writer in Czechoslovakia during this period. His fame came overnight with his first play *Majitelé klíčů* (The Owners of the Keys), which was successfully staged in 1962 at the Prague National Theater under the direction of an experimental legendary director, Otomar Krejča. This absurdist play of paradox and irony was staged by a number of additional theatres in the same year. It also came out in a printed version with Kundera's afterword, in which he gave his own interpretation of the play.

A strong motif of hiding and betrayal prominently figures in *Majitelé klíčů*. As its title suggests, the key to this play are *the keys*, two sets of keys to an apartment, shared among four family members: a young couple, and the wife's parents. The storyline is set in the Nazi period in a small town, Vsetín, and its major theme is unfulfilled ambitions and disappointments in a family where narrow-mindedness, rigidity, and pretentiousness are contrasted with the young husband's secret life. The husband must hide his participation in the resistance movement and his murdering of a Nazi concierge of the house they live in, to protect his former girlfriend Věra against her seizure by the Gestapo. When forced to make a decision—either to admit he was a killer, or to flee with his former girlfriend—he decides for the latter, leaving behind his young wife and in-laws. They continue arguing about the ownership of the keys while the grand picture of murder and betrayal is unfolding right "under their noses," and eluding them entirely. The enormous success of this play was due to its open ending and the various possibilities that inspired the audience and critics to extensively discuss the plot, significance, and symbolism of the play. In a stale atmosphere of hardline oppression, the play was refreshingly new and original with Milan Kundera's talent shining through, despite its conformity to the prescribed socialist realism guidelines of the time.

As a person, Milan Kundera has been full of controversies and half-spoken statements. He believes that a *life opus* could be changed, or its parts erased, just like in *an opus* of musical composition. His frankness is sometimes breathtaking, but because it is embedded in his novelistic context, the reader doubts its authenticity. Does the narrator refer to himself, or does he just play with his characters and readers? For instance, when Kundera reveals that he was anonymously writing a horoscope for R. (a female editor of a magazine for young people), and that she was summoned for interrogation by the police one year later, Kundera writes: "I realized I had been chosen to be a mailman who delivers warnings and punishments to people, and I began to be afraid of myself."[54] This simple sentence suggests that he has been well aware that this was not the first time for him to "deliver warnings (*the suitcase*) and subsequent punishments (imprisonment)." Several pages further, he explains the reason for his emigrating from his home country. His secret meeting with R. made him realize that he became "a bearer of ill tidings and could not go on living among the people" he loved and "wished them no harm."⁵⁵ To what degree is his statement truthful? To what degree does it play the part of fictional agency?

In his heart, however, he has remained the genuine Milan Kundera, a Moravian, who has longed to be included in the "ring dance" of his Communist youth and, as he claims, who feels that he has been falling ever since. On the flip side, he wishes to hide his *Czechness*, just like Sabina succeeded in hiding "the fact that she was a Czech" once she had moved to America. She refused to be labeled a martyr who had suffered under the Communist regime and struggled against its oppression, being forced to leave her torn and bleeding country. She refused to let her paintings be labeled a representation of martyrdom and "a struggle for happiness," the way her art was judged at exhibitions in Germany and America. Needless to say, Kundera embodied Sabina's emotions into his own feelings, or just the contrary—he endowed Sabina with his foremost thoughts and feelings about his home country, political system, and immigration while living in voluntary exile (or as he calls it, "his real homeland now"). In this respect, he could be compared and contrasted with Alexander Solzhenitsyn, the author of *One Day in the Life of Ivan Denisovich*, and *The Archipelago Gulag*. Solzhenitsyn loved his native Russia, and after two decades living in forced exile, he returned home in 1994 to help build a new Russian orthodox society. But unlike Solzhenitsyn, Kundera gave up on his love for his homeland, claiming allegiance to France, all the while profiting from the historical background of Czechoslovakia, the country which he avoided calling by its name, using either *Bohemia*, or specifically regional *Moravia*. Adjusting his Czech characters accordingly, he made his novels challengingly readable, intriguing, and valuable in the West.

There are two types of immortality, as he tells us in his novel *Immortality*: the so-called *minor immortality*—being remembered by people who knew the person, and *great immortality*—being remembered by people who never knew the man personally.⁵⁶ His statement, inevitably, implies that *minor immortality* is passing, short-lived within one, two, perhaps three generations, while *great immortality* can last for centuries, even millennia (Boccaccio, Thomas Aquinas, Cicero, Aristotle, etc.). Surely enough, the narrator tells us that *great immortality* is a path for artists and statesmen, determined from the very beginnings of their journeys. Using his division, one could say that Kundera himself began with a prospective *minor immortality* in Communist Prague, and then the political environment—lucky for him personally (albeit cruel to him and to millions of his compatriots)—led to his prospective future *great immortality*. He began to fly high above his small country, an embodiment of "small mentality," as he has referred to it.

NOTES

1. Kundera, *Art of the Novel*, 145.
2. Kundera, *Art of the Novel*, 145.
3. Kundera, *Life Is Elsewhere*, 118.
4. Kundera, *Life Is Elsewhere*, 119.
5. Kundera, *Life Is Elsewhere*, 120.
6. Kundera, *Life Is Elsewhere*, 85.
7. Kundera, *Life Is Elsewhere*, 89.
8. Kundera, *Unbearable Lightness*, 122.
9. Kundera, *Life Is Elsewhere*, 85.
10. Kundera, *Life Is Elsewhere*, 77.
11. Kundera, *Unbearable Lightness*, 199.
12. Kundera, *Unbearable Lightness*, 6.
13. Jordan Elgrably, "Conversations With Milan Kundera," *Salmagundi Magazine*, no. 73, (Winter 1987): 3–24.
14. Kundera, *Unbearable Lightness*, 76.
15. A number of articles concerning the "Kauza Kundera" see Kundera as indirectly responsible for the arrest of the additional people found guilty in the Dvořáček case, but the prison reports clearly indicate that the StB already knew about the Touš family (father and son, and their associates) who helped many other defectors to cross the border. The likelihood is that if Dvořáček had not been caught, the Touš family would have been punished nonetheless.
16. Fred Misurella, *Understanding Milan Kundera* (Columbia, SC: University of South Carolina Press, 1993), 85.
17. Misurella, *Understanding Milan Kundera*, 99.
18. Misurella, *Understanding Milan Kundera*, 99.
19. Misurella, *Understanding Milan Kundera*, 103.
20. Maria Němcová-Banerjee, *The Terminal Paradox, The Novels of Milan Kundera* (New York: Grove Weidenfeld, 1990), 106.
21. Němcová-Banerjee, *The Terminal Paradox*, 106–7.
22. Alexander Solzhenitsyn, *Cancer Ward*, trans. Nicholas Bethell and David Burg (New York: Farrar, Straus and Giroux, 1974), 432.
23. Kundera, *Laughable Loves*, 34.
24. Kundera, *Laughable Loves*, 17.
25. On p. 80 in Adam Hradilek and Martin Tichý's report, "Osudová mise Moravcova kurýra" (Fateful mission of Moravec's agent), published in *Paměť a dějiny* (Rememberance and history), no. 1 (2009), Militká says: "Tu nešťastnou středu navečer jsem se vracela na kolej, když ke mně na chodbě přistoupili dva studenti. Odvedli mne do prázdného pokoje a tam mi řekli, že pro toho, koho čekám, si přišla policie a abych byla zticha a nesnažila se utéct." (That unhappy *Wednesday* [italics added] in the early evening, I was returning to the dorm when in the hallway two students approached me. They took me to an empty room and there they told me that the police came for the man I was waiting for, and that I should remain quiet and should not attempt to flee.) However, the day *Wednesday* is peculiar; the calendar of 1950 indicates that March 14 actually was a Tuesday, not a Wednesday (author's translation).
26. Kundera, *Laughable Loves*, 38.
27. Kundera, *Laughable Loves*, 34.
28. Kundera, *Unbearable Lightness*, 195.
29. Kundera, *Unbearable Lightness*, 177.
30. Kundera, *The Joke*, 37.
31. Kundera, *Unbearable Lightness*, 177.
32. Kundera, *Nesmrtelnost*, 343.
33. All partial or full quotations in these paragraphs are taken from E.L. Doctorow's article, "Four Characters under Two Tyrannies: The Unbearable Lightness of Being," in *Critical Essays on Milan Kundera*, ed. Peter Petro (New York: G.K. Hall & Co., 1999), 26–30.
34. Kundera, *Nesmrtelnost*, 350.
35. Kundera, *Unbearable Lightness*, 95.

36. Kundera, *Unbearable Lightness*, 95.
37. Kundera, *Unbearable Lightness*, 27.
38. "A Talk with Milan Kundera," Interview with Milan Kundera by Olga Carlisle, 1985. http://www.kundera.de/english/Info-Point/Interview_Carlisle/interview_carlisle.html
39. "A Talk with Milan Kundera."
40. Kundera, *Unbearable Lightness*, 219.
41. Kundera, *Unbearable Lightness*, 218.
42. Kundera, *Unbearable Lightness*, 189.
43. Kundera, *Laughter and Forgetting*, 88.
44. Kundera, *Laughter and Forgetting*, 87.
45. Kundera, *Laughter and Forgetting*, 101.
46. Kundera, *Laughter and Forgetting*, 91.
47. Kundera, *Laughter and Forgetting*, 92.
48. Kundera, *Laughter and Forgetting*, 92.
49. Kundera, *Laughter and Forgetting*, 92.
50. Kundera, *Laughter and Forgetting*, 4.
51. Kundera, *Laughter and Forgetting*, 227.
52. Kundera, *Laughter and Forgetting*, 33.
53. Kundera, *Laughter and Forgetting*, 8.
54. Kundera, *Laughter and Forgetting*, 99.
55. Kundera, *Laughter and Forgetting*, 105.
56. Kundera, *Immortality*, 48.

Chapter Four

Czech Destiny or Fate?

CZECH FATE

Kundera's inquisitive, analytical, and erudite mind was far too expansive to remain content in a small nation. In his 1968 essay "Český úděl" (literally *Czech lot*, known in translation as "Czech Destiny"—though *úděl* semantically implies "heaviness of bearing one's lot," and thus is closer to *fate*), Kundera expresses his skepticism over the "smallness;" (i.e., small mentality—*malost, malá mentalita*) of the Czechs that has developed historically. For instance, he sees "the very embodiment of the spirit of Czech smallness"[1] in the insipidness of the third Communist President Antonín Novotný. In addition, in "Český úděl" he mentions his own play, *Owners of the Keys*, and labels it as anti-Czech because it attacks passivity and complacency of Czechs. In the play, the former Army Major instructs his son-in-law about how Czechs have expressed their political resistance. They have always preferred attending their sport organization to building barricades, the character of Army Major explains. Workouts in Sokol gym have done more for Czechs than ten revolutions.[2]

While Kundera's essay begins with skeptical criticism, it changes its tone once he admits he discovered the greatness of the Czech nation during the unforgettable experience of the Soviet-led invasion of Czechoslovakia in August 1968. When visiting France in the post-invasion period, Kundera participated in innumerable conversations and debates, and to his own surprise, he positively praised Czech patriotism for, what he defines as "a rare nation that has withstood such a test and has shown such steadiness, reason and unity."[3] Further, in "Český úděl" he claims that in retrospect, he saw August of 1968 cast "a new light on our entire history,"[4] and his skeptical criticism was illuminated from a historic angle. In his view, this angle is connecting the current Czech nation with heroic warrior traditions of Jan Žižka and the Hussite movement. In the essay, Kundera also praises Czechs for their "gigantic achievements" in the nineteenth century. They transformed themselves from a nation that had been semi-literate and semi-dissimilated from their Czech identity into a European nation with its own identity despite its unrelenting attempts of systematic Germanization.

In his essay of the same title "Czech Destiny?" (with a question mark), Václav Havel replied to Kundera with a witty irony. Havel's essay was published several months later (February 1969) in the literary magazine *Tvář*. In the name of the entire Czech nation, Havel ironically cheers Kundera's approval for the August 1968 stance. He calls Kundera a "lightly skeptical intellectual dandy," who has always been prone to seeing the shortcomings of Czechs. He accuses him of illusions and a romanticized notion of Czech destiny. Specifically, Havel challenges Kundera's idea of Czechs becoming the center of world history for the first time since the Middle Ages. Due to their Prague Spring movement, "socialism with a human face" in 1967–68, Kundera sees Czechs striving for freedom of the press and eradication of the omnipotent secret police as heroic accomplishments. However, Havel considers them basic rights of any civilized society. Havel also argues with Kundera's idea that the Prague Spring movement was far ahead of its time, and for that reason it was destined to be misunderstood and doomed to failure. This essay debate turned into a serious polemic, Kundera replying a month later to Havel with an essay entitled "Radicalism and Exhibitionism."

Kundera and Havel took critical but contradicting positions in the immediate post-Prague-Spring period; nonetheless, prior to the Prague Spring Reform Movement, they both paved the way for Czechoslovakian liberalization reforms. Kundera's speech at the Fourth Congress of the Czechoslovak Writers initiated the Congress's adopting a resolution that called for rehabilitation of the literary tradition and establishing free contacts with cultures of the West. In the polemical discourses after the crash of the Prague reform movement, Kundera mostly romanticized passive patriotism by celebrating past glories while Havel emphasized the need of addressing problems of the present. Kundera, a Communist, believed in reform, but Havel, a non-Party member, was skeptical about rebuilding the system by reform alone.

During the 1970s normalization period, Havel remained in Prague and became the leading voice of the writers' dissident movement. He was frequently imprisoned for expressing his opinions. Kundera moved to Paris and became the leading novelist. He insisted on his novels bearing existential messages only; however, he was viewed by critics and readers as a vigorous anti-Soviet advocate. In 1989, Havel led the Velvet Revolution and its Civic Forum, and shortly after he became the President of the newly established democratic Czechoslovakia. Setting his differences aside, Havel invited Kundera to join his cabinet, which was largely composed of former writers, dissidents, journalists, and artists. But Kundera declined. In relation to his non-return, he later wrote: "In November 1989, I was overcome with happiness over the ending of occupation, but also with melancholy: for me the change came too late; too late to be able to—and wanting to—turn my life upside down once more, to change my home all over again."[5]

But even today Kundera's and Havel's diverging perspectives remain representative of the Czech culture around the world. Their works, along with Milos Forman's Czech films, are most authoritative in defining the international image of the Czech Republic. In addition, significant was Kundera's attempt to redraw the Cold War boundaries of Europe, an issue that he addressed in his essay "The Tragedy of Central Europe," published in the English translation in the *New York Review of Books* on April 26, 1984. The crux of his argument is his proposed incorporation of "small nations" formerly under Soviet control into Central Europe ("A Kidnapped West," in the Czech original "Únos západu"), where these nations, according to him, belonged historically and culturally, rather than to the Eastern block of Soviet Satellites, whose culture and mentality were somewhat alien to them.

CZECH MENTALITY

There is no doubt that at the nascence of the "Kauza Kundera" in 2008, Iva Militká could be incognizant of Kundera's multifaceted contributions of the past half-century to the international community. In her October 2008 interview, Militká blatantly shifted the guilt of denouncement onto Kundera, saying: "I have known for 15 years that Milan Kundera 'had his fingers in it' (was involved in the denouncing)."[6] When asked how that knowledge made her life easier, she replied in a vernacular manner: "Mně houby záleží na Kunderovi"[7] (I couldn't care less about Kundera), explaining that it didn't bring her any good. On the contrary, once her name appeared in the media, it made her ill at ease because people learned about her involvement in the case. "Why should they know?"[8] she asked, and replied: "It's none of their business."[9] She revealed that she didn't follow Dvořáček's trial, that she never apologized to his parents, never offered any help to his family, or said that she was sorry when he, her dear childhood friend, was released from prison in December 1963. She baldly admitted that she stopped coming to her hometown because she didn't want to run into the Dvořáček family—it would make her feel uncomfortable. All this she did despite knowing that Dvořáček's father was seriously ill for many years and the whole family was going through unspeakable hardship; according to her, Dvořáček's younger brother who had escaped to Canada had drowned with his children. She simply didn't seem to care about the family. Only one thing mattered in her mind: the fear that Dvořáček would divulge her name and those of her parents and relatives who helped him escape to Germany, and they would be arrested. When asked why she thought the police never persecuted her, she defended herself, saying: "I didn't have a part in it (denouncing), I never was interrogated, and there are no documents about me with my name or my signature on them."[10]

These interviews have a comedic effect; like a story in a Kundera novel. As we know from the publicly available police report, Kundera only singled out Dvořáček's *suitcase* and three names to the police, with no further detail. The actual denouncing—telling the police Dvořáček was an Army deserter and an illegal escapee to West Germany—was done by Militká *alone*. But in her interviews, she ignores this fact; she skips it altogether, speaking only of the two students who locked her in a room. When quoting the police report, the *Respekt* editors purposely cut out the information with Militká's name and made it sound as if Kundera alone was responsible for providing *all* the information, including Dvořáček's illicit activities. Their report is as cryptic as can be, a statement that shifts the responsibility onto another actor by omitting crucial details, like a police report that read "a black car (passed by and the next car) hit and killed the man" where "passed by and the next car" is omitted.

How could Militká claim her non-involvement in the case? Her name has appeared in several police documents and in Dvořáček's prison reports; though he spoke of her in a positive light, never saying a single word to compromise her well-being or freedom. While the purpose of the series of interviews with Militká was to clear her name and to transfer shame and guilt onto Kundera (like heavy stones that would push him down to the ground, as he might say), they produced an oxymoronic effect. Even if she excused Kundera's action based on his youth (he was twenty), her *denominator of morality* and her *code of shame* seem to indicate clear remnants of her brainwashed communist past and dogmatic thinking. Claiming that she has felt guilty well over fifty years and yet never lifted a finger to apologize and help her friend's family, whose destruction she initiated and ultimately caused, is absolutely tragic and absurd. Ironically, all those years, she was convinced that Dlask, her boyfriend (and later her husband), went to the police with the information and she was undisturbed by that belief. When interviewers suggested that it must have been difficult for her to live with that knowledge about her husband, her reaction was: "To nevím, nemluvili jsme o tom"[11] (I don't know, we haven't talked about it). Her answer as to why she told Dlask about Dvořáček has been equally quibbling. She replied that she didn't have a choice—she needed to tell him. After all, what if her boyfriend had stumbled upon a strange man in her room that night? That was her final reaction.[12]

Between March 1950 and October 2008, Militká had over half a century to reflect on her deed, but her mind seemed frozen in the time of Stalinist thinking, despite the many political changes and versatile views that evolved over that sixty-year period in Czechoslovakia (and later the Czech Republic). The editors of the October 15, 2008 interview with Militká apologized for removing readers' comments that followed the text. Some comments, they explained, were too inappropriate to be posted online. One can speculate that the removed comments were speaking in favor of Kundera and against the self-justifying Militká with her weak arguments. Anyone who instinctively recognizes right from wrong understands that she contradicted herself and that her self-defensiveness was purposely aimed against the writer of world renomé. Her arguments, it seems, could not convince readers to take her confused statements at face value. [13]

However, this is not to say that Kundera should be exempt from responsibility. If his participation in the case cannot be documented by live witnesses, selected details in his works speak for it. Militká said that soon after March 14, 1950, Dlask and Kundera stopped seeing one another, their friendship was over. But sixty years later, she still would speculate as to whether Kundera went to the police to protect her, Dlask's girlfriend. Kundera might have met her only a handful of times, especially since Militká claimed that the two, Kundera and Dlask, weren't particularly close friends. But the triangle's relationship remains veiled in puzzling mystery: Kundera's hand-written dedication to Dlask and Militká in his first-published volume of poems in 1953 remains proof of a certain degree of loyalty among the trio. In her interviews, Militká would not mention to what extent she knew Kundera personally; she would only refer to him in the connection with Dlask, admitting familiarity with his name. In his own defense, in the 2008 phone interview, Kundera denied knowing her, but she did not publicly react to his reply. Thus, the gaps are numerous since both Kundera and Militká refused to provide concrete details, claiming that they simply did not remember. For instance, Dlask's reaction to Dvořáček's arrest remains unknown. Yet, if Militká was convinced for decades that it was her husband Dlask who denounced Dvořáček, one would expect a verbal exchange on the topic to occur between them.

The information that Militká provided has been inconclusive, showing a visible disconnect between her answers and Kundera's involvement. During her interviews, questions were structured to avoid small but crucial evidential details. The opening of the "Kauza Kundera" has truly been a *family affair* that within days grew into an international spectacle. Not only has Militká been related to Mr. Hradilek, the researcher and coauthor of the detailed report in the *Respekt* weekly, but also to one of her interviewers. Kundera seemed to have become "the common property" of the Militká-Hradilek team, just as the famous trumpeter Klima, who became "the common property" of Ruzena and the staff nurses in Milan Kundera's *Farewell Waltz*. The trumpeter's portrait was hanging on the wall, and "whenever his name came up they all chuckled to themselves as if he were an intimate acquaintance."[14]

"BEAUTIFUL DEMOLITION"

As pointed out, the image of a *suitcase* and its destructive effect that runs through many of his novels speaks convincingly for Kundera's real-life involvement. Some critics have underlined his frequent portrayals of real-life denouncing; however, the generic cases that these represent stem from publicly known facts, and any writer could have adopted them as topics for his or her creative works. But how many people have known about a *suitcase* being deposited in a dorm that had caused a man's arrest, which subsequently became a symbol of destruction in their prose?

It appears a bit too obvious that the two things (a *suitcase* in real life and a *suitcase* in the novels) would happen entirely independently and would have no relation to one another. Would someone have known, for instance, Kundera's novels in the 1970s so perfectly well that he could reconstruct the police report around the *suitcase* with the precision fitting the novelist's works? It seems unlikely especially since his novels were hardly available in Czechoslovakia, being published outside of the country in translation. And how many police officers (or people with an access to police files) in 1950 would type a statement using the name, address, and birthdate of a young man of whom they had never heard? How many students would go to the police and pretend to be a certain Milan Kundera, without having his ID booklet (*občanský průkaz*), but providing his correct address, date of birth, and knowing that this act could have serious repercussions in the climate of the Stalinist terror? And ultimately, would Kundera be so fascinated, if not obsessed, by an event that he did not experience and, perhaps, had only heard of in passing?

Some critics suggested that he might have gone to the police, but over time had forgotten about it. This is very unlikely, because scientific research demonstrates that long-term memory is remarkably stable, especially if it is rehearsed. Going to the police station is not an everyday act for an ordinary citizen, and thus the event would be retained by episodic memory. The names of people, however, could be forgotten because they don't necessarily bear special significance, often are completely arbitrary, or appear quite common. Thus, it might be possible that Kundera has forgotten the name of *Dvořáček*, especially since he never met the man. However, it is very unlikely that he would have forgotten the names of *Dlask* and *Militká*, especially since evidence points out that he was in touch with them in 1953.

FRENCH FICTIONAL MENTALITY

Part Five of Kundera's *Immortality*, entitled "Chance," opens with Agnes feeling blissful after having spent two nights alone in a hotel. Her *suitcase* open, it is packed with her clothes, and on the top of her folded skirt lies a book of Rimbaud's poetry. The poems reminded her of earlier times with her husband. They both liked Rimbaud's verses tied to simple wonders of nature, expressed in semantics of a language that was gradually fading into obsolescence by the generation of Agnes and Paul's daughter, Brigitte. Once she closes *her small suitcase*, Agnes descends the staircase and gets into her car, tossing *the suitcase* onto the backseat.[15] This would be her last trip to the Alps before moving for good to Switzerland, her place of birth. Agnes's decision to leave her husband and change her life makes her "continuously and madly happy."[16] But before she tells her husband and daughter about her decision, she needs to reflect on her upcoming life changes, and decide how to break the news to them.

This part of the novel is permeated with the nostalgic scent of death. Agnes would not make it home from her two-night trip in the Alps or to Switzerland. Readers soon learn about her accidental death caused by a suicidal girl, unrelated to Agnes or anyone else in the novel. Like in other instances, sheer chance and unlucky coincidence cause a death, a *suitcase* foreshadowing the dramatic ending of a character. Agnes remembers her father dying, holding his hand when he "entered the last phase of his death agony." He told her, "Don't look at me anymore."[17] At the same time that Kundera draws the reader into the darkness of dying, he produces one of the most beautiful lyric passages in literature in describing Agnes's death. Her death is preceded by her connecting with nature in the mountains, and permeated with verses of Rimbaud, a poetic admirer of nature.

Part Five of *Immortality* contains a number of situations involving chance and shame. In addition to the motif of a *suitcase*, a motif of *glasses* dominates, indicating Agnes's tumultuous relationship with her younger sister, Laura. There are differences between the two sisters: Laura, their mother's favorite child, is stronger, more sensual and emotional than Agnes. Rational and calm, Agnes is the favorite daughter of their father. In a fierce argument about their father's photographs that he was tearing up (along with his memories) before dying, an angry Laura put her dark glasses on.[18] During another argument, Agnes throws Laura's glasses onto the floor to humiliate her sister. The dark glasses, a symbol of injury and displeasure, break. Laura feels injured, not only by the success of her 'happily married' sister (she perceives her marriage to be a happy one), but also by her younger lover, Bernard. Uninvited, she visits him in his villa in Martinique; however, he gets angry, throws a couple of things into his *suitcase* and leaves. Laura is on the verge of attempting to commit suicide because of her lover's desertion.

But Laura does not die, nor does the suicidal girl who causes Agnes's death. Sitting in the middle of the highway, the girl's head is on her knees. Several cars swerve into a ditch to avoid running over her, including a couple and their children who met their death. The suicidal girl disappears, the loud noise of motorcycles reminding her of existence in the real world. She hitch-hikes with no success. Feeling alienated with the cold world around her, she takes a different route, reaching a smaller, "quieter road." Driving on the highway at the same time, Agnes is disturbed by speeding motorcycles and decides to get off to continue on a "quieter road."[19] Inevitably, the chance (or coincidence) brings the two together: Agnes meeting her death in an attempt to prevent the suicidal girl's death.

To make this scene "vividly real," Mr. Kundera enters this part of the novel with his double, Professor Avenarius. They engage in a metaphysical discussion on reasons that the girl could have had for wanting this "terrible end, making other people die!"[20] The narrator expands his semantic clarification of *reason*, as a reaction to fictional Mr. Kundera's opinion: "Only a reason deprived of reason can lead to such an unreasonable horror."[21] The narrator proposes two meanings for reason: a) one's "ability to think," based on the Latin *ratio*, and b) "the cause," implied in the German *Grund* ('ground,' or 'basis'). Here, Mr. Kundera, the author, steps in, perhaps re-vealing his reason (another of his viewpoints slanted within his usual reason-ing) for his real-life reporting of the *suitcase* to the police: "Such a *Grund* is inscribed deep in all of us, it is the ever-present cause of our actions, it is the soil from which our fate grows."[22] Peter Kussi, the translator of *Immortality*, uses the word *fate*; in the Czech original, Kundera uses *osud*, which means either *destiny* or *fate*. Mr. Kundera—*he* being his own character in the nov-el—continues his reasoning on the account of *Grund*. It's "hidden at the bottom of each of his characters," and he is "more and more convinced that it has the nature of a metaphor."[23] With these ideas Kundera might be hinting at his own *Grund*, inscribed in his own *id* and represented by the metaphor of a *suitcase*. In fact, the fictional Kundera—that is, the real Mr. Kundera in *Immortality*—says to Professor Avenarius that the *Grund*, containing "the nature of a metaphor, is the most important thought that ever occurred to him."[24]

Professor Avenarius, Mr. Kundera's alter ego, plays the role of a manager of chance. He declares Bernard, a broadcasting announcer by profession and Laura's lover, "a complete ass," delivering a piece of paper as a diploma, all incognito. He does this because he likes Laura and intends to free her from him. Embarrassed and humiliated, Bernard distances himself from Laura, refusing to discuss the issue or to admit his shame over the insult. Avenarius, a producer of bad deeds, clashes with a policeman over vandalism. He is arrested on the street where he had been slashing the tires of parked cars with a knife, getting into an argument with a passerby woman. On the one hand, he seems to be attuned to Mr. Kundera's high-minded ideas on novel creating, on philosophy of a human face and its disappearing either into the earth or into the ashes, as well as on the deprivation of all rights of the dead (rights are granted only to a living person). On the other hand, Avenarius seems to be behaving like a scoundrel who cares little about the harm he is causing to others. And as the coincidence has it, his tire slashing affects Paul exactly at the time when he needs to urgently reach Agnes before she passes away in the hospital. His tires punctured, Paul loses the most valuable time, the last moments together with his wife. When he arrives in the hospital with his daughter Brigitte, they find Agnes's body covered with a white sheet.

TWO OR MORE FACES, AND DENOUNCING

The image of a multifaceted character, having *two faces* or *many faces,* frequently runs through Kundera's works, with the author's emphasis on their contradicting nature. In many situations, the idea of two (plus more) faces is expressed by surprise, shock, and betrayal; in others by discovery, but in most cases it is simply a hidden side of the characters. "Is having two faces such a triumph?"[25] asks Jean-Marc in *Identity* when he sees Chantal interacting with her former sister-in-law. The face of Chantal is unfamiliar, a thinly disguised "simulacrum" of the Chantal he loved. The classic picture of a many-faced character has been known since *The Joke.* After some insistence of his peers, Ludvik accepts and internalizes the idea that he is "a man of many faces."[26] They accuse him of individualism and intellectualism because of his behavior and "strange kind of smile."[27] He accepts their assessment because he can't see how he, the individualist, could be correct about himself and yet the others who represent "the spirit of the times—the Revolution itself" could be wrong. The narrator gradually builds on the idea of Ludvik's multiple faces. They keep multiplying—from earnest to witty, and cynical to insecure (being unsure of himself)—to the point that Ludvik no longer knows which of his faces is real. After some reflection, he admits that they were all real because he was too young to know who he was and who he wanted to be.[28]

In addition to his personal discovery, Ludvik's different faces reflect a development of the political and social environments that he was exposed to. Today psychologists would subject his multiple faces (personality) to the Five-Factor Model, known by its acronym OCEAN (openness to experience; conscientiousness; extraversion; agreeableness; and neuroticism, versus their counterparts: cautiousness; carelessness; reservation; coldness; and confidence) to examine which of the dimensions are intrinsic, and which are predominantly caused by social pressure under Communism. Ludvik's personality is like the layers of an onion: on the surface a thin skin, his "strange kind of smile," and deep inside, at the core, his real individuality covered up by multiple layers, one on top of the other. Ludvik is multilayered, not just two-dimensional like many characters in Kundera's fiction. Even Sabina uses a similar method in painting that she calls "Behind the Scenes."[29] On the top layer of her paintings is "an impeccably realistic world," but in the cracks of the canvas, there is something "mysterious," imprecise, unknown.[30] After learning about his death, Sabina sees her former lover Tomas as Tristan through a crack of her painting, not as the Don Juan that he appeared to be on the surface.[31]

Kundera likes to foreground the double dimensionality of his characters forward, as if they would be entirely blank without it. Inevitably, their *doubleness* serves its purpose. For instance, Jean-Marc first enjoys the idea of Chantal's *doubleness*: in reference to her job in funeral advertising, he pictures her as "a spy, a masked enemy, a potential terrorist." However, in a conflict with her sister-in-law, he discovers in her "a collaborationist." The fact that Kundera takes recourse in a "political terminology" descriptor and gives an eerie conclusion to Jean-Marc's thoughts, makes the reader ask whether he is providing a clue to his author's personality. To what extent does he describe Chantal, and how much of it belongs to its creator, Milan Kundera? Through thoughts of Jean-Marc, he says about Chantal: "A collaborationist who serves a detestable power without identifying with it, who works for it while keeping separate from it, and who one day, standing before her judges, will defend herself by claiming that she had two different faces."[32] And, of course, when Chantal is introduced in the first paragraph of *Identity*, she arrives in a Normandy coast town with *a small valise.* Before she goes for a walk on the beach, she leaves her *suitcase* in her hotel room. This time, the heroine doesn't encounter her death; that's what is understood from the last image of Chantal and Jean-Marc's profiles seen under the light of a bed stand lamp despite many layers of previously compiling visual images that aimed at the surreal. She ends up in a confusion of hallucinating dreams of orgies and fire ("she is in flames, utterly naked"), Jean-Marc desperately searching for her on the train she took to London. The description of this passage evokes a hopelessness of a human being faced with loneliness; inevitably it reflects the author's feelings to some degree. Jean-Marc feels like "a marginal person, homeless, a bum,"[33] but he must help Chantal; though, he doesn't know how, "he is the only one who can help her, he, he alone, because she has nobody else in the world."[34]

These pages set in mournful grayness imbue the whole novel with the author's turmoil. This was his second novel that he wrote in French, completing it in France in the fall of 1996 at the age of sixty-seven. His French characters lack the natural flow and depth of Czech characters, and this is not only due to his writing in French, Kundera's non-native language, but also to the absence of the vibrantly rich human relationships that he had while living in his home country. Loneliness, sadness and pessimism are so deeply set at the core of *Identity* that one almost feels a deep sorrow for its creator. The motif of saliva through which he describes human beings as "one single community of salivas, one humankind wet and bound together,"[35] seems to be a rather forced abstraction that does not evoke readers' compassion. It is a novel of "boredom," and indeed the author presents its three degrees: "passive, active and rebellious" boredoms.[36] The author's vision and perception of the world have descended to a level of human exhaustion: there is very little that is exciting around us and we are more and more distant from one another. Of course, death is present, too. Framed by Chantal's working for an agency advertising funerals (and implicitly promoting death), the novel feels like a novel for the dead. It falls short of expressing the paradoxical vignette most likely intended by Kundera: the cheerfulness of advertising versus the gravity of death. Chantal buried her five-year-old son, yet we don't learn why he died. The focus of the child's death centers on the irreplaceability of an individual: Chantal refuses her former sister-in-law's advice to make another child in order to forget the dead one.

But there is also a death of Jean-Marc's old friend, F. The two were close friends since high school until one day later in life, at a meeting at work, when his colleagues attack Jean-Marc and F. didn't defend him. This scene is a simplified betrayal like the one that Kundera described with compassion and persuasion in *The Joke*. Unlike Ludvik, Jean-Marc only loses his job, which he doesn't care for much; however, he deeply cares about being betrayed by his friend. His friendship with F. has ended, but at Chantal's wishes, he visits him in the hospital. Kundera connects their past friendship with the idea of mirroring images of oneself of the past and from the past: F. reminds him of the disgust that a teenage Jean-Marc felt when seeing a movement of the eyelid over the cornea of a girl's eye.[37] Jean-Marc doesn't remember this and doesn't care "about the mirror of himself from the past his friend is holding up to him." He feels a strange joy when he realizes he doesn't have to see F. anymore. When he learns that F. has died, he isn't upset, just relieved.

As awkward as the reading of these pages feels, one cannot forget the author's friendship with Dlask, who passed away around the mid-1990s (his grandson, Matěj Hradilek, provided the year, 1997), and allegedly revealed Kundera's name in the "Kauza Kundera" to his wife, Iva Militká in 1992. Did some drastic exchange of opinions implying betrayal occur on March 14, 1950 between Kundera and Dlask that had affected their friendship, and Kundera's attitude toward Dlask for good? Within this context, the idea of "feeling a strange joy" when Jean-Marc's friend dies only reinforces this suspicion.

In most of his novels Kundera is preoccupied with the idea of denouncing. Not only that Chantal has two faces but that she is also depicted as an imaginary informer. When she seeks a graphologist service to find out if the author of secret love letters to her is Jean-Marc, a young graphologist—in whom she recognizes a waiter from her previous unpleasant encounter in a café—tells her: "This is not an informer's office."[38] She feels shame ("her mantle of flames turned into a mantle of shame"[39]) like a traitor who denounced the man she loved to the police.[40] In one of his letters, Jean-Marc anonymously wrote, "your valise looked to me like something artificially added on to your life."[41] The *suitcase* that was "artificially added" to Kundera's own life has made the persistent line *suitcase-police-denouncing* vividly present throughout his novels.

The notion of *two faces* has been explored in other literatures as well. For instance, Italo Calvino's novel *Il visconte dimezzato* (The Cloven Viscount) introduces two surreal characters of viscount Medardo, after he was split into two halves in the territory of Bohemia, in the times of wars and plague, the bubonic black disease. One part of the viscount, Gramo, exemplifies evil and causes damage but is entitled to privileges, including life in a castle. Buono, the other part, leads a simple life in the woods, bringing good and helping villagers. Mistrustful locals don't like either part of the viscount; the *two* parts eventually die in a fight over their *one* bride. Severely wounded, Gramo and Buono are sewn back together into one, and Medardo marries his bride. While the ending of Calvino's novel is fairytale-like, its idea is not unlike Kundera's notion of good and evil existing in one person (as he claims, it is in all of us). But Kundera's characters don't find life "living together happily ever after" as individuals, couples, friends, a community, or a nation. His characters, good or bad, contain a streak of viciousness, and their lives remains open to constant changes and human struggles. In this sense, Kundera's philosophy is close to Milos Forman's, whose characters exhibit a similar attitude: ignorance of their surroundings, pain, pessimism, deviousness, and occasionally brutality.

It is typical for Kundera's literary form to digress from a storyline to engage in philosophizing over a topic, often on several pages. In *Identity*, he has opted for the topic of friendship as a reflection of mirroring oneself in the past. Jean-Marc's friendship with F. has gone sour over betrayal, and he is discussing it with Chantal as a part of a daily conversational exchange. Unfortunately, as much as Kundera attempts to hide his authorial voice, it is present, too strong to believe that it is a natural voice of his fictional characters. Its stiffness is underlined by Chantal's passivity; her short questions and comments in the form of interruptions of Jean-Marc's soliloquy feel more like fillers used in a literary context by debutant writers than her spontaneous reactions. Jean-Marc (Kundera) sees the premise of friendship today in its transformation from traditional values of *helping friends* to "a contract of politeness, of mutual consideration."[42] Jean-Marc explains to Chantal that friendship used to spring from "an alliance against adversity, an alliance without which man would be helpless before his enemies."[43] In his eyes, it no longer exists today: it is institutionalized by consumer advocate organizations that offer help, and it has lost its power to be stronger than any ideology.

This dialogue that was born from the death of F. and turned into Jean-Marc's monologue begins with his disappointment over his own legacy to friendship: "between the truth and a friend, I always choose a friend."[44] To justify his statement, Jean-Marc gives an example of the great and natural friendship of Alexandre Dumas's four musketeers—D'Artagnan (the Gascon gentleman) and his three friends from the King's regiment, Athos, Porthos, and Aramis. The musketeers valued friendship above the truth, he tells Chantal. When required by the kingdom (an agency representing the truth) to fight on opposite sides, against one another, they retained their friendship despite the institutional interference. The romanticized and nostalgic feeling of lost friendship that Kundera experienced when working on *Identity* is not an unusual phenomenon.

FRIENDS IN NEED

Milan Kundera's friendship in Moravia was formed in his earlier years of adolescence, and while it has survived (as evident from his own references), it has acquired a distant and quite different form due to natural processes of human aging and Kundera's leaving his home country, relatives and friends, traditions and values. In 1990, after receiving a letter from Brno signed by Jan Šabata, the head of a new publishing co-op, Kundera writes nostalgically: "Suddenly, in front of my eyes I saw Jan's father, Jaroslav, whom I admired when I was seventeen and when he was nineteen. And in front of my eyes, I saw young Milan Uhde, and the road in the fields between Brno and Královo Pole, on which we walked, having lengthy discussions together, at the time, when I wasn't yet twenty-five and he twenty. It seemed to me that the circle was closing."[45] Jan Šabata offered Milan Kundera to take care of his books forbidden over the past two decades to be published in Czechoslovakia. As Kundera writes, this letter put him into a happy but melancholic mood over the lost but beautiful time of the past.

Milan Uhde seems to remain a friend of Kundera. When the "Kauza Kundera" erupted, he defended his friend by saying that, if he were in Kundera's position of the university dormitory head in the political climate of 1950, he would have gone to the police, too. This admission by Uhde inadvertently implied that he found it quite possible that Kundera had gone to the police. But when asked if he had ever denounced someone, he objected, saying he would never report even a minor incident. He explained that after listening to a broadcasting of a son denouncing his own father, he became petrified by such a brutal act.[46] But even if Kundera's friendship with Uhde remains, the two friends, both writers, live in two separate worlds. It is an open question of how many of Kundera's friends from his childhood and adolescent years have remained his genuine friends today. Regardless of what the friendship and truth are, there is a great amount of mysterious information about Kundera circulating among Czechs of his generation. For instance, the January 29, 2009 *iDnes* online issue reported Ladislav Vorel's past conversation with Petr Chudožilov, a former dissident and one of the Charter 77 signatories, about Kundera, saying that he apparently based *The Joke* on his own experience, claiming that he denounced his friend Jan Trefulka. As sketchy as this information sounds, one might conclude that the conversation would have taken place before 1975, the year Kundera left for Paris, for allegedly Chudožilov told the dissident Vorel: "If you don't believe me, just ask Kundera. He surely won't deny it. But can you imagine doing something as low as this and then to write a book about it?"[47] One only wonders how Chudožilov arrived to such a conclusion. Unfortunately, the distribution of these *he said she said* reports can be relatively wide and their information easily consumed once it gets into frequently read newspapers and periodicals. In this particular case, there is no evidence to support this statement, and in addition, it proves that both dissidents have been only superficially acquainted with *The Joke*, and possibly with the rest of Kundera's novels.

IT'S *THE JOKE*

As a piece of literary art, *The Joke* is one of the most brilliantly written novels of the twentieth century. Not only does it offer moving personal stories of several characters, but at the same time it clarifies the process of changing one political system to another and the impact of that change on the everyday life of man and his family, reaching the corners of philosophy, religion, history, music, folkloric traditions, and cultural values. From the viewpoint of musical polyphony, it gives a voice to four characters (Ludvik, Jaroslav, Kostka, and Helena), leaving Lucie—one of the most cherished characters—without a voice; thus, keeping her only as an allusion, a mystery. Throughout the novel, readers constantly stumble upon asking which of the portraits of each character is "real." Of course, there is no such notion as one permanent and single image of a character: each is subjected to his or her own perceptions and to a variety of perceptions by other characters. Nothing in the novel is static; everything is in flux. As David Lodge said in *Critical Quarterly*, Kundera has subjected the aesthetics of *The Joke* to a "radical rearrangement of the spatio-temporal continuity of the narrative line—what the Russian formalists called the deformation of the *fabula* in the *sjuzet*."[48] In his critical foreword to its 1968 French edition, *La Plaisanterie*, published immediately after the crushing of the Prague Spring, Louis Aragon, a journalist, spokesperson for Communism and a prominent figure in French avant-garde poetry, hailed *The Joke* as "one of the greatest novels of the century."

The musicality of the novel is already noticeable in the table of contents. Divided into seven parts, the novel is structured within the reflection of Ludvik's perception: A-B; A-C; A-D; A-C-B, or Ludvik-Helena; Ludvik-Jaroslav; Ludvik-Kostka; and the seventh part, longer, and intense, Ludvik-Jaroslav-Helena. In addition, the author establishes the technique of a tempo (speed) in each part by proportioning the number of pages (length) in each chapter with the number of the chapters, subjecting them to musical terminology. For instance, Part One "Ludvik" is very short (nine pages and no chapters = *adagio*), Part Two "Helena" is also very short (ten pages in three chapters = *allegro*), Part Three "Ludvik" is long (eighty-eight pages in fourteen chapters = *moderato*), Part Four "Jaroslav" is short but dense (thirty-eight pages in ten chapters = *presto*), etc.

While Kostka's voice takes only one ninth of the novel length in Part Six (forty pages in twenty chapters, thus possibly *prestissimo*, [i.e., faster than *presto*]), it presents one of the most uplifting Christian teachings via Kostka's views, only to be undercut by his human imperfection, a lost battle of the soul versus the body that turns his teachings into a paradox by his act of Lucie's seduction. In *The Joke*, it is not only Kostka's act but almost every character's intended act, be it positive or negative, that is shaken and turned upside down, including the title of the novel, and culminating into an unwanted antinomy, leaving everyone bewildered or bewitched.

In Part Six of *The Joke,* "an old, ugly and cheap" *suitcase* belongs to Lucie. Hidden in a heap of hay in an abandoned barn in a countryside village, it is discovered by a farm director and examined by both the farm director and the local *policeman*. Once they open the suitcase, they find four nice new dresses and some underwear. The men know it belongs to a homeless girl who has recently appeared in their village and has stimulated local children's fantasies about the existence of a fairy. This chapter is narrated by Kostka, a Christian believer. As a student, he initially stands on the side of "Communist minority," but is questioned about his religious faith. At the intervention of Ludvik, who defends his difficult position, Kostka is permitted to continue his studies but decides to leave the university, realizing that Communist and Christian teachings don't bond together, each getting more and more contradictory. He accepts a position on a farm, and takes Lucie, the homeless girl, under his supervisory and spiritual guidance.

This part of the novel is shockingly fascinating. From Ludvik's viewpoint readers already know details about Lucie's life that Kostka doesn't know, and through Kostka, they learn new and surprising details about her, and about Ludvik. The new information includes a paradox of the previously established information, and a chain of paradoxes encircles readers' minds into a conviction to form yet another opinion of the character. Lucie, who Ludvik believes to be a virgin after she refuses him, confides in Kostka that she was a part of a male gang and each member used to frequently rape her. When finally she offers her love to Kostka, he rejects it (her soul), realizing that he has been afraid of her love, not knowing what to do with it, given he had a wife and son in Prague. But he desired her physically (her body) from the moment he met her, calling himself "a seducer in a priest's robe." Her soul abandoned and lonely, Lucie is destined to suffer in silence. She marries a man from the village, who becomes a brute, drinking and beating her up. Like in many other situations, the *suitcase* determines Lucie's destiny, opens unknown horizons for her but ultimately leads to her downfall. She is alive, but her lot is tragic. She becomes a hairdresser and moves to the next village to be close to Kostka, her spiritual teacher and strength in her life.

Not surprisingly, the theme in this part of the novel is *forgiving*. Using Kostka's words, the author states that people don't know how to forgive, that forgiveness is out of their power, and that "to annihilate a sin exceeds a man's strength" and only God's "mysterious and supernatural power can erase men's sins, make them into nothingness."[49] This passage speaks once more of Kundera's conviction that he owes nothing in terms of explanation or justification in the "Kauza Kundera." Chapters 17 and 18 are a powerful witness to Kundera's talent and thoughtfulness. It is a rare occurrence in contemporary Czech literature that authors would express their thoughts on religious faith, and write as clearly, smoothly, spiritually, and convincingly as Kundera. It is rather Russian writers who have been devotedly religious-expressive, introducing faith in their fictional characters. Kostka's call to Ludvik to examine his own attitude of revenge for the injustice that was done to him by his university peers and by society is a reminder of Alexander Solzhenitsyn's character in *The First Circle* of the Stalinist inferno. Gleb Nerzhin, a political prisoner finds strength, personal happiness, and freedom in the un-free world of prison. When his wife Nadia visits him, she realizes that she is the one who suffers more by living a free life in Stalinist Moscow, and that the prison suits her husband well: "Seen from the outside it appeared an unhappy one [life], but Nerzhin was secretly happy in that unhappiness. He drank it down like spring water."[50] In his mind, Kostka speaks in the same vein to Ludvik, reproaching him for becoming "bitter to the depths of his soul" because he was put in the mines with "the politically dangerous soldiers" and because "the sense of injustice" guides him at every step. Giving the example of Jesus and his disciples, Kostka encourages Ludvik to view his experience as a mission, as a "great opportunity" to better himself. He wraps up his mental exercise aimed at Ludvik with an idea that the people thrown into unwanted situations are "merely the unwitting messengers of a higher will," often responding to "disguised instructions from above."[51]

These God-driven ideas on accepting one's lot, no matter how difficult the fate may be, and profiting from it by acquiring an outlook of wisdom and self-betterment, could easily be interpreted as Kundera's message from the "above" to Dvořáček.

In Part Three "Ludvik," the narrator provides skillful details of his life in the camp for the "black insignia" and describes the hardship in the mines of Ostrava; a Moravian city covered by black soot, with such physical and psychological detail that it appears the author experienced that hard life in reality. Initially, this description might have confused some critics: it was all mingled in a nebulous veil of Kundera's "autobiographical novel." However, now it gives an impression that Kundera was guided by the invisible upper hand to live through *in writing* what Dvořáček had to live through *in real life* due to their coincidental constellation dominated by a *suitcase*.

THE (REAL LIFE) JOKE?

Dvořáček's dream of reaching the sky as a pilot collapsed in the life paradox of reaching down into the ground as a miner. It is in close proximity to the collapse of Ludvik's dream of becoming a positive builder of a new society when he is reduced to a political worker in the coal mines. Ironically, after his second illegal escape from Czechoslovakia on September 10, 1968, Dvořáček and his wife landed in British Columbia, and he continued working as a miner of copper ore in the Britannia Mine in Squamish, near Vancouver. His son Patrik, born in Canada, is quoted in Adam Hradilek and Martin Tichý's report "Osudová mise Moravcova kurýra" (A fateful mission of Moravec's agent), speaking of his father's perpetual exhaustion, which led to divorcing his Czech wife of several years. Either he worked (in the mine), slept, or ate, nothing else, said his son. In the second half of the 1970s, Dvořáček moved to Sweden and married his brother's former classmate, Markéta Dvorská. (In 1954, after learning of his fate, she pretended to be his brother's fiancée in order to be able to visit Dvořáček in prison.) If fearless Dvorská were a fictional character in Kundera's novels, she would represent the other spectrum of Militká's fearful but depersonalized force[52]—in Kundera's words—a "totalitarian kitsch" that he defines in *The Unbearable Lightness of Being* as "the aesthetic ideal of a single political power."[53]

In Sweden, Dvořáček spent some thirty-five years, and half of this time he worked in food service in a Gothenburg hospital. One can only hope that surrounded by the love of his second wife, his life was finally peaceful and enjoyable in this picturesque and dreamily charming European city. Fictional Ludvik arrives to the conclusion that "a beautiful demolition" that he wanted to achieve as an act of vengeance is fruitless. After brutally seducing the wife of his former friend (and later his enemy), he realizes the futility of his act because "one's destiny is often complete long before death,"[54] and *all wrongs will be forgotten* for *no one will redress them.*

KUNDERA, THE AUTHOR OF POTENTIAL POSSIBILITY

As many coincidences as govern Kundera's novels, it is not a coincidence that he has become one of the greatest novelists of our times on the international stage. On a brighter note, a more positive attitude toward Kundera and an interest in his works have grown in recent years in the Czech Republic. In 2008, his friend, Ladislav Smoček, convinced Kundera to allow him to set his 1966 play *Ptákovina* (The Blunder) in the Prague Činoherní klub, and it has been staged successfully until now. Kundera says that of his four plays he has been most attached to *Ptákovina*. He worked on the play in a Slovak spa town, Trenčianské Teplice, writing every morning for several hours over one week.[55] *Ptákovina* is based on a drawing of a rhombus ◊, a quadrilateral in geometry (or a diamond in spoken English), which is often painted as graffiti on buildings, walls, and fences in the Czech Republic, with a short vertical bar in the middle of the rhombus. It is a graphic representation of the female vagina, mostly drawn by teenage boys but understandable to every Czech and Slovak. The word *ptákovina* (a blunder, farce) is unique too, containing nuances of colloquialism and eroticism of *pták,* (a bird), slang for *penis.* These erotic undertones are linguistically and culturally preserved only in Czech and Slovak; thus, the essence of the farce could not reach other audiences. The play is set in a school environment where boredom clashes with power and indecency. The school director draws the rhombus on the blackboard, and the school head needs to find and punish the culprit. One of the pupils is secretly spying, another pupil falsely admits guilt and his ears are cut off, and the director gets involved in a sexual intrigue with the school head's wife. These motifs prove to be further evidence of Kundera's attraction from the very beginning of his creativity to depict eroticism, betrayal, and denouncement, set in a frame of humor and political farce. It works perfectly when applied to Czech characters, depicted with their humanly multidimensional nature against their country's backdrop. It has ignited the imagination of Western readers and inspired them to adore Kundera, this Czech "intellectual dandy."

Kundera did, in fact, return to the Czech characters in *Ignorance* (albeit written in French), and thus revived the energy and intimacy of his fiction. Except for a few enthusiastic voices, critical reviews of his previous *Identity* were unflattering or flat, pointing at its French characters as quite *un-French*, almost generic. They could have been situated in any European country and be of any nationality. On the contrary, in *Ignorance*, he explores identity against a larger canvas of Europe and time-space. On the surface, the two Czechs, Irena and Josef, appear to be ordinary folks, not evoking much sympathy; however, underneath they open up to a world of intimacy of delusions, ironies, and contradictions, and call for readers' compassion. The story itself, based on the idea of Odysseus's great return to Ithaca after two decades of wandering, is less significant than its theme of memory. Wrapped in and driven by coincidence of a random meeting of Irena and Josef at the Paris airport when each is "returning" to Prague after twenty years, the motif of coincidence recurs from the distant past. In their youth they randomly met in a Prague bar. At that time, attracted by Irena, Josef gave her a little ashtray that he took from the bar, and invited her to his flat. Tempted, Irena accepted the ashtray, a little souvenir of their mutual attraction, but refused his invitation because she was dating Martin, her future husband. This brief episode left a profound mark on Irena but none on Josef.

In preparing to immigrate with Martin to Paris, Irena packs the ashtray into her *suitcase*. Inevitably, the appearance of the *suitcase* indicates upcoming death, and the ashtray—a tangible connector between Josef and Irena—aims at a double death. In fact, not too far into their arrival in France, Irena's husband dies, and Josef's Danish wife passes away in Denmark, a country of his immigration. A political denouncement enters on the stage of *Ignorance* as well; this time it is muted and unobtrusive, but present in its full force. It is Martin's old friend, a bachelor, whom they visited shortly before their departure and "spent some emotional hours with together. Only later, in France, did they learn that the reason this man had been so attentive to them over time was because the police had selected him to inform on Martin."[56] Irena is extensively preoccupied with her image of being entrapped by a secret police—in her dreams her old friends work for the secret police, and might denounce her. She feels that even Gustaf's contacts in Prague could be a potential threat to her until she realizes that the barrier between the two worlds, Communist and the free West, is as impenetrable as wrought iron.

The theme of unpleasant consequences resulting from coincidence is spread throughout the novel like snowflakes in a snowstorm. A high school girl, Milada, falls for Josef, "a detestable snot whose only desire was to torture her."[57] He attempts to seduce her at the time her school has scheduled a skiing trip in the mountains. This scenario is reminiscent of Ludvik's planning to seduce Marketa, who is sent to the Party school training exactly during the weeks of Ludvik's planned seduction. Milada, out of despair over losing her boyfriend, decides to end her life. Wandering into the purity of snow-brilliance reflected in the sun, she consumes sleeping pills. She survives, losing one ear to frostbite. This incident affects her life—she is left destitute to loneliness and bitterness, abandoned by Josef for good. In fact, middle-aged Josef remembers nothing; he learns all this from his diary of his youth, which his family kept for him among his few possessions after he had emigrated.

From a methodology approach, many of these themes have been worked out in Kundera's previous novels. In the earlier years of his creativity, Kundera used to elaborate on a theme—mentioned in passing in his previous works—by developing it into a full topic, story, or novel. For instance, the idea of *slowness* appeared first in connection with Lucie in *The Joke* when Ludvik meets her in front of a movie theatre. In *Slowness,* he expands this idea philosophically and touches upon issues ranging from the perception of the speed of life in modern times versus the eighteenth-century slow-paced lifestyle, and indulgence in erotic affairs. In the period of his Czech creativity (partly including his French creative period, up to around the year 2000), Kundera's topical approach was a *progression*, but since then, during his exclusively French period, his approach had turned into a *digression*. It is not only that the narrative in his novels becomes compact, if not simplified, with a unity of plot, but in a sense, also redundant. Some topics and motifs, elaborated before artistically and convincingly, often in a polyphony of voices, are now presented in a reductionary way. The idea of memory is one of them.

The situation of a male student attempting to seduce a naïve girl exactly at the time period when circumstances prevent them to be together was seen in Ludvik and Marketa in *The Joke*. The attempt to commit suicide by downing over-the-counter medication was dramatically described in Helena's case after she had understood that Ludvik didn't love her. These women, teenage Milada and mature Helena, are ready to take their lives because their "love objects" abandon them. The idea of memory in *Ignorance* is contrasted with the idea of forgetting in *The Book of Laughter and Forgetting*. Kundera's characters either wish to forget their past (Mirek), avenge it (Ludvik), or recover it (Tamina). Regardless of what their intentions are, their past, painful or endearing, has been present, living with them in their memories. But twenty years later, the author of *Ignorance* forces the reader to believe in the idea of selective amnesia for his relatively young character (about fifty-five years old), Josef. Kundera cleverly approaches the idea, saying that: "Josef's memory was malevolent and provided him nothing to make him cherish his life in his country," and for that reason, "he crossed the border with a brisk step and with no regrets."[58] The idea of memory in *Ignorance* is an extension of memory that we encountered in Jean-Marc and his old friend F., but it is dressed in a more elegant coat. It refers to a memory of displaced individuals who lost the prospect of developing their memories along with their loved ones in one steady environment, such as a couple living in one apartment and sharing similar experiences and therefore retaining similar memories. However, "memory capacity varies among individuals,"[59] Kundera instructs their readers, explaining that two people cannot have the same recollections. His authorial contemplation on quantifying memory by using "the ratio between the amount of time in the lived life and the amount of time from that life that is stored in memory,"[60] is fruitless, as he acknowledges it even before getting into details, using a paradigm of his previously seen "a hundred-millionth" in *The Unbearable Lightness of Being* in reference to differences in female bodies.

The crucial information about memory that one might get in *Ignorance* may, actually, be the reference to Kundera's own memory and Kundera as a person. It seems that he has been hunted more persistently than his fictional Josef by that "little snot so that never (even if only in a bad dream) would he be mistaken for him, be vilified in his stead, be held responsible for his words and his acts!"[61] And that "very brief chapter of his life came to an end, and, having neither sequel nor consequence, was relegated to the dim cupboard of cast-off items."[62] Kundera published this novel a full decade after the new regime took place in his homeland. By that time, political lustrations had shown who had been good and who had been naughty under the iron gaze of Communism. It seems that nothing bad came out about him in relation to the 1950 episode when researchers dutifully examined secret police files; so he could finally feel confident that his secrets would continue to remain secret.

Nonetheless, he has remained vigilant, defending his position in view of existential inquiry and political judgment. In his authorial voice, speaking for himself, his characters, his readers, and for all émigrés, Kundera throws in a thought about life left behind. It has "a bad habit of stepping out of the shadows, of bringing complaints against us, of taking us to court."[63] And once more, he skillfully covers his thoughts under a blanket of inquiry: Who were the *guilty parties*? Finding an immediate answer, he assures us that everyone was guilty, including Mr. Kundera: "Everybody was hunting down the guilty and everybody was being hunted down."[64] And to avoid his readers' confusion, the author resumes his fiction in a most natural manner. Yes, Josef has remained a friend of N., the former "Red Commissar" that everyone was afraid of, especially Josef's sister-in-law who hated him fiercely. But N. helped Josef in a moment of his political *faux-pas*; he raised his hand in Josef's defense, and now, if necessary, Josef would raise his hand in defense of N. Josef and N. have remained true friends despite the contortion of history. N.'s belief in Communism had roots in the philosophy of Karl Marx but Josef's sister hated N. as an abortionist of free society to enslavement of Communist-driven-ideology society. Josef has always disliked her. Now twenty years later he realizes that she only cares about private property being taken away from her by the state; however, she has no feelings of regret for appropriating a painting that was given to Josef by a persecuted dissident, and bears his personal dedication to him. Josef's view of his own past life in his homeland and of his relatives, who still live there, could be put into the ashtray that he had given to Irena, and thrown away. He has no

respect for himself, for the past, for his brother who—as an opportunist—
joined the Party to complete his education in medicine, or for his relatives,
who have disposed of him as no longer existing. Josef is standing alone, a
single body against the camps of his antagonists and of his antagonistic
memories and dismal discoveries. And as Mr. Kundera convincingly assures
us, the memory is the key to everything that happened in the past. Who then
could today accuse him of going to the police on March 14, 1950, with a
report? Mr. Hradilek who published an article about the incident in the *Respekt* magazine? No. Mr. Kundera has no memory of such an event, and he is
not lying. His selective amnesia has erased everything that needed to be
erased from his memory. Whatever he wanted to say and admit, he has done
it in his novels.

    Thus, the correct answer to Mr. Kundera's identity is to read his novels,
reflect on their characters and ideas, and clear one's memory of the bad
memories.

DVOŘÁČEK, THE CREATOR
OF POTENTIAL REALITY

In Kundera's view, the secret of human life lies in the proximity of the border
that can be easily crossed and behind which feelings (faith, love, fear, etc.)
lose their meaning. His words ring true in his works of fiction. They are also
applicable to the "crossing of the real border" of the two friends, Dvořáček
and Juppa. Most likely, Kundera has never looked into the lives of the two
men, and yet he knows well that they, like he, have not been freed from the
constraints of the invisible force that pulls people in only one direction within all the possibilities that the universe offers—the life that they must go
through before they die. In evaluating Dvořáček's and Juppa's destiny, one
could conclude that Dvořáček was unlucky, while Juppa, who wasn't caught
during his secret missions between Germany and Czechoslovakia, was the
lucky one. However, Juppa's family had no news of him or from him for
almost two decades. Only in the late 1960s during the political *détente*, did
he send a note to his parents and brother saying that he was well, living in
Germany. In the Prague Spring period of 1968, his family was permitted to
travel to Austria to meet with him. They learned that his life was far from
happy. In 1950, he was seriously injured in a car crash, his head suffering the
most from the impact. Unable to continue his work for the secret service, he
moved with his German wife to Chicago, where he held odd jobs, including
working in a crematorium. At his wife's and her family's insistence, the
couple returned to Germany two years later in 1956, and Juppa regretted it
ever since. Back in Germany, he was pressured by the secret service of both
camps, the Western and Eastern, to join them. As a result, he suffered a

mental breakdown and spent a considerable amount of time recovering in medical institutions. In 1969, his brother Vlastimil succeeded in visiting him one more time before Husák's government closed down the border. Their next meeting, which took place in 1990, revealed visible signs of Juppa's fateful life. After his wife's death, he felt lonely, and being without children and close relatives, he became withdrawn, sad, and suspicious to the point of being paranoid, his brother revealed to Mr. Hradilek.[65] The emigration filled his life with sadness and disappointments, not happiness and professional success as he had hoped for. It was a paradox of expectation that could add to the coloring of Czech émigrés tossed around Europe in Kundera's *Ignorance,* and *The Book of Laughter and Forgetting.*

FICTIONAL REALITY ON RASKOLNIKOV'S TERMS

The implicated sadness of Dvořáček and Juppa is subconsciously but masterfully expressed in Jakub's view of his "revealed denial of beauty" when he meets Mrs. Klima in the spa town in *Farewell Waltz.* Stunned, Jakub realizes that he had missed *beauty* in his life. He meant a feminine beauty that he noticed in Mrs. Klima, a youngish, physically flawless former actress. She became a messenger of his *discovery of beauty,* sent to him, unfortunately, only several hours before his leaving his native land. He muses on his own experience with women, realizing it was "thirst for revenge, or sadness and dissatisfaction, or sympathy and pity" that drove him to them. Like Ludvik, Jakub recognizes that the feminine world for him merged with "the bitter drama of life in his country, where he had been both victim and persecutor."[66] When naked in front of a dressed Lucie in a small room that one of the miners let him use for the night, Ludvik was "seized by an insane rage," feeling similarly to Jakub: being possessed by that *hostile force* that had "senselessly deprived him of everything: women, friends, studies, Party, happiness."[67]

One of the reasons why Milan Kundera's novels are so appealing to worldwide readers is his deep human sensitivity, expressed in a simplistic beauty, even though often wrapped in black-and-white humor and critical judgment. Milan Kundera is a man of profound feelings and suffering. He lives for and through his writings, identifying with every single character that he brings to life in his novels and plays. For instance, when Jakub reflects on leaving "a place where he had been born by mistake, and where he didn't really belong," he is also painfully aware that "he was leaving his only homeland, and that he had no other."[68] On the way out of his country, Jakub speculated on whether or not his blue pill caused Ruzena's death, his thoughts being aligned with guilt that he struggled with. He admitted that the issue wasn't whether his pill was poisonous or not, but the fact that he was convinced of its lethal composition and did nothing to retrieve it from Ruzena. That made him a murderer, he realized, and in addition, a murderer without a motive. "Nothing was to be gained by it . . . its only sense was to make him see that he was a murderer,"[69] reflected Jakub about himself. This fictional statement sounds familiar; it is, as if it was Kundera's allusion to himself in the case of Dvořáček's *suitcase* reporting.

The whole Chapter 18 of the "Fifth Day" in the last part of the novel offers additional insight into Jakub's rationalizing on human nature and the right to live and kill. Jakub attempts to defend his possible murder in terms of Raskolnikov in Fyodor Dostoevsky's *Crime and Punishment*. He killed to prove that he was capable of the act of killing, asking: "Does a man have the right to kill an inferior human being, and would he be strong enough to bear the consequences?"[70] What makes Kundera's ideas challenging in comparison with Dostoevsky's is his placement of a character into a *potential possibility*. The readers know that Raskolnikov is a fictional character and within that *fictional setting*, he *really killed* the old pawnbroker. But Kundera places his fictional character within a *potential possibility*: Jakub does not know the truth and that *potential possibility* of indirectly killing Ruzena allows him to play with all possible ideas. For instance, the narrator uncovers Jakub's thoughts on "all human beings" who, according to him, have a secret desire of the death of another human being. But it is the physical difficulties associated with the killing and the punishment that would follow that prevent them from committing murder.

Reflecting on Raskolnikov, Jakub attempts to convince himself that the Dostoevsky character couldn't bear his act of murdering because his conscience as a believer in God was strongly presented in him. But Jakub, considering himself to be enlightened and free from religious beliefs, feels no remorse for the potential death of the nurse Ruzena. Approaching the border, he is relaxed and self-content. He assumes but *does not know* that the nurse is dead, and feels that his "deed was weightless, easy to bear, light as air." This idea of assuming but not knowing, the so-called *potential possibility*, has been repeated in Kundera's works from early on until his last novel, *The Festival of Insignificance*. One might presume that it relates to his *private feelings* of the "Kauza Kundera." If this "light as air" weightlessness is, in fact, a conscious reference to the 1950 episode, then its honest response is to be found in the following thought: Jakub wondered "whether there was not more horror in this lightness"[71] than it was in Raskolnikov's agony, expertly described by Dostoevsky on numerous pages of the novel. As pointed out, Kundera elaborated on the "horror of lightness" as a philosophical premise based on Parmenides's idea of positivity vs. negativity in *The Unbearable Lightness of Being*; hence, the descriptive "unbearable" in its title.

Farewell Waltz is a parody, questioning the right of man to exist on Earth and to procreate. Its tension drives the plot and culminates in the *police* inspector's questioning the spa town actors to determine who could possibly have murdered Ruzena. His interrogation concludes the novel on the note of a detective story without finding a culprit. The police inspector suggests a suicide; after all, Ruzena had a fight with her boyfriend and being distraught, she swallowed an assumed sedative, which could have contained poison. Bartleff, an American of local origin, and a presumably deeply religious but phony parodistic character, rejects this proposition. He and the nurse Ruzena just spent a beautiful night together, he claims; he made her happy and she was beginning to live. To exonerate Ruzena from self-induced death, Bartleff proposes to be named her murderer for, in his view, "there is no greater sin than suicide."[72] The interrogation during the private meeting of several participants reaches absurd proportions within the parodistic tone of *Farewell Waltz*. For instance, Dr. Skreta, who has been curing his infertile patients by artificially inseminating them with his own sperm without their knowledge, rejects a societal justice in the name of a higher justice, and thus feels he has been "living beyond justice."

The context of interrogation is cleverly set within the frame of two men and one woman; thus, only three people (Dr. Skreta, Jakub, and Olga) know about the poisonous pill being in Jakub's possession and ultimately taking Ruzena's life. When Olga says to Dr. Skreta that she knows he once gave the lethal pill to Jakub, he bluntly denies it: "That's absolute nonsense. I never gave him anything of the kind."[73] According to the police report in the "Kauza Kundera," only three people—two men, Dlask and Kundera, and one woman, Militká—knew the secret of the *suitcase*, which might suggest a possible allegory of the poisonous pill in *Farewell Waltz*. They keep their secret to themselves, just as Olga, Jakub, and Skreta will not reveal the secret to anyone else. It is only the narrator and readers, who along with Skreta, Jakub, and Olga, know of the pill in Jakub's hands as revealed earlier in the novel.

Evidently, Kundera enjoys inserting interrogations in his novels and playing around with them. In the "Symposium" of his *Laughable Loves,* a novel written in seven stories, a predecessor of the five-act novel, or five-day play *Farewell Waltz*, the beautiful-bodied but ugly-faced nurse Alzhbeta, is found unconscious in her hospital staff room. Her strong desire for sexual intercourse with male doctors would not even insure the attention of Dr. Havel, the Don Juan conqueror of women. Trying to perform a striptease in front of the night shift doctors, Alzhbeta is found lying in her room, unconscious with the smell of gas around. With the prompt assistance of the doctors, resuscitation, and blood transfusion, she is revived. The discourse on why Alzhbeta intended to commit suicide takes place, and becomes a reminder of theoretical possibilities within the interrogation of philosophical questioning. Flaishman, the ward intern, is convinced by Dr. Havel that Alzhbeta was interested in him, and wanted to take her life because he did not respond to her erotic and emotional calls. Flaishman feels guilty and "emphatically blames himself" for ignoring her and almost causing her death. Again, the narrator flirts with the idea of responsibility and guilt. The chief physician instructs Flaishman that a "man is responsible for his ignorance: he is obliged to know rather than to ignore, and that ignorance doesn't absolve him from his guilt."[74] The chief physician accuses Dr. Havel of rejecting the nurse, while accepting all other women. His idea is rebutted by Dr. Havel's theory of psychological nature, claiming that Alzhbeta fought with "the impossibility of stripping, impossibility of making love and impossibility of living."[75] Only the Woman Doctor's theory is the most practical and truthful: Alzhbeta turned the stove on to boil the water for coffee and, in the meantime, fell asleep. Once the stove flame mixed with overflowing water, it died and gas filled Alzhbeta's room; a mundane reason, a simple pretext that gave a wave for grandiose philosophizing. The theories, one clashing with another, give the narrator a fascinating freedom to enter a world of *potential possibility*. Who can prove the truth in "the adult world, which is full of uncertainties"?[76] One can almost hear Kundera laughing behind the *façade* of the serious: one day researchers will argue, philosophize, give hundreds of reasons, and prove and disapprove whether he was *the one* who went to the police and why.

HISTORY REPEATS

The allegations of Kundera being involved in the 1950 episode have brought comparisons with Günter Grass, Louis-Ferdinand Céline, Martin Heidegger, and possibly other prominent figures who have some dark spots on their conscience from their past. Günter Grass, the 1999 Nobel Prize-winning German novelist and social critic is best known for his first novel, *The Tin Drum* (1959). In 2006, he publicly revealed that as a teenager he served in the *Waffen SS*, the most notorious branch of the Nazi party. Grass, who was regarded as a representative of the German conscience of recent history, stunned the world with his confession. In his 2000 interview with *The New York Times*, he said that being a product of the Hitler youth generation, he believed in its agenda and goals until the end of the war. Only after the war did he understand the magnitude of the Nazi destructive force. In the *New York Times* article of August 17, 2006, "Günter Grass under Siege after Revealing SS Past," Alan Riding quotes Joachim Fest, a prominent Hitler biographer: "I do not understand how someone can elevate himself constantly for 60 years as the nation's bad conscience, precisely in Nazi questions, and only then admit that he himself was deeply involved."[77] If Grass's name had been substituted with Kundera's and the Nazi's period with Communist's, this would shed light in theory as to what the reaction to Kundera's open admission about his involvement in the 1950 events would be. Kundera must have been well aware of this *potential possibility*.

Marie Reslová, a Prague theater critic, has been one of the few observers who interpreted the 1950 police report correctly. She compared "this bizarre denouncing" that led to the discovery of a *suitcase* by the police to absurdism in Kundera's comedy *Ptákovina*, in which a seemingly innocent blunder exploded into a tragedy. The report only becomes serious, she writes, with the sentence in which Militká reveals that Dvořáček was an Army deserter and an illegal *émigré*. Reslová's short article implies a possibility of Kundera's reporting of the *suitcase* as a farce. This theory should be taken into consideration, especially because the framework of a "farce unwantedly turning into a tragedy" is Kundera's well-known literary strategy. In his first novel, *The Joke,* the farce—Ludvik's postcard of political message to Marketa—marks tragically Ludvik's destiny. The paradox of something entirely frivolous and intended as laughable that culminates in tragedy is embedded in most of Kundera's works, if not in all. It was first introduced in stories of *Laughable Loves*. Each of the seven stories provides a situation, which stems from a farce but ends up darkly flipped, though with some hope and laughter within comical tragedy.

A good example is "The Hitchhiking Game," which truly speaks to young people as a warning sign for their relationships. It begins with an innocent game of a young man's girlfriend: while he is filling up his gas tank, she walks along the road in the direction of their trip, and a few moments later waves at his car pretending to be a hitchhiker, stopping him as if he were an unknown driver. The game begins with the thrill that it brings out—her seductive flirting and his playing a flirting aggressor. However, soon the young man arrives at the conclusion that his girlfriend's seductiveness is inside of her, that she is different from how he had perceived her. The ending is paradoxical not only in the young man's discovery but, above all, in the girl's discovery that she, in pretending to be a free and sexually liberated person, enjoys the erotic encounter "beyond that permitted boundary" that "she had dreaded the most: 'love-making without emotion or love.'"[78]

Even Reslová ends her opinion piece ironically, saying that we will learn Kundera's intention only if *he decides to remember* the event. "But why would he do it?" she asks and concludes: "Most likely he is convinced that it's none of the public's business." However, Reslová dismays her piercing remark with her conclusion: "In a way, he is right."[79] This last sentence is selfishly nuanced; it isn't irony.

In his opinion piece on Günter Grass in *The New York Times* of April 14, 2015, Jochen Bittner addresses an issue of similar nature. He states that many Germans have regarded Grass as "our national poet and our conscience," but he admits that Grass "did not speak to him" personally because he created his works when "strong ideology and determined judgment counted more than the hard work of examining what is actually going on around us." Bittner continues saying that it's no longer "moral judgment" that is, above all, demanded from writers today, but it is "clearheaded analysis of our ever-accelerating world."

Do Bittner and Reslová perceive today's world as so corrupt that they don't recognize values of moral direction? Or on the contrary, do they believe that technology, which has been taking over man, will become a substitute for human thoughts and feelings with no need for morality? Rather, technological inventions and their applications in the real world make it easier than ever for human beings to take advantage of one another, especially the most vulnerable. Society needs a compass for a *global sense of morality* in the technologically complex, unequal, and chaotic world. Without it, the human race will be overrun by programmed behavior dictated by technology, and by its definition will become another ideology, a technological form of ideology, or *technological ideology*. This idea subjects the role of literature in questioning the past, present, and future, and this is *Kundera's claim to literature.*

It only suffices to remind another Czech author, Karel Čapek, and his utopian play, R.U.R. (Rossum's Universal Robots), the inventor of the word *robot* that he had derived from the Czech *robota,* "forced work." The word has been adopted by the majority of the world's languages into their everyday vocabulary. Čapek's play is about the machines, *robots*, that have become so perfect, acquiring the look and mind of humans, that they ultimately take over human society by destroying it. Artificial intelligence scientists actually predict that this could happen to the human race unless people preserve the values of humanity. The cognitive scientist, Steven Pinker, also believes that "a human-made information processor could, in principle, duplicate and exceed the powers of the human mind."[80] However, he assures us that most likely this will not happen in practice since the human race will lack the technological and economic motivation necessary for its realization. The implication of human morality and human reasoning supported by the sense of morality is, inevitably, implied in Pinker's statement.

Bittner attacks Grass as a critical moralist who put himself above everyone else, ignoring the rules that he demanded from others. Kundera has been accused of the same attitude despite his absolute denial of his involvement in the "Kauza Kundera." The German newspaper *Die Welt* compared him to Grass, claiming that as a "moral institution of authority," Kundera is finished. However, Grass's revelation contrasts with Kundera's denial. With few supporters, Günter Grass has been mostly vilified, while Kundera's camp has divided into his many supporters and fewer accusers. Grass is mostly accused of keeping the information secret for six decades and less for being recruited by the SS in the last month of the war. If Kundera is accused of any wrongdoing, it is on the same grounds—withholding the information for over six decades rather than for the act itself—reporting Dvořáček's *suitcase.* Since the "Kauza Kundera" remains an open subject without a final nod by its alleged culprit, Kundera has been receiving significant support. Eleven internationally recognized writers came to his defense, including four Nobel laureates, Orhan Pamuk, J. M. Coetzee, Nadine Gordimer, and Gabriel García Márquez.

But as proven in the case of Céline and Heidegger, Kundera's legacy is destined to remain tainted regardless of the future outcome of his acknowledging guilt, if any outcome is ever reached. Louis-Ferdinand Céline's broad influence on modernism and existentialism in world literature, and particularly French, has been overshadowed by his support of the Nazi ideology during WWII, and his exhibition of anti-Semitic feelings. Likewise Martin Heidegger, a German phenomenologist and existentialist, whom Kundera refers to often in his works, and whose ideas have been embraced by leading post-modernist theorists of the twentieth century, including Derrida and Foucault, was involved in the Nazi movement. This negative aspect continues marking his *résumé* despite being acknowledged as one of the most original and influential philosophers of our times.

Regardless of his silence, unfortunately, Kundera is too weak to blow away the dark cloud floating over the clear, bright sky of his literary canon.

NOTES

1. Milan Kundera, "Český úděl," *Listy*, nos. 7–8 (December 1968): 2. English quotes from "Czech Destiny" in Tim West's translation, 1–6. https://www.academia.edu/2503513/Czech_Destiny_Milan_Kundera_
2. Kundera, "Český úděl."
3. Kundera, "Český úděl."
4. Kundera, "Český úděl."
5. Kundera, *Nesmrtelnost*, 344.
6. "Rozhovor: Že v tom měl Kundera prsty, vím už 15 let," an interview with Iva Militká on October 15, 2008 in *Aktualne.cz*. https://nazory.aktualne.cz/rozhovory/rozhovor-ze-v-tom-mel-kundera-prsty-vim-uz-15 let/
7. "Rozhovor: Že v tom měl Kundera prsty."
8. "Rozhovor: Že v tom měl Kundera prsty."
9. "Rozhovor: Že v tom měl Kundera prsty."
10. "Rozhovor: Že v tom měl Kundera prsty."
11. "Rozhovor: Že v tom měl Kundera prsty."
12. Information on Militká's recollection was gathered from Rozhovor s Ivou Militkou-Dlaskovou in *Sbírka rozhovorů*, ÚSTR, 26. 5. 2008.
13. For instance, Militká claims that early in the 1990s, her husband said to her *only* that he told Kundera about Dvořáček the following: "On [Dlask] mi zase neřekl nic—jen že to tehdy řekl Kunderovi. (Again, he [Dlask] didn't tell me anything—only that, at that time, he told Kundera). She contradicts herself in the next sentence: "Znamenalo to ulehčení, že to nebyl on, kdo došel na tu bezpečnost." (It was a relief that it wasn't he [Dlask], who went to the police). How did she know in the early 1990s that it was Kundera and not Dlask who went to the police if her husband didn't give her that information, and the police report was not discovered until 2008? In his article, "Kauzu Kundera začaly vzpomínky pro vnuka" (see reference in Note 52), Jiří Šťastný quotes Militká from *MF DNES*: "Byla jsem naivní. Za ta léta jsem si často vzpomněla, co jsem svou hloupostí způsobila," (I was naïve. Over those years I often recalled what I had caused by my stupidity). Further Šťastný explains that Militká mentioned her

unexpected meeting with Dvořáček to her boyfriend, Miroslav Dlask. According to her, Šťastný writes, Dlask revealed to Kundera *everything* [italics added]. The original text says: "Ten podle ní vše vyzradil Kunderovi." These quotes show the confusion of what Militká (and interpreters of her case) claim. Did Dlask tell Militká *only* that he had told it to Kundera, or did Dlask tell Militká that he had told Kundera *everything*? In addition of various interpretations of details of the case, there are Czech cultural and linguistic grounds that make the understanding additionally unclear. Culturally, the Czech language, and especially its spoken variants, thrives on fillers and ambiguous words that native speakers enjoy using, and are often unaware of. Here an example would be *vše, everything*. This phenomenon makes Czech not only difficult to understand to non-native speakers but it also makes Czech literature difficult to translate, preserving the original flavor of the culture. This is another reason why Kundera, among a group of excellent Czech writers, is one of the few, if not the only one (perhaps along with Vaclav Havel), that is highly appreciated. In writing in his native Czech, Kundera avoids superfluous words and expressions, colloquialisms, and spoken variants of literary Czech. Additionally, for that reason, his stories, excerpts from his novels, or entire novels are very appealing to learners of Czech to read. Because of his logical structure and message, his sentences are understood with a greater easiness than, for instance, a text in a popular magazine or a local newspaper.

14. Kundera, *Farewell Waltz*, 6.
15. Kundera, *Immortality*, 219–20.
16. Kundera, *Immortality*, 224.
17. Kundera, *Immortality*, 249.
18. Kundera, *Immortality*, 95.
19. Kundera, *Immortality*, 251.
20. Kundera, *Immortality*, 237.
21. Kundera, *Immortality*, 237.
22. Kundera *Immortality*, 237.
23. Kundera, *Immortality*, 237.
24. Kundera, *Immortality*, 24.
25. Kundera, *Identity*, 115.
26. Kundera, *Joke*, 32.
27. Kundera, *Joke*, 32.
28. Kundera, *Joke*, 33.
29. Kundera, *Unbearable Lightness*, 63.
30. Kundera, *Unbearable Lightness*, 63.
31. Kundera, *Unbearable Lightness*, 124.
32. Kundera, *Identity*, 115.
33. Kundera, *Identity*, 151.
34. Kundera, *Identity*, 162.
35. Kundera, *Identity*, 54.
36. Kundera, *Identity*, 15.
37. Kundera, *Identity*, 10.
38. Kundera, *Identity*, 102.
39. Kundera, *Identity*, 102.
40. Kundera, *Identity*, 103.
41. Kundera, *Identity*, 61.
42. Kundera, *Identity*, 48.
43. Kundera, *Identity*, 47.
44. Kundera, *Identity*, 46.
45. Milan Kundera, *Valčík na rozloučenou*, (Brno: Atlantis, 1997), 319.
46. This Milan Uhde's quote appeared in a number of reports in October 2008, including *Lidové noviny,* as well as in Jana Prikryl's article on Milan Kundera of May 20, 2009: https://www.thenation.com/article/kundera-conundrum-kundera-respekt-and-contemp
47. Ladislav Vorel, "Co mi kdysi o Milanu Kunderovi vyprávěl spisovatel Petr Chudožilov," *idnes* (January 29, 2009), http://zpravy.idnes.cz. According to Mr. Hradilek's correspondence with the author of this book, another document is kept in the Prague National

Archives containing the information on Kundera's involvement with the police. This document can be only accessed with Milan Kundera's permission; therefore, it most likely will remain confidential information. One can only speculate whether this document refers to Dvořáček, or someone else, such as Jan Trefulka.

48. David Lodge, "Idea of the Author," *Critical Quarterly* 26, nos. 1–2 (March 1984): 111.
49. Kundera, *The Joke*, 234.
50. Alexander Solzhenitsyn, *The First Circle*, trans. Thomas P. Whitney (New York: Bantam Books, 1976), 181.
51. Kundera, *The Joke*, 242.
52. On October 30, 2008, *Zprávy idnes.cz* published online Jiří Šťastný's opinion piece in which he quoted Militká: "Byla jsem hrůzou bez sebe. Když běžel proces, celá rodina jsme se báli, co řekne. Kdyby řekl, že se u nás schovával, tak jsme šli všichni do kriminálu," and she added: "Mirda ale neřekl nic." (Horrified, I was beside myself with fear. During the trial, our entire family was frightened of what he would say. Had he said that he was hiding [before his illegal escape to Germany] in our place, we all would have gone to jail, adding: But Mirda [Miroslav Dvořáček] didn't say anything.). http://zpravy.idnes.cz/kauzu-kundera-zacaly-vzpominky-pro-vnuky-fi1-/domaci.aspx?c=A081030_083148_domaci_jte
53. Kundera, *Unbearable Lightness*, 251.
54. Kundera, *The Joke*, 317.
55. Milan Kundera, "Ptákovinu jsem měl vždy moc rád," reviewed by Ivan Matějka, *Literární noviny* (September 4, 2015). http://www.literarky.cz/literatura/recenze/20540-milan-kundera-ptakovinu-jsem-ml-vdy-moc-rad
56. Kundera, *Ignorance*, 134.
57. Kundera, *Ignorance*, 86.
58. Kundera, *Ignorance*, 76.
59. Kundera, *Ignorance*, 126.
60. Kundera, *Ignorance*, 122–23.
61. Kundera, *Ignorance*, 87.
62. Kundera, *Ignorance*, 87.
63. Kundera, *Ignorance*, 90.
64. Kundera, *Ignorance*, 92.
65. Adam Hradilek a Martin Tichý, "Osudová mise Moravcova kurýra," *Paměť a dějiny*, no. 01 (2009, footnote): 85. Apparently, there is an evidence, as Mr. Hradilek revealed in a conversation, that during one of his secret missions in Prague, Juppa was about to meet with Iva Militká, but noticing her coming to their meeting pregnant, he turned away and the meeting did not materialize.
66. Kundera, *Farewell Waltz*, 174.
67. Kundera, *The Joke*, 111.
68. Kundera, *Farewell Waltz*, 205.
69. Kundera, *Farewell Waltz*, 193.
70. Kundera, *Farewell Waltz*, 193.
71. Kundera, *Farewell Waltz*, 195.
72. Kundera, *Farewell Waltz*, 199.
73. Kundera, *Farewell Waltz*, 207.
74. Kundera, *Laughable Loves*, 97.
75. Kundera, *Laughable Loves*, 120.
76. Kundera, *Laughable Loves*, 124.
77. Jochen Bittner, "Günter Grass's Germany, and Mine," *The New York Times*, The Opinion Pages (April 14, 2015): https://www.nytimes.com/2015/04/15/opinion/gunter-grasss-germany-and-mine.html
78. Kundera, *Laughable Loves*, 86–87.
79. All the quotes are from Marie Reslová, "Policejní záznam jako divadelní scéna," *Hospodářské noviny* (October 16, 2008): 11.
80. This quote is from Steven Pinker's passage, "Thinking Does Not Imply Subjugating" taken from *Edge*.org (2015): "What Do You Think About Machines that Think?" Pinker begins his reasoning with the following paragraph that could clarify Jochen Bittner's concern for

"clearheaded analysis of our ever-accelerating world": "'Thomas Hobbes's pithy equation 'Reasoning is but reckoning'" is one of the great ideas in human history. The notion that rationality can be accomplished by the physical process of calculation was vindicated in the twentieth century by Turing's thesis that simple machines are capable of implementing any computable function and by models from D. O. Hebb, McCullough, and Pitts, and their scientific heirs showing that networks of simplified neurons could achieve comparable feats. The cognitive feats of the brain can be explained in physical terms: to put it crudely (and critics notwithstanding), we can say that beliefs are a kind of information, thinking a kind of computation, and motivation a kind of feedback and control." The idea of morality then falls into the category of 'feedback and control.'"

Chapter Five

The Betrayal

BETRAYAL OF THE BETRAYED

Betrayal within betrayal is a theme that underlines Milan Kundera's works. In their study, social psychologists T. Shackelford and David Buss maintain that man has become accustomed to the possibility of being betrayed by others as a part of evolutionary development. They suggest that man has been attuned to detect different types of betrayal in relationships by means of an inborn "cheater-detector;" however, to understand betrayal, it is necessary to understand the context of the relationship within which betrayal occurs.[1] Nonetheless, over human history, betrayal has been regarded as a major sin. In Dante's *Divine Comedy*, the souls of those who betrayed their friends and guests suffer eternal damnation in the third zone of the ninth circle of *Inferno*, and traitors who committed crimes with societal consequences are relegated to the final and coldest circle of hell to remain forever frozen in a lake.

In most Kundera's novels, betrayal concerns the psychology of characters who lack self-esteem, are unhappy about themselves, are angry because they feel injured in love or in their profession, and seek some sort of revenge. The impulse to take revenge in response to betrayal is a powerful catalyst that leads Kundera's characters to action. *The Joke* is infused with betrayals, small and big, regarded as paradoxes. But in *Life Is Elsewhere* betrayals are wrapped not only in a layer of history, but are also enhanced by outside forces and inner impulses, often cruel, that characters must face but cannot easily overcome. Attuned to characters' mindsets, the reader wants to feel compassion for and to understand them but instead he often feels only pity, sorrow, or disgust for both, the betrayed and the betrayers. A series of betrayals presented in *Life Is Elsewhere* is a painful reminder of how vulnerable a human being truly is and how far his self-deprecation can lead, becoming a destructive force for others.

JAROMIL, THE BETRAYED

Jaromil is involved with a girl, called a redhead in the novel. She is a salesperson in a local store. A substitute for her girlfriend, whom Jaromil was attracted to initially, the redhead strokes and bolsters Jaromil's low ego at every turn. In physical and mental ability, she is far from the student he met at the poetry discussion and with whom his love affair ended as quickly as it started because he failed to perform sexually when the opportunity presented itself in her apartment. Jaromil's lack of confidence has deep roots in his family structure. His prodigious poetic inclination is more induced by his grandparents and his mother than springing from Jaromil's natural and spontaneous talent. For most of Jaromil's life, his absentee father has no influence on him, and Jaromil grows up under the strong feminine spell of his mother and grandmother. Unbeknownst to him and his mother, his father has a secret love affair, a type of great love to which both Jaromil and his mother aspire and strive to pursue, each on their own terms. Jaromil's father betrays his wife and his son for the love of a Jewish woman. Ultimately Jaromil's father perishes in a concentration camp for a single glance at his beloved—a brief moment to see her in Terezín, the notorious ghetto that the Nazis established "as the first circle of Inferno" for deportation of Jews. Jaromil's mother, a lonely woman who lives for her unfulfilled dream of great love, desperately chases after her dream just like Jaromil. They become a pathetic duo, his mother pathologically attached to her son, at moments fusing with him almost as if he were her lover, exhibiting the Jocasta complex. Jaromil is chained by his mother's leash and held back from developing naturally as an adolescent and young adult. He feels both love and hate for his mother and for his redheaded girlfriend, and Jaromil's mother feels hate and jealousy once she is introduced to the redhead. The relationship of the unfortunate triangle is intensely described in a scene where Jaromil and his girlfriend are making love in his room, when his mother barges in, "driven into her son's room by intoxicating anger."[2] In her state of emotional ecstasy, she "feels an urge to see her son's girlfriend completely naked"; she wants to merge with her son and his redhead's naked bodies, to hold them closely to her bosom, the way she used to hold Jaromil when he sucked the milk from her breasts.

In as much as readers find some scenes in *Life Is Elsewhere* insanely provocative and uncomfortable, they understand Jaromil's deficient childhood and his conflicted feelings for his mother and his girlfriend. After all, he struggles to find his place in society, like most young people do. The novel is challengingly flavored with vignettes of real-life poets, providing specific details of their rise and fall. The narrator introduces a range of lyrical poets from the romantic period to modernism of the late nineteenth and early twentieth centuries. Most of these poets shared a dream of death perceived as beautiful, in fire and in the heat of their fame in their short lives. Their lives are governed by a strong female influence from which they attempt to get away but instead get trapped in, usually lasting till their end. The poets, whose brief lives the narrator describes, range from Byron, Shelley, Keats, and Lermontov to Mayakovsky, Wolker, and Halas. They died young, either in duel, from illness, or in some other unusual circumstances, but typically not in the heroic fashion they had desired. They represent a variety of European poetic trends from the earlier romanticism to Parnassianism, and symbolism to Czech poetism. It is as if Jaromil, the fictional poet, mingles with them; though, compositionally, his function is inside the novel's plot and theirs is outside of it. The slogan, "youth, poetry and revolution is one and the same,"[3] ties them all together.

Set against the canvas of the European poetic giants and their turbulent lives, Jaromil's irrational behavior can, at times, be justified as his uncontrollable lyric impulse. The narrator tells us that lyrical poetry is an expression of the intensity of the poet's own emotions: whatever he feels, he writes down without the need for explaining, justifying, or proving anything. It is only his inconsistent feelings that count, changing from one day to the next. Jaromil's poetry is published but doesn't receive much attention and yet, he "so passionately thirsts for fame and glory" (just like Mr. Kundera had since his childhood). And the glory arrives in the police uniform of his school friend, a janitor's son. He invites Jaromil to the police station, showing him weaponry and pictures of police officers with dogs, and in the center of these real, rough men, there is Jaromil's poem pasted on the bulletin board. Over several glasses of beer in a tavern, the janitor's son reiterates how much he loves Jaromil's poetry, reciting his poem by heart. Finally, he invites Jaromil for a special poetry night for young policemen in a villa near Prague.

A sophisticated reader notices the clue before the narrator spells it out: the policeman is trying to win Jaromil over to engage him as a spy among university students. Is this a subtle allegory to the supervisory role that young Kundera held in the Kolonka dormitory while a student at FAMU? The ironic narrator occasionally steps in with a comment to justify Jaromil's naiveté and immature way of thinking. Admiring the manhood of his friend, the janitor's son, who is already married and keeps classified secrets from his wife, Jaromil agrees with his friend and the actions that the police had been undertaking. When he hears of a dark-haired Jewish man's arrest, a former leader of the Marxist youth group, he believes the arrest must have been made for a good reason. Jaromil is aware the arrests were happening, the narrator explains, "but he did not know that there were tens of thousands of them, including many communists, that many were tortured; and that their

guilt was mostly fictitious."[4] As pointed out earlier, Kundera finished writing
this novel in 1969, two decades after the Dvořáček episode, and the narrator's interceptions might suggest that this was how Kundera felt in 1950, as a
young man, a student of Jaromil's age. A large dose of ignorance of what
was really happening behind the *façade* of Communist propaganda, that inevitable reality partly swept under the rug away from the public eye, was
quite common among young people who searched for idealism; be it in love,
poetry, revolution, or Marxist teaching. In real life, Militká's words resonate
with a truthful ring of blissful ignorance, ironically echoing sixty years later.

READERS' REACTION

In his contribution "Genre and Paradigm in Milan Kundera's *The Book of
Laughter and Forgetting*" in *Critical Essays on Milan Kundera,* Herbert
Eagle, a University of Michigan Slavic scholar, suggests that Kundera distances himself from his "fictional creations by openly speculating with the
reader about the character's 'real' motivations and general lack of self-
awareness (which we, with Kundera, view quite ironically)."[5] The argument
contrary to Mr. Eagle's statement is many-sided. If we, the readers, view
Kundera's characters "quite ironically," it is only because the author leads us
with his style and imposing narrative voice to acquire particular perceptions
of our views of his fictional personae. However, this all might have been
acceptable (though, at times too overwhelming) prior to the discovery of the
police's document mentioning Milan Kundera. Since then our perception is
less ironical, more speculative, and even more inquisitive. Despite his absolute denial, we might have evidence that he has been denying *the undeniable*
and that his speculations on his characters' real motivations might be *his own
irony* of himself, embodied in his characters, of the periods he lived in and
placed them in. His "real" motivations might also reveal some angles of his
"real" identity more than he had ever intended. The cruel laughter (and irony)
in *Life Is Elsewhere* is evidenced in the very first sentence of the novel, posed
as a question: "Exactly when and where was the poet conceived?"[6] The poet,
of course, is Jaromil (and, to some extent, an allusion to Kundera himself, at
least as a young Communist poet, disguised under the frolics of his fictional
persona). All the characters in the novel, with the exception of Jaromil, lack
their Christian given names. Jaromil's mother receives a skeptical name *Maman*, and the girlfriend is called "the redhead," an attribute that contains a
demeaning connotation (in the Czech original, *zrzka* is viewed pejoratively
as a person with non-pleasing colored hair, easily harassed for the atypical
ginger color of her hair). Thus the reader, like the narrator and author, distances himself from her the moment she enters the scene of the novel. Jaromil is trapped in the farce of his own inadequacy. Standing on the balcony of

his Maman's house in pajamas, fever and cold shaking his body, he is trapped in watching the crowds of young Czechs instead of participating in their celebration of the arrival of the 1948 Communist Revolution. But he is also trapped in an intimate situation of eminent erotic excitement with a beautiful filmmaker; his arousal prevented by a trivial pretext—his ugly shorts his mother had prepared for him to wear; or in his inability to handle a condom in a bedroom scene with the university student described in the earlier pages of the novel.

The irony and laughter stop once the narrator takes us to Jaromil's state of humiliating rage when waiting for his redhead girlfriend, angry at himself for his failure of sexual performance with the beautiful filmmaker. His humilia-tion is additionally aggravated by the recently completed shooting of a docu-mentary about him as a great poet that the filmmaker worked on with the assistance of his mother. During the shooting, his wishes were ignored, and he was treated like a puppet, forced to obey the orders of the filmmaker and his mother. Pacing now in front of his girlfriend's home, he pities himself for ending up with "leftovers"—an "incorrigibly ugly," freckled and simple girl, who in addition to all her faults, doesn't respect him, as demonstrated by being grossly late to their date. She is one of seven children, and Jaromil, the only son born into a petty bourgeois comfort on his mother's side, sees her family as an animalistic nest—like a large "family of rabbits."

The several pages in which Kundera masterfully and intensely describes Jaromil's anger and mental rage running through "his head like alcohol," detail his feelings, and awaken both understanding and pity for him. The redhead apologizes for her lateness with an excuse that infuriates him even more. She was with her friend, who had broken up with her fiancé and was very upset, and needed to be consoled by her. Jaromil feels that the redhead reduced him to a position of a second-hand customer, elevating "an obscure girlfriend—the very essence of insignificance"—above him. He forbids her to touch him, calling their love affair off, at the same time realizing that his "self-tormenting hate" is futile, that he is unfair to the girl, too cruel to her, that giving her up, the only girlfriend he has, would create an abyss for him, "the abyss of solitude and of self-condemnation." The narrator reiterates that "all this knowledge was impo-tent against the splendid intoxication of anger."[7]

Attempting to save the tense situation, the redhead ultimately admits that she was lying. She was with her brother, Jan, she tells him; those were her last moments with him because the next day, he was leaving the country illegally. As she suspected, Jaromil forgives her lateness but urges her to call the police to inform about her brother's intentions. As obnoxious as she finds his reaction, she makes an effort to dissuade Jaromil from his suggestion so he would forget about it altogether. But he insists, blending the political with the personal: "So a brother means more to you than I do?"[8] He proclaims her brother his enemy, and by that definition she becomes his enemy too: "The fate of the revolution and my fate are one and the same. Anybody who is against the revolution is against me."[9] The redhead is willing to agree with Jaromil. She assures him that his poetic slogan "Love means all or nothing"[10] is close to her heart; she assures him over and over again that she couldn't live without him, she couldn't go on if he dies. Inebriated with the idea of one woman's devotion—tears rolling down his face—Jaromil is overwhelmed by a feeling of the transcendental greatness of their love and their "union with infinity." In that ecstasy of forced, confused, and painful passion, their lovemaking takes place. They are still promising to love each other over death until the redhead errs in her assumed role of total devotion and repeats that she would be terribly sad and lonely if he died. At that instant, Jaromil realizes that he has been betrayed and trapped, that he mistook her sadness for her pledge for death. Humiliated to the utmost degree, he calmly dresses, and then strokes the redhead's cheek. Looking into her eyes, he asks: "You want to go to the police yourself?"[11]

This statement is like a narrative thunderclap. The reader shivers, the fictional girl stutters. Using the rhetorical technique of repetition, the narrator achieves the urgency and the level of seriousness of his character's statement: "Are you going to tell the police yourself?"[12] Up to the point of their lovemaking, the narrator leads the reader to believe, or at least to hope, that their reconciliation will occur. Inasmuch as he is detached from Jaromil's manipulative and—to an extent—irrational behavior, the reader feels a close affinity to fictional Jaromil and his redhead, watching their intimate encounter in minute detail. The few lines of their interaction are so powerful and so skillfully written that they evoke anger and fear in the reader himself. At the intersection of this exchange, the narrator's ironic treatment of the characters subsides, and the level of reality is established. Jaromil tells his girlfriend that if she does not want to go to the police, he will take care of it himself. The redhead is so confused that she is unable to speak. After they kiss, Jaromil departs.

BACK TO REAL LIFE OR JUST IRONY?

The fictional rhetoric "I'll take care of it myself,"[13] has been quoted in several documents in an altered version in reference to alleged Kundera's reaction concerning the Dvořáček episode. Matěj Dlask, Militká's grandson, wrote that when Miroslav (Tása) Dlask told Kundera about Dvořáček, Kundera said: "Neboj se, Táso, my to zařídíme." (Don't worry [lit. don't be afraid], Tása, we'll take care of it).[14] Matěj Dlask claims that his grandmother, Iva Militká, quoted this sentence when she told him for the first time about the March 14, 1950 incident. However when asked later, Militká wasn't sure if this information was truthful—apparently, she could no longer remember it. It is possible that this reference might have floated around as taken from *Life Is Elsewhere*; though, one has to bear in mind that its Czech original, *Život je jinde,* was first published in 1969 by Toronto Sixty-Eight Publishers, a small publishing company of Czech dissident literature, run by Josef Škvorecký (best known for his novels *The Cowards, and The Engineer of Human Souls*) and his wife Zdena Salivarová. If the Toronto edition was accessible in Communist Czechoslovakia, it was only in a few copies distributed underground. The second edition came out only recently, in Brno Atlantis in 2016. Thus, the question remains to what degree the alleged statement, "Don't worry, Tása, we'll take care of it," and Kundera's fictional statement by Jaromil to the redhead, "I'll take care of it myself" (following Jaromil's assumption that the redhead won't go to the police herself to denounce her brother) are related. Due to various levels of denials in the Dvořáček episode by both Kundera and Militká, this "mystery" will, most likely, remain unsolved. However, in his first book of verses "Člověk zahrada širá" (Man, a Wide Garden), a gift to his friends, the married couple Dlask and Militká, Kundera handwrote a dedication, using Dlask's first name as *Mirek* (and not *Tása*), which could indicate that *Mirek* was what he used to call his friend. Since this poetry book was published in 1953, and given to Dlask and Militká after its publication, this is yet further evidence that Kundera *did know* Militká (and should be able to remember her)—a fact that he denied in his interview in 2008.

Kundera's life has been influenced by paradox, a thematic device on which his works are constructed. His handwritten dedication to Dlask and Militká paradoxically states that he is giving them the book in memory, to remember (implying: not to forget) one another. In other words, the thing that counts is the retention of the memory, not the reading of his book:

> *"For Mirek and Iva to remember (not for reading) Milan."*
> *Mirkovi + Ivě*
> *na památku*
> *(nikoli k čtení)*
> *Milan.*

In the series of Milan Kundera's involvement in the Dvořáček episode, this dedication is the fourth *obvious* evidential case, following: a) the 1950 police report; b) Jerman's 1951 oral report, published in 1952; c) the idea of betrayal and denouncement, and the presence of a *suitcase* and *policemen* in the body of Kundera's creative work, including his poetry, plays, and novels; and d) his friendship with Dlask and Militká evidenced by his dedication to them of his first poetry book (despite his recent denial of knowing Militká). Most likely these four *obvious* facts are not the only ones. *Subsidiary* facts are his: a) strictly instructing his readers on how they should read his novels;

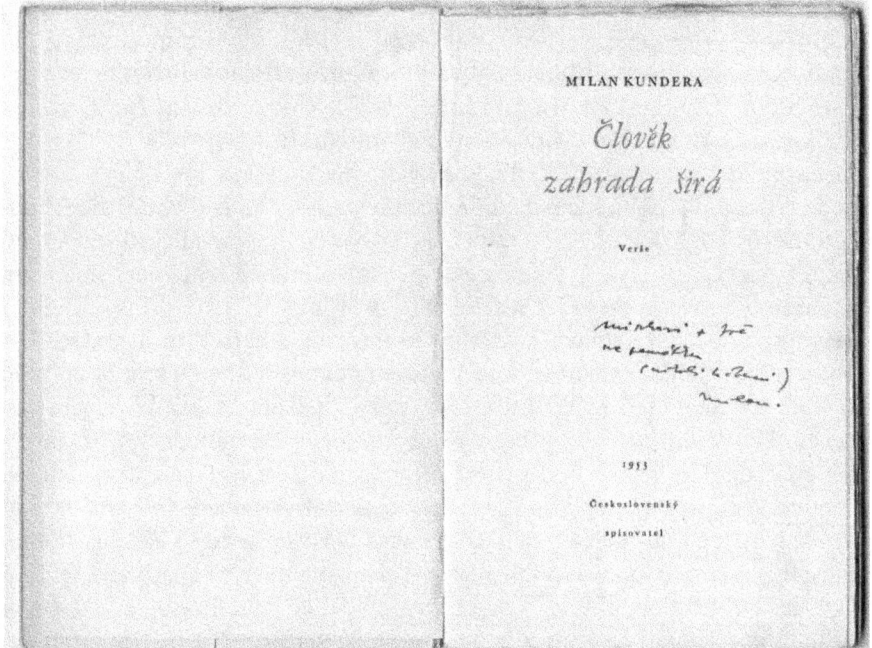

Figure 5.1.   Published with Adam Hradilek's permission

b) his refusal to give interviews, especially after 2008; c) before the 1989
Velvet Revolution, his refusal to be treated as a dissident writer (it would
have brought out additional digging into his Communist past); d) his travels
to his homeland incognito; e) his biography reduced to one simple sentence—born in Czechoslovakia in 1929 and living in France since 1975; f)
his refusal to translate and publish (or republish) his earliest works, poetry,
and plays that reveal his Communist favoritism and admiration for the Soviet
Union; etc. All this could be summarized in one short sentence: *Milan Kundera has been obsessively guarding his past and his private life to the point
of the irrational.* His identity shines through his work, and despite his re-
nouncing the approach of deconstruction of his work with the purpose of
searching for his past and identity, it remains the only tool for uncovering it.
That is, unless he, himself, reveals his full and truthful persona and/or biography to the public.

   The evident question is to what degree Milan Kundera could be judged by
the public. If one takes into account John Locke's argument that personal
identity is based on consciousness, and that only oneself has access to his or
her consciousness, the public judgment may not be valid; in fact it would be
erroneous. In Locke's sense that identity is a matter of psychological conti-

nuity even after death (consciousness can be transferred from one soul to another), Kundera's personal identity would remain imprinted for eternity in his fictional characters, and hence, immortality would remain an eternal obsession. However, the notion of identity is a complex issue. In the eighteenth century, Locke's theory was criticized by the English theologian Joseph Butler and the Scottish philosopher Thomas Reid, who argued that if consciousness presupposes identity, it cannot constitute it.

The French phenomenologist and hermeneutist, Paul Ricoeur (1913–2005), has developed narrative and narrative identity, which has remained of interest to psychoanalysts and scholars in the fields to which narrative versions are applicable. His idea is that human identity is essentially expressed through one's narrative, persistent in connectedness of time: who the person was in the past through his/her own perception and what potentialities this self-perceived person has now and will have in the future. In his essay, "Narrative Identity," Ricoeur clarifies: "The problematic of connectedness, of permanence over time, or, in short, of identity, finds itself raised to a level of lucidity and also perplexity in fictional narratives that is not achieved by stories immersed in the course of life . . . According to my thesis, the narrative constructs the durable character of an individual, which one can call his or her narrative identity, in constructing the sort of dynamic identity proper to the plot [*l'intrigue*] which creates the identity of the protagonist in the story. It is primarily in the plot, therefore, that we must search for the mediation between permanence and change, before being able to transfer it to the character."[15] In this respect, the purpose of this book, encapsulated in the book title, is to elucidate the narrative identity of Milan Kundera, the man, through the means of his "durable character" and "mediation between permanence and change," has been performed by the deconstruction of his novels and plays, and reference to "identity."

FICTIONAL VERSUS REAL-LIFE BETRAYAL

The fictional betrayal of the redhead by Jaromil at the level of the political has its core in an emotionally charged sexual misunderstanding and, in its essence, is a reminder of the real-life political betrayal of Dvořáček by Militká. Jaromil's denouncement of his girlfriend's brother to the police is caused by Jaromil's perception of her betrayal of him (if he dies, she would only miss him; she was unwilling to die for him) and because of that, he will denounce someone that is close to her but someone that he doesn't know personally, basing his decision only on his girlfriend's information. Conclusive from her interviews, Militká betrayed Dvořáček by giving her boyfriend Dlask information about Dvořáček on an emotionally charged (if not sexual) ground, too (what if Dlask had found a man in her room?; after all, in March

1950 she still considered Juppa, Dvořáček's friend, to be her boyfriend and still planned to follow him to Germany). Dlask betrayed Militká by passing the information to Kundera, who went to the police concerning a *suitcase* belonging to a man that he didn't know personally, basing his decision on his friend's girlfriend's information. The erotic in both situations leads to the political and its farcical twist is embedded in the fact that *the truth* is not evidential but based on hearsay only. The betrayal itself has several degrees of intensity and several layers of betrayals.

In the next part of the novel, Part 6: "The Middle-Aged Man," the reader learns that the redhead lied to Jaromil about her brother—he had never planned to escape to the West. She had a lover, a man in his forties (a widower, and a former pilot who fought against the Germans in England), and was spending the afternoon with him, which was why she was late to the meeting with Jaromil. The redhead betrayed Jaromil by having a lover, but he never learned about her betrayal. Militká betrayed her boyfriend Juppa by having an affair with Dlask, and Juppa did not know about her betrayal either: she did not want Dvořáček to know about her involvement with another man and for that reason she needed him to avoid meeting Dlask. Thus, a parallel at the level of the fictional inspiration could be clearly noticed. Militká claimed that she returned to her room on March 14, 1950 at 6:00 p.m., and Jaromil was supposed to meet with his redhead at 6:00 o'clock too. When the redhead returns from the prison three years later, she waits until 4:00 o'clock to see her former lover, the middle-aged man. As documented, 4:00 o'clock was the time when Kundera showed up at the Police Station in Prague 6 on March 14, 1950. In fact, the 6:00 o'clock timing also plays a decisive role in the random meeting of Tereza and Tomas in *The Unbearable Lightness of Being*.

The day after the unfortunate lovemaking, Jaromil went to the National Security building. In the lobby he turned in his ID according to protocol, then continued to the upper floor to inform his janitor's son's friend about the planned escape of his girlfriend's brother. The narrator describes Jaromil as a proud, big man, "filled with destiny, carrying his fate on his shoulders, feeling as if climbing on the higher level of his own life." The same day, at 6:00 p.m., he was waiting for his redhead in front of her building. But her landlord informed him that she had not returned from work yet, and that two men were looking for her around 5:30 (around the same time as two policemen were waiting for Militká in the dormitory). Jaromil figured out that the two men were police officers, and while he feared the unknown, he felt pride for "setting in motion the real events." The next day, when he returned, the landlord told him that the *two men* took the girl away. Not until that moment did Jaromil realize that "he had *entered the realm of tragedy*." The fictional Jaromil is overcome by the very same *feeling of tragedy* as Militká was, watching *two men* from a dormitory window taking away her friend Dvořáček.

Jaromil returns home and writes the "greatest poem of his life;" his fantasy is uncontrollably present with the redhead: he sees her defenseless, surrounded by policemen, interrogators, and guards, taking advantage of her sexually whenever they please. But it no longer matters to him for his redhead girlfriend will remain in his mind as *his creation*. He has influenced her destiny, and from the time she is taken away she is acting the way he wants her to act in his imagination, the way he wants to see her: the way he creates her. The narrator uncovers Jaromil's thoughts by covering the redhead's body with an imaginary curtain, a quote from the romantic poet, John Keats: *"You must be mine to die upon the rack if I want you."* [16]

Kundera inevitably shows the reader how a single event could be easily propelled by the fantasy and imagination of its creator to the realm of abstract, beauty, and fiction. The author's life narrative of being a poet and young righteous Communist, who went to the police in Prague 6 to provide information on a *suitcase* that was brought to the dormitory by "some sort of man," constitutes an early exemplar of Kundera's narrative identity. Referencing to and paraphrasing a sentence in *The Unbearable Lightness of Being*, one could say that the Dvořáček episode imprinted such a deep trace on Kundera that it *only increased his desire to remain faithful to* it. This paraphrased thought belongs to Franz and is expressed through the fictional narrator: after Sabina leaves him without a trace, Franz feels a desire to remain faithful to her. This form of betrayal suits him perfectly. Sabina becomes his imaginary goddess, his *unearthly love* that propels his future engagement in the kitschy Grand March in Cambodia to protest Communism, and as the reader predicts that his participation in the protest will lead to Franz's death.

The Czech philosopher, Václav Bělohradský, called *Life Is Elsewhere* one of the greatest novels of the twentieth century. Milan Uhde, Kundera's friend, pointed out the significance of this novel, unprecedented in Czech literature: Kundera's settling his own accounts with Communism and with poets trapped in the Communist doctrine. [17] However, this novel is more than that; it has a magic key to the "Kauza Kundera" (and to the author's identity) and, most likely, for this reason Kundera delayed its publication in the Czech original until all the players of the March 14, 1950 incident were gone. Militká had passed away about two years before *Život je jinde* has reached bookshelves. The reviews written by Czechs instruct readers to read the novel according to Kundera's wishes; they warn them against making any parallels with the author's life. Lacking proper and honest criticism, these schematic Czech reviews, ironically, sound as though they were subjected to Stalinist censorship.

Commenting on his own work has been Kundera's long-standing tradition. In this respect, in *The Curtain* he quotes from Witold's Gombrowicz's

letter in response to one of his readers' complaints about the author's comments to his novels. Gombrowicz replied that his intention was to comment
"as much as he can and for as long as he can" to be a "complete writer."[18]
Naturally, the same stance is Kundera's credo. As a writer, he feels entirely
fused with his work; as he says, *he is his work.* As a reaction to plagiarism,
Cervantes proclaims a similar idea concerning his fictional Don Quixote, "he
was born for me alone, and I for him. He knew about action, I about writing.
He and I are simply one single entity."[19]

In addition to Part 2: "Xavier," Part 6: "The Middle-Aged Man" is the
most significant and revealing in terms of understanding Kundera's psyche.
In his authorial voice, Kundera admits that the poems Jaromil wrote and
recited at police cultural meetings have been long forgotten. He emphasizes
that "the authors themselves would deny ever having written them. For they
are ashamed, everyone is ashamed . . . "[20] He goes on, justifying his and
other poets' actions of the time, saying that it wasn't only a period of terror,
persecutions, political trials, and executions, but also of lyricism, expressed
by poetry. That epoch was "ruled hand in hand by the hangman and the
poet."[21] *Revolver Revue* cites Zdeněk Pešat who said that Kundera had
phoned him after the "Kauza Kundera" had erupted, and explained to him
that nowadays no one would be willing to understand those times. "At that
time, events were happening like in a detective story, and I wasn't used to it,"
Kundera said. "I was an ordinary student, despite being a member of the
Faculty Committee for several months . . . "[22] In spite of not wanting to
admit his participation in the event of March 1950, Kundera does admit it
indirectly to his old friend, who was bedridden, nearing his end (he died in
March 2010). If his conscience was one hundred percent clear, would he
even bother to justify the times that today "no one would be willing to
understand" and seek his friend's support?

Nonetheless, Kundera's denial sounds like the same old story. The phenomenon of denial is receiving wider attention in today's psychology. Freud
and a number of other psychologists have categorized denial as a defense
mechanism against negative realities that threaten man's ego. Research cases
and studies suggest that if trustworthiness is violated within a social group,
an apology on the part of the violator is more hurtful to him than denial. In
Beyond Revenge: The Evolution of the Forgiveness Instinct, Michael McCullough contends that "denial is part of the uneasy bargain we strike to be
social creatures" and that "we cut corners to get individual advantage, and we
rely on the room that denial gives us to get by."[23]

The redhead, in Part 6, of *Life Is Elsewhere*, now called *a girl*, argues
with her former lover, the middle-aged man, when visiting him after being
released from prison. Three years prior, she saw him the last time; she came
to tell him that she was to break up with him because of Jaromil (ironically,
this was the reason why she was late to the meeting with Jaromil). Now,

three years later, she sits in the same chair, is dressed in the same clothes, but denies everything. She has never said anything of this kind, she assures her former lover. And Mr. Kundera steps in in his role of a narrator, helping the girl out and agreeing with her. No, she wasn't lying, he explains and gives a little lecture about "those rare souls" (into which category he inevitably belongs himself, although he does not admit it) who "mistake their ethical wishes for reality."[24] The choice of denial by *these rare souls* is a natural reaction when they recognize they should have not said (or done) something, and while they remember everything perfectly well, they *deny those particular recollections the right to exist.* Therefore, they are not lying, only defending and protecting themselves, like the narrator defended and protected the fictional girl. This suggests that Mr. Kundera would similarly defend and protect himself in case he would be accused of something he should not have said or done. To present this concept poetically and to elevate it above rationality, it can be perceived the same way as Leoš Janáček viewed his approach to a musical composition: *only the note that has something of essence to say, has the right to exist*—an approach that Kundera has been using throughout his entire work. Clearly, he applied it to his own reaction in the "Kauza Kundera." Yes, from his own perception, denying any knowledge of the March 14, 1950 episode and of its players, Mr. Kundera was not lying; he has simply denied *those particular events and actors the right to exist in his personal recollections.* To speak in McCullough's term, he "relies on the room that denial gives him to get by."

When the reader meets the middle-aged man, he sees him opening his *suitcase* (valise) and taking out "a pair of wrinkled overalls." It is in this part of the novel that he tells the girl about Jaromil's death and how he died: he got sick and died an ordinary death, not by fire as he had dreamed. He, a Communist poet, died, and his tombstone bears the inscription with an epitaph that Jaromil once showed to his girl. She let her middle-aged lover read it, and he found Jaromil's poems to be in poor taste. In this part, the reader also learns about the girl's brother's whereabouts. He is still in prison, and she feels the burden of her guilt that had brought disaster onto him and her whole family. She feels the very same weight of guilt as Militká did once she learned what a disaster she had caused to her childhood friend, Dvořáček, and his whole family!

From the Preface written by Milan Kundera for the 1986 Penguin Books edition of *Life Is Elsewhere*, we know that Jaromil was a sensitive young poet and simultaneously a monster. He must die because of his monstrosity. And his girlfriend, the redhead, must reckon with the fact that Jaromil no longer lives. Thus the cause of all her disasters no longer exists. It all becomes "a nightmare, nonsense, unreality," says the narrator, and he means *unreality* for the girl, his fictional character, as well as for himself, the real player, Mr. Kundera. Inasmuch as the poet Jaromil, whose monstrosity was brought to the surface by a monstrous regime, must be gone, so gone must be the young lyrical poet Milan Kundera—all that part of his past, during which he was celebrating the monstrosity of his time. Both the fictional poet and the real poet of the 1950's period become fused in *nonexistence, in void.* That is why Kundera would like the public to see the beginning of his creative period only since the publication of *The Joke* and *Laughable Loves.* Everything published before (unless it has seen his heavy hand of editing) is a *nightmare, nonsense, unreality.* But no matter how much he wishes to shed his narrative of the past, the connectedness—bridging his narratives in time space—forms his narrative identity.

NO RIGHT TO RECONSTRUCT THE FICTIONAL?

Kundera's novels are his personal creations, and as Jason Wirth explains, he "writes in solitude but of the greater world of human affairs, as if one were one of the Leibnitz' monads, expressing the universe from the oblique and irreducibly singular perspective."[25] From his niche of solitude, he "mirrors the universe" in his own way, which (regardless of whether he admits it or denies it), reflects his life experience to form "the universe of his novels." He rejects the idea of making a novel out of moral and political ideas, reducing them to "discussions of ideas."[26] His concern of fictional reconstruction to recreate the real being is a serious concern to him. "No one has the right to pretend to be reconstructing a human life that no longer exists,"[27] concedes Charles, one of the five Parisian friends, in *The Festival of Insignificance* after hearing the story-joke about Stalin and his shooting twenty-four partridges. To a great extent, this is a reduction of Kundera's concept of *immortality* in his *Immortality.* As time moves on, Charles says, we die and live only in the memory of close friends, people who knew us, until we become the "old dead" providing the space for the "young dead" and "we vanish into the void,"[28] no one remembering us any longer. The concept of the old dead versus the young dead has been masterfully presented in a funny and touching interaction of a young man with an older woman in "Let the Old Dead Make Room for the Young Dead" of *Laughable Loves.* Now, the idea of immortality no longer has significance; it is replaced with the theatrical aspect of marionettes. *The very rare* deceased will live longer in people's memories; however, lacking the authenticity of their contemporaries, they will be reduced to hearsay remembrance messages, to *puppets.* The author's anxiety of becoming one of those puppets in his posthumous life seeps through.

FORMAN'S AMADEUS: GENIUS VS. MEDIOCRITY

The theme of a life of insignificance, a human struggle between mediocrity and fame, has been cinematographically presented in its powerful melodic beauty in Milos Forman's *Amadeus,* based on Peter Shaffer's play of the same title. The film has retained its popularity not only for its everlasting theme of mediocrity versus genius, but also for Salieri's carrying the guilt of alleged wrongdoings that he had committed to Mozart. Unlike Kundera, who discourages his readers from judging fictional characters on the basis of their own morality, Forman's idea of guilt and morality pervades the story.

The film is set in a mental asylum as a flashback of Antonio Salieri's recollections. Aging Salieri is a former composer at the Court of Austro-Hungarian Emperor Josef II, and he confesses to a priest—or rather accuses himself—of murdering Wolfgang Amadeus Mozart because of his jealousy and envy of Mozart's musical talent. Thomas J. Slater evaluates the theme: Mozart lives for composing music; it is his identity and life. His music may lack form but it has substance for he is able to elevate the common and average to greatness and his melody is divine. However, knowing the extent of his own talent, potential, and fame, Mozart becomes arrogant, refusing to abide by the rules of the Court. Shrewd and envious Salieri represents mediocrity; his music contains form but lacks substance and he reduces his grand ideas to commonness. He conspires against Mozart by betraying him for his own benefits and fame. While believing he is deeply religious, he holds resentment for God because he feels God betrayed him by endowing him with less talent than Mozart's. He is convinced that God is mocking him: Salieri feels he has sacrificed everything (physical pleasures included), so that his music would become the most supreme eternally. But young Mozart enjoys earthly pleasures: marriage, women, drinking and partying, and yet possesses the supreme talent. In the end, both Salieri and Mozart pay for their selfishness, rejection of Christian spirituality, and lack of understanding of oneself and one another. Mozart's body is thrown into a grave for commoners, and Salieri, calling himself "the highest priest of mediocrity," rides in a wheelchair through the hallway of a mental asylum, chained, caged, and visibly deformed patients forming his audience.[29] Mozart's laugh accompanies Salieri's sad procession: Salieri's music is forgotten and he lives in guilt and misery to witness it; Mozart's music lives on, gaining fame and recognition, and ultimately becoming immortal—the same posthumous phenomenon that Kundera labels *immortality.* The immortality in *The Festival of Insignificance* that Kundera comes to terms with is reserved for very few select people, like Mozart.

THE SIGNIFICANCE IN INSIGNIFICANCE: GUILT

The Festival of Insignificance seems to be indicative of the author's gradual progression of acceptance. Alain, whose mother wished that he had not been born and tried to drown herself when she was pregnant with him, suffers from a lack of self-esteem as a grownup. He imagines his mother in a number of situations, talking to her in his mind; her image present with him for most of his daily life. He has one concrete memory, though, etched in his mind: ten years old, he is by the pool. His mother meets briefly with his father after years of separation and before she leaves, she comes to the pool to say goodbye to her son, her gaze intensely resting on her son's navel until she touches it with her index finger. Since this was Alain's last memory of his mother, he lives under the spell of her *inexplicable mix of compassion and contempt*,[30] struggling with her rejection and attracted by the look of girls' navels (the way their jeans' waistline lies below their navel, and the way Parisian girls walk, exposing it), a connection between his lost mother and the zone of erotic seduction.

In this novel, Kundera's political ground is represented by Stalin and one of the members of his inner circle, Kalinin, after whom the Prussian native town of Immanuel Kant, Königsberg, was renamed *Kaliningrad,* once it was annexed to Russia. Kalinin's enlarged prostate makes him interrupt his own speeches, and even Stalin's oratories, but the moment the political is left behind, the theme running through the novel is guilt. Denial has evolved into guilt. "The person who apologizes is declaring himself guilty," says Alain. "And if you declare yourself guilty, you encourage the other to go on insulting you, blaming you, publicly, unto death."[31] Pondering over the theme of guilt by paraphrasing Shakespeare's *to be, or not to be* of Prince Hamlet's soliloquy, *to feel guilty or not to feel guilty*, comes up as a result of a trivial circumstance. Alain, jostled by a fast-walking girl on the street, apologizes; instead of accepting his apology, she shouts expletives after him. The philosophical issue, inevitably, remains unresolved. Who jostled whom, if both are jostled? Both are involved: the jostlers and the jostled. This short novel published in the French original *La fête de l'insignifiance* six years after the "Kauza Kundera" certainly points to the progression of Kundera's identity. Gone is the idea of greatness and everlasting immortality; it is replaced with a contrasting idea of insignificance; (i.e., forgotten in the blink of an eye). Is that a result of the jostling of Militká and Kundera? "The one who manages to make the other one guilty will win. The one who confesses his crime will lose,"[32] reveals the narrator in Alain's words, and concludes by Charles's statement: "One should not apologize."[33] The novel came out around the time Militká passed away.

As previously seen, Kundera's novelistic ideas go through a cycle of repetitions. In the context of philosophical interpretation, Kundera's use of repetition could be summarized as a reflection of Martin Heidegger's *interpretive* concept, first introduced by Kierkegaard and reiterated in his *Repetition: An Essay in Experimental Psychology*. In an essay, "Heidegger on Repetition and Historical Understanding," Calvin O. Schrag quotes from Heidegger's *Being and Time*: "*Repetition is the handing-over and appropriation (Überlieferung)*—that is to say, a going back to the possibilities of the *Dasein* that has-been-there."[34] Here repetition is understood not as a compilation of facts, incidents, and historical events but as an interpretation of existential possibilities: "Repetition enables one to achieve an understanding of one's personal past, as well as of the tradition out of which the personal past itself emerges."[35] This interpretation may well fit Kundera's own *Dasein*—his self-understanding of *being the human being*—within the frame of guilt and insignificance. Schrag further clarifies that Heidegger's notion of repetition is "a matter of understanding the past rather than identifying with it. Historical understanding takes the path of projecting possibilities through which new meanings within one's past are released."[36] It is these new meanings and new existential possibilities that Kundera faces and addresses in *The Festival of Insignificance*.

The concept of a person's life being a trap was introduced in his *The Art of the Novel*: a man being born without his own consent and trapped in a body that he has not chosen, his destination eventually coming to an end whether he likes it or not.[37] Kundera reinforces this idea in *The Unbearable Lightness of Being*, presenting his own authorial viewpoint and emphasizing that the purpose of the novel is an investigation of this human trap. The reader accepts his opinion readily because it is the author's opinion—he speaks from the parabatic standpoint. However, when the same idea comes from the lips of his characters, it feels forced, reminding the reader that the author *forces* his own opinions onto his characters. In *Slowness*, Vincent tells Julie out of the blue, without explanation: "The only thing left for us is to revolt against the human condition we did not choose."[38] In the literary context, Vincent's thinking is tied to a showmanship of dancers and living condition under the light of cameras. He didn't choose to live under cameras and if this has become a human condition, he should revolt against it. Alain's mother holds onto the same philosophy in her son's imaginative talk, arguing the reason for human rights in *The Festival of Insignificance*. In Alain's mind, she feels horrible about bringing him into the world because he didn't ask for it. Alain carries his ideas further, attributing his mother dislike for "defenders of human rights."[39] What do they want to defend if they cannot defend the basic condition of human beings? If they can't defend facts like being born ugly and carrying ugliness all their lives? If they cannot defend the gender they were born with, their hair and eye color, the country and the area they were born into? In a sense, Mr. Kundera tells us that human beings feel betrayed all their lives, and revolting against their condition might exceptionally bring only a brief period of relief, such as his own revolting against his "Czechism" and transforming himself into a Frenchman.

Erik Erikson (1902–1994), the noted developmental psychologist and psychoanalyst, was the first to use the concept of identity, and is largely responsible for the popularity of the word and the concept, especially for *identity crisis*. His theory on ego identity calls for "the ability to experience one's self as something that has continuity and sameness and to act accordingly"[40] as a prerogative for reaching some degree of authenticity within a social environment and in social behavior. In Milan Kundera's case, his "continuity and sameness" oscillate within a variety of environments, political and philosophical thoughts, but his authenticity is chiefly accomplished by his writing, creative and critical, that has provided him with "continuity and sameness." This idea overlaps, to some degree, with Foucault's theory on one's identity seen as a continuous but shifting (non-static) discourse of oneself with others.

IS IT ONLY CZECH ENVY?

Laughable Loves, a collection of seven stories (in German and Spanish retaining a reference to a "book" in its title; thus, making a better allusion to a novel) is a prelude to a further evolution of topics in Kundera's novels. As the title suggests, the stories contain a dose of laughable twists of erotic implications, not necessarily light in their nature, but more or less harmless. The themes of betrayal, two- or multiple-faced characters, and revenge play out heavily in *The Joke*, and the theme of denouncement is markedly pronounced in *Life Is Elsewhere* and *Farewell Waltz.*

The effects of governmental oppression of the life of an individual, induced by the higher Soviet power, are evident in Kundera's novels written in France, *The Book of Laughter and Forgetting,* and *The Unbearable Lightness of Being,* both placing the author at the pinnacle of his fame. The political climate of the mid- to late 1980s indicated a détente in Eastern Europe with the growing political prominence of Mikhail Gorbachev in the former Soviet Union. This political easing perfectly coincides with Kundera's creative trajectory and his identity. Under the impact of approaching upheavals in the Eastern bloc, Kundera must have been aware of being possibly deprived of his political arena of anti-Communist canvas, a background against which he placed his characters. The antagonists of the two novels (both written in Czech while living in France) were a natural extension of the pro-Soviet ideology, which spread into Kundera's former country where he, for the most part, placed his characters. These fictional antagonists have embodied spying, policing, executions, Soviet tanks, emigration, strong fear, and general unhappiness. The types of personae (usually Czech), who went with the ideological flow of pre- and post-normalization period of the late 1960s and during the 1970s, were threatening anti-regime novelistic protagonists like bogeymen. They instilled fear in them and interfered with their professional lives but left their erotic, intimate encounters largely untouched within the sphere of privacy. A good example of this representation is Tomas, once reduced to a window washer. His daily task of window washing was constantly filled with new erotic encounters with housewives and women, willing to satisfy his thirst for discovering that "one-millionth part" of their bodies.

It is in this climate of easing strained relations that Kundera changed his direction. In the sense of Ricoeur's definition, Kundera's identity is affected by the "search for the mediation between permanence and change." Not welcoming political changes in his novels, he instead turned his back on them, embracing European, mostly French, characters in *Immortality*. In this novel it seems that he put his hopes into being hailed as one of the great European novelists, someone who has continued the traditions of Cervantes, Broch, or Kafka; his fame, like theirs, embodied in his immortal *chef-d'oeuvre*. However, to Western critics and readers, this novel felt somewhat forced for the first time. Stripped of politically charged antagonists, his characters now oppose one another in their mundane problems, rather than facing the overarching machine of Communism. The political opposition of an ordinary man fired up the imaginations of Western readers and left them feeling fully satisfied because the protagonists fought against the true and tangible evil that needed to be eradicated. But what kind of force does one oppose in a free society? How does the author replace the evil machine of Communism with the free-society machine of Capitalism?

This is where the paths of Czech and Western readers have diverged. It wasn't only that Czechs might have resented Kundera's success in the West as many critics have pointed out. It was rather their understanding that Mr. Kundera, being endowed with a colossal literary talent and also with cunning shrewdness, in the eyes of many Czechs, has acted like a chameleon: first distorting and manipulating their Czech reality into convenient ideas worthy of Western readers' worship, regardless of the level of reduction of history, and then, when freedom has finally arrived to his native land, turning away altogether.

In this respect, Ladislav Jehlička, an editor at the Vyšehrad publishing house, a man of deep Catholic faith who spent a decade in Communist labor camps as a political prisoner, published a highly critical and disparaging article on Kundera's trajectory, "Lehká jsou jen hovna" (Only Shit Is Light). In its title he uses Vladimír Holan's ending verse of his poem "For the Enemies," and concludes that there is no difference whether feces float in Prague in the Vltava River or in Paris in the Seine. Purposely written in the rich vernacular of folk approach, Jehlička recounts Kundera's trajectory in the most rudimentary way: "He has only switched his gears: first he worshiped Soviets, now he curses them; first he was a Communist, now he is an anti-Communist, and all that he does equally naturally, equally self-confidently, equally theatrically, seeing himself the same way in either mirror"[41] (of conscience). Referring to Paul Eluard, whom Kundera blamed for the refusal to defend Holan when the poet fell under political scrutiny, Jehlička compares Kundera's rising to Eluard's: he has been all the same whether he wrote a pro-Communist poem about Julius Fučík, or his verses *à la* "Kdykoliv si Stalin zapaluje dýmku, nad celým světem svítá," (Whenever Stalin his pipe lights, the whole world in glare ignites).

Jehlička published his critical piece in 1998 and he only analyzes three novels: *Laughable Loves, The Book of Laughter and Forgetting*, and *The Unbearable Lightness of Being.* However, his approach is systematic. By stripping sexual scenes of philosophical and political rhetoric, he shows Kundera's characters naked, comparing their erotic antics with protagonists of third-rate literature, typically marketed to postpubertal girls and hormone-driven adolescents. Likewise, stripping Kundera's literary scenes of the author's reflective insertions and of a politically evocative canvas, Jehlička indicates to what extent Kundera plays on purpose with metaphysical ideas for which there are no straightforward answers, how he turns them upside down over and over again, how he deviates from real historical facts and elevates topics of "insignificance" to grand issues of existence.

In his pre-publication article for *Slavonica* (2018), "Mystification as an artistic strategy in Milan Kundera's work," Jan Čulík proposes that "Kundera's texts should be viewed as provocations, as mystifying agnostic games which are deliberately built up from seemingly convincing, authoritative statements." Čulík supports Milan Jungmann's assertion that Kundera's characters are "born not of flesh and blood" but rather serve as *functions* to transform an intended idea or a theme into a fictional surrounding. In his analysis, Čulík elaborates on "discrete aspects of Kundera's use of mystification," and thus unwittingly, he advances Jehlička's theories on Kundera's "fake" aesthetics while presenting them in a literary, rather than colloquial, discourse.

Kundera's use of repetitions and of the everyday (the seemingly trivial) has its aesthetic function in his novels. The use of repetition as a mnemonic device is common in poetry, and its significance in prose is equally essential. Gilles Deleuze (1925–1995), an influential post-modern French philosopher, held the opinion that repetition acquires a new outlook as everything constantly changes and thus, in a flux of perpetual changes, no repetition is the same but rather different and new. James Williams's study on Deleuze's difference and repetition is concerned with relationships of interchange between "actual events" and "virtual events," and with the loss of actual identity of things via repetition by acquisition of another actual identity.[42] Kundera's approach to the aesthetics of repetition is a conscious choice not only in his novels but also in his perception of his own identity.

ELONGATED LÍTOST

Kundera's linguistic and historical adjustments to fit his literary context to suit his ideas and connecting them with behavioral attitudes of his characters are of some concern, though. In this respect, the word *lítost*, comes to mind. Due to its introduction in his *The Book of Laughter and Forgetting*, *lítost* has become frequently quoted in prestigious magazines and journals, including *The New York Times*. According to Kundera's assertion, *lítost* has no equivalent in any other language. In the English version of *The Book of Laughter and Forgetting*, *lítost* is spelled *litost*, which defeats the purpose presented by Kundera. He begins by pointing out its first long stressed syllable *lí-* that sounds like "the wail of an abandoned dog." But even at a superficial glance, a linguistic argument comes into play for the following reasons: a) the initial syllable is stressed in all Czech words; b) if containing a long vowel (indicated by the length mark, the so-called *čárka*, above vowels *á, é, í, ó, ú, ý,*), the syllable becomes long and is pronounced in an elongated way. Unfortunately, in English spelling, *litost* loses its length and meaning, becoming meaningless. Just like in English *leak* vs. *lick,* the vowel length often changes the meaning: *bílí,* 'white' (an adjective in the masculine animate plural form) vs. *bili,* 'they beat' (the past tense and participle of masculine animate plural verbal form 'to beat'). Literary Czech contains a number of words and their derivatives beginning with the *lí-* syllable, embracing a variety of meanings: *líbat* (to kiss); *lízat* (to lick); *lízátko* (lollypop); *lívanec* (pancake); *lístek* (ticket); *lípa* (linden tree); *líný* (lazy), etc. In addition, spoken Prague Czech reduces certain words with the prefix or stem *lé-* into *lí-*: *lépe* (better) becomes *líp; létat* (to fly) becomes *lítat; vylétnout* (to run out, to fly out) becomes *vylítnout,* etc. Evidently, English exhibits similar oral features of long *lí-* syllables by indicating their length by two vowels: *leeway, leave, leach, Lee,* etc.

In the Part Five, "Litost," of his novel, Kundera demonstrates the application of *lítost* to his characters: Kristyna, a butcher's wife, who in her naïve fear of getting pregnant refuses a student, her young lover of limited practicality but with an abundance of philosophical eloquence about poetry, Schopenhauer, and Czech poets who appear under pseudonyms of real poets, such as Goethe, Petrarch, Lermontov, etc. Both Kristyna and her lover become overcome by *lítost* in various situations because of differences in their social and intellectual backgrounds and their failed lovemaking due to an absurd misunderstanding: she was afraid of a possible pregnancy, and he mistook her fear for the immensity of her romantic love for him that prevented physical love.

While the idea of *litost* drives the plot in "Litost," it is important to emphasize the author's fictional embellishment of the meanings of the word *litost*. It might be acceptable in poetics but it is misleading in linguistics. Even considering the ironic position of the author, many of Kundera's readers validate the meaning of *litost* based on Kundera's description in his novel: a combination of many feelings, including "grief, sympathy, remorse, and indefinable longing," and a state of "torment" that is evoked by "the sudden sight of one's own misery," a torment that leads to desiring revenge. Kundera concedes that he cannot "imagine how anyone can understand the human soul without it." But once stripped of fictional poetics, *litost* reverts to one of the abstract words used infrequently in Czech. Its use is common in idiomatic expressions, such as *k mé lítosti* (to my sorrow, to my sorrowful disappointment), *je mi líto* (I am sorry, I regret), but in most cases, it is replaced with the verb *litovat* (to be sorry), and its verbal noun *politování* (pity, sorry) used in the sense of expressing compassion. Elevating an ordinary word to a poetical platform, Kundera has charmed his sophisticated non-Czech-speaking readers at the expense of linguistic havoc. Dictionaries provide a range of equivalents for *litost* from remorse, repentance, compassion, sorrow, grief, commiseration, sympathy, pity, to regret, which indicates that *litost* is ambiguous and a less precise word than its English equivalents.[43] Depending on the context, it might be difficult to find the exact meaning; however, *litost* has little to do with "understanding of the human soul" as Kundera attempts to convince his readers. Wouldn't he indirectly imply that only people speaking Czech can "understand the human soul" and, above all, that language-disabled people are devoid of that ability?

There are a variety of examples of purposeful cultural, historical, and linguistic distortions in Kundera's novels. Among readers, there are relatively few Western "experts" whose profound knowledge of Czech, life experiences in the country, knowledge of the history and mentality, and grasp of cultural nuances allow them to fully see these nuance-ridden distortions. The peripheral sphere of this mixed bag in Kundera's novels has often enticed intellectuals with its metaphysical meaning. Czech readers accept it either as a distorted banality or the aesthetic beauty of banality at the level of pop-culture psychology and philosophy. Kundera is fully aware of the power of the everyday, and its potential impact on his readers. He addresses this issue in his essay *"The Power of the Pointless"* in *The Curtain*: "The everyday. It is not merely ennui, pointlessness, repetition, triviality; it is beauty as well." The comical outlook is an interpretation of one culture that can easily be rendered as intellectual philosophizing in another culture.

In this respect, a quote from Jason Wirth's book, *Commiserating with Devastated Things*, clarifies this attitude. Referring to his undergraduate philosophy studies, he says that he "was quickly captivated" by *The Unbearable Lightness of Being:* "I was immediately taken by the philosophical sounding title and the opening discussion of Nietzsche's eternal return as the existential DNA of Tomas—that things do not return again and again makes them appear light and trifling and thereby 'in this world everything is pardoned in advance and therefore everything cynically permitted' . . . " At the same value, Wirth admits that "Kundera is not in the business of producing knockdown philosophical arguments, nor does he repackage classical arguments in the sweeter guise of fiction. In Kundera's practice of the novel, thinking was simultaneously more dangerous, complex and exciting."[44]

The trivial and the often unnoticed (monotonous, uninteresting every-day, repetitive things perceived as boring and pointless) acquire "the magical charm" once set within the poetics of a story or a novel. As Wirth implies, it is the allure of highly provocative thoughts that Kundera attaches as an apanage to the utmost ordinary (hat) and to the rejected (shit) in order to revert it into the extraordinary and exciting. The perception, liking or disliking, and understanding of his novels depends on how one views their aesthetics.

Czechs, proud of their complex historical heritage and simultaneously seeing the other side of the coin, do occasionally resent the simplification and distortion of their past that provides the fictional existential canvas for his characters and literary benefits for the author. For instance, Kundera's reference to his acquaintance with R. speaks for this occurrence. In Part Three, "The Angels" of *The Book of Laughter and Forgetting*, R. was one of Kundera's young friends, who were too young to be yet on the lists of persecuted Czechs, the list maintained by Russians. Many of these young friends intended to help him earn a living by proposing to publish his work under their names and passing the earnings on to him. In the novel, Kundera writes that he couldn't accept their offers because the offers were too many for him to handle and, in addition, it was too dangerous for young people. He wouldn't want to see their names on the Russians' lists because the secret police would want to starve them, reduce them to poverty and force them to make public retractions, him included. But he accepted R.'s proposal to write horoscopes for her youth-oriented and popular magazine. Mr. Kundera speaks convincingly about his female friend R. being devoted to him, and putting her life at stake for him, especially when he describes their last meeting in a borrowed apartment after their ruse was discovered by the secret police.[45]

Readers assume that all this happened in Mr. Kundera's life because he enters the novel as its author, referring to himself, the real man. But alas, there are contemporaries who knew him well during this Prague period, interacted with him on a daily basis and knew other people who were in touch with him; however, no one ever seemed to know R. or hear of her, "a shy, subtle and intelligent young woman." In his article, "Lehká jsou jen hovna," Ladislav Jehlička clarifies her mysterious existence. First he addresses the issue of Kundera's inflated, if not incorrect, statements about Russians. The Russian KGB had no interest and involvement in the petty political intrigues of Czechs and Slovaks; it was their own Czechoslovak government, national and secret police that got involved when they judged it appropriate. In reality, it was the very same agency to which young Kundera brought his information about Dvořáček's *suitcase*. In the particular case of Kundera's secret writing of horoscopes, it was done for the well-known magazine, *Mladý svět* (Young World), and the deal was arranged and covered up by its twenty-three-year-old editor, P.P. (Mr. Jehlička gives only his initials). The horoscopes were signed not by P.P., but by a man from Brno, and the honorarium was sent to an undisclosed Brno address. When the secret StB agency discovered Kundera's involvement in horoscope writing, the young editor P.P. lost his position at *Mladý svět,* and remained unemployed for two years until he was hired by a democratic weekly, of which Jehlička was the editor at the time. Jehlička further emphasizes that while an author has the right to present real events fictionally, he should do it with decency and concerns about his characters. He finds Kundera's ending of the fictional meeting with R. cheaply constructed, distasteful and theatrically exaggerated. He asks: What author would write about having "a wild desire to rape a woman," to throw himself on a person, who in fear is relieving herself into the toilet bowl, her stomach and intestines contracting with anxiety and shame? Kundera is not concerned about R., but only about his sexual urges, Jehlička concludes. He sees Kundera standing on the side of the devil's laughter: it is Kundera's life philosophy and his innermost faith, and the above example merely reflects this in practice.[46]

Kundera wrote and published this novel in a time of severe political tensions between the West and the East, and it was read as yet another testimony of the evils of the Soviet regime. But Kundera was no Solzhenitsyn. In his anti-regime novels, Solzhenitsyn was depicting humiliated anti-Soviet-Stalinist-regime characters as morally strong, while Kundera was depicting upper-hand pro-regime characters as immorally weak.

CHARACTERS IMMORALLY WEAK?

We may look for the response in *The Festival of Insignificance* in Stalin's vision of the world as represented in Schopenhauer's idea by *representation* and *will*. Kundera's Josef Stalin assures his comrade, Zdanov, of the necessity of *imposing one single representation on everyone* to instill order in the chaos of the world; after all, there are as many visions of the world as there are individuals living on the globe. And to introduce a single representation for everyone, one has to possess a strong will to convince people to believe him. Inevitably, Kundera's fictional Stalin boasts with his own *grip of a great will,* laughing "with pleasure in his voice."[47] Behind his laughter an attentive reader hears the echo of Kundera's pleasurable laughter. Doesn't Stalin's will resonate with Kundera's will to impose upon his readers to achieve *one single representation* of his works?

Kundera's novels are heavily charged with self-references, disguised in the actions and thoughts of his fictional characters. They are poking and laughing at the reader everywhere, and the author is wholeheartedly laughing behind the scene. Why would he not? How could the reader not see Kundera himself in Khrushchev's reaction to Stalin's boasting? "Still, Comrade Stalin, even though people have always believed anything you say, these days they no longer believe you at all."[48] There is no longer a need for Kundera to drag *his suitcase* into the theme of *insignificance*; however, he still does, possibly for the sake of consistency of self-explanation and preserving his narrative identity. Its carrying by his characters is always present, often cleverly and innocently hidden in between the lines, yet outlined and documented enough throughout his works. In *The Festival of Insignificance,* it appears in the hands of friends, Charles and Caliban. After setting a table in the salon for a cocktail party in the apartment of their friend, D'Ardelo, Charles, and Caliban retired into a small room, opened a *suitcase* (valise) and took out two white jackets to put them on. The author concedes that they did not need a mirror; just looking at one another, they laughed; they had a feeling they were putting on "the white costumes" for fun, not for work. Is the author aiming to tell the readers not to take his mirror image seriously? By now, his readers learned about D'Ardelo pretending to have cancer and about his supposed upcoming death within three months; about the recent death of Madame La Franck's partner; and about Charles's mother being seriously ill and nearing the end. The mirroring of one character in another, often in the author himself, has been a technique Kundera has had recourse to in a number of novels. In her article on *Slowness* in *Critical Essays on Milan Kundera*, Karen von Kunes writes: "A closer look at *Slowness* reveals the novella as a mathematical design based on the appearance of two masks within the *commedia dell'arte,* the device of the so-called twin-sided mirror."[49] When Charles and Ramon discuss Stalin's story of the twenty-four partridges in Nikita Khrushchev's memoir, Kundera enters his own observation about Stalin from his visit to the Soviet Union in 1954 into Charles's mouth, saying, "he had become the greatest criminal of all."[50]

The idea of secret policing creeps in, too. It comes in the form of a small, bald man, who at the cocktail party gazes at the three friends, Charles, Ramon, and Caliban. It is Caliban, who fears being watched by the man. He has a reason: at the social events, he has been pretending to be a Pakistani, concocting a nonexistent language for his own amusement. And the author amuses himself by Ramon's reference to Caliban, an allusion to the "Kauza Kundera" eruption. If the small bald man discovers that Caliban is hiding his true identity, that he is not a Pakistani but an ordinary Frenchman, he will think that Caliban has "some shady reason" to play this game, and will alert the police, Ramon says. "You'll be interrogated! You'll explain that your Pakistani character was a joke. They'll laugh at you: What a stupid alibi! You must certainly have been up to no good! They'll put you in handcuffs!"[51] This passage is a redundancy of the infamous scene in *The Joke*. It is jotted as a suggestion; it is not developed into serious plot, and may only serve as another statement why Mr. Kundera will continue ignoring the "Kauza Kundera." Almost every human interaction in Kundera's works departs from various perceptions: one character sees what the other misses. And who is right and who is wrong? As Ramon makes his friend D'Ardelo instantly a "secret lover" of Madame La Franck by inventing an absurd lie, D'Ardelo makes a fool of Ramon by lying about being struck with an incurable disease. They both ignore the truth, taking each other's lie as a true and valuable statement.

From the first page of day one to the last page of Milan Kundera's current writing, it's all betrayals. It is a pleasurable game of light invention and heavy application; it is a paradoxical game that flipped his insignificance into immortality by turning in a *suitcase*. The gravity of the *suitcase* reported to the Prague Police was so heavy that it has made its bearer think poetically and philosophically, artistically, and, above all shrewdly; however, *creatively shrewdly*. Kundera belongs to the few "rare ones" who possess the gift of flipping heaviness of human conscience into lightness of laughable life. But one cannot really reproach him for that or even blame him. If Kafka didn't write about Gregor changing into a vermin that he, himself, found hilariously silly and worth a good laugh with Max Brod and his group of close friends, there would be no libraries filled with criticism on *The Metamorphosis, The Trial, The Castle,* and his other writings that were looked upon first with skepticism and artistic reluctance.

After all, even Ladislav Jehlička, as much as he had ridiculed Milan Kundera's novels and his two-sided personality, admits that his somewhat kitschy writing, based on a theatrical pose, has not necessarily been his fault alone. Since the National Revival of the Czech language in the nineteenth century, Czech literature has been overestimated. There was not much to celebrate for a writer whose small nation gave up on fighting and remained apathetic to politics since its defeat in 1620 in the Battle of White Mountain during the thirty-year war that ravaged Europe. The pride of Czechs injured, they welcomed any boost to their national ego and celebrated anyone who took the courage to set down a simple story. Czech literature has remained *national in its scope*, and aside from its worn-out names that international readers know, such as Čapek, Hašek, Hrabal, Havel, there is little to offer which would excite international readers' minds. Giants like Russian Tolstoy, Dostoevsky, and Pasternak, or French Balzac and Flaubert, or even

Italian Dante and Boccaccio are absent in Czech literature. And while Czech criticism glorifies its own "literary giants," the fact remains that few people read them outside of the small territory and its surrounding countries, despite translators' and publishers' efforts to bring them to global readership. All over again and again, it is Milan Kundera. No one else but Milan Kundera.[52]

NOTHING BUT BETRAYAL

As emphasized, betrayal is an everlasting theme in Kundera's work. In *Immortality*, Agnes is betraying her husband Paul by seeing from time to time a failed painter, nicknamed Rubens (whose personality is hidden until Part Six of the novel, "The Dial," and who possibly is another alter ego of Kundera, an unrecognized painter himself). Once when she is kissing him in the lobby of a hotel, a stranger takes a picture of them. Agnes tries to obtain all the pictures and negatives to destroy them for "she could not bear the idea that somewhere there remained a document testifying to her acquaintance with the man she had met there."[53] In this passage, Kundera's anxiety seems to blur with Agnes's: "she could not rid herself of anxiety because one second of her life, instead of dissolving into nothingness like all the other seconds of life, would remain torn out of the course of time and some stupid coincidence could make it come back to haunt her like the badly buried dead."[54] Being always vigilant, Mr. Kundera had no clue how prophetic his words would become twenty years to the day, in March 2008.

In *Slowness*, his first novel in French, Kundera cleverly ties the idea of betrayal to the eighteenth-century social climate of hedonism, bringing in Epicurus's idea of pleasure—the absence of suffering: "one is happy to the degree that one can avoid suffering."[55] Kundera builds *Slowness* according to the triptych, three stages of lovemaking, as presented in Vivant Denon's 1779 novella *Point de lendemain* (*No Tomorrow*). With three additional reprints by 1866, *Point de lendemain* became an erotic bestseller of the time, reflecting its spirit, values, and artistic tradition. Kundera assigns the admiration of the hedonistic tradition to his protagonist Vincent, but before he introduces him, he dwells on Choderlos de Laclos's epistolary novel *Les liaisons dangereuses* (1782). Laclos's novel summed up a long tradition of libertine literature, in which the theme of seduction and betrayal has been set in a frame of social pressure-cooker games, a system of psychological control, in which seduction became a tool of expression of power, and put stress on its players, women in particular, because they needed to resist it to preserve their good name in the society. This revival of Epicurean hedonism, or "*la doucère de vivre,*" has its roots in the inability of the French army to display its potency in military affairs at the threshold of the eighteenth century, which France entered with its bankrupt kingdom; so the upper-crust of

society turned to private affairs. The social games of erotic conquest produced a major literary figure—the seducer, who in the manner of Molière's
Don Juan (1665), in a play in prose of daring message of the time, defies the
ostensible rules of church, state, and social mores. These games developed
their own rules, which have been subjected to codification and theory in at
least a dozen novels and created a fertile soil for Laclos's masterpiece. In
fact, Laclos's novel has never ceased to fascinate artistic creators, who, in the
following centuries, produced a variety of its interpretations.[56]

Kundera himself was fascinated by *Les liaisons dangereuses*, and in the
1950s introduced this slim volume in his FAMU lectures, and subsequently
its content left a deep mark on his student, Milos Forman, who several
decades later, in 1989, released its film version, *Valmont*. Inspired by Chris-
topher Hampton's dramatization of Laclos's novel that he saw in London in
1987, Forman approached the stage director Hampton, inviting him to cooperate on his film. While he promised, Hampton betrayed Forman in the sense
that he collaborated with Stephen Frears, a British film director, on a version
retaining its original title and exhibiting less artistic freedom than Forman's
Valmont. Hampton's feature *Dangerous Liaisons* (1988) received greater
recognition than Forman's film, primarily because Forman's release came
out second, after Hampton's, at the peak of the revolutionary time in Europe
when the public on both continents was absorbed in the politics of the disso-
lution of Communist Europe rather than in the amorous intrigues of eighteenth-century decadent French nobility. However, all three interpretations of
Laclos's novel, Hampton's, Frear's, and Forman's, share the theme of social
pressure of love intrigues and manipulation, ostensible and forced emotions
and sincerity. Their art is expressed in cultivated eloquence and the utmost
rhetorical skills that all characters must muster to succeed in being accepted
in upper-crust society. In fact, one can notice an interesting parallel of the
late eighteenth-century French society of hedonistic pleasures with late twentieth-century Communist Europe. Each society was decadent in its own right,
seeking refuge in solipsism and self-gratification of erotic pleasures that
culminated in the rebellious spirit of the revolution: in 1789 in France and
two centuries later, in 1989 in Czechoslovakia. Had Forman grabbed the
opportunity to make his notorious seducer Valmont a revolutionary fighter,
instead of leaving him a pitiful victim of a duel over his pride, he might have
produced a powerful feature that would talk directly to the hearts of Czechs
and Europeans by its obvious analogy.

Kundera's approach to the theme of *Les liaisons dangereuses* was either
wiser or more calculated than Forman's. Published five to six years after the
revolutions changed the maps of Communist countries within Europe, Kundera's *Slowness* focuses on the physical speed at the dusk of the twentieth
century. Kundera perceives it as a "form of ecstasy the technical revolution
has bestowed on man."[57] In a sense, Kundera must have felt betrayed by the

political upheaval in his native country that he had not predicted would happen in his lifetime, and that had shattered his line of creative vision: his characters marching upright through their lives, their bitterness and daily struggle caused by the public machinery of Communist politics but their lives sugarcoated by their erotic privacy. Up to this point, it was "the cold impersonality" of a political system, but now it has become "the cold impersonality of technology," both creating a "flame of ecstasy." And yes, Mr. Kundera glorifies the "good old times" of the eighteenth-century lovemaking process, during which the French upper class enjoyed the slow motion of sexual encounter, divided into several stages of erotic seduction and yet, full of betrayals, which his fictional characters seem to enjoy as much as *la chose*—the thing, the lovemaking itself.

Kundera calls the utilitarianism of today's sexual encounter "the religion of orgasm,"[58] and presents its goal as a quick "explosion of ecstasy," comparing it to the speed of a fast-driven car. A driver chases his vehicle outside of an awareness of time, the past and the future, only concentrating on the speed of his car and thus, being in a state of ecstasy, he is unaware of his life and surroundings. In as much as *Slowness* begins on a grand scale of Epicurean hedonism, with Milan Kundera and his wife Véra stepping into the novel within the first lines and with their critical view of speeding cars passing theirs, it progresses into a Super Bowl of a comedic theater farce in *"le genre de sottie."* As the author suggests through the words of his wife Véra, this novel might be "A Big Piece of Nonsense for Your Own Pleasure."[59] She reminds her husband that his mother used to warn him against seeing life as a joking journey: "Milanku, stop making jokes. No one will understand you. You will offend everyone and everyone will end up hating you."[60] This interaction in the novel between the author and his wife, during which she speaks and he remains docile, bowing his head and agreeing, could be overlooked, had it not been for its conclusive message. Véra suggests that unless he gets serious, he will be left "naked to the wolves" for the wolves "are waiting for him" to devour him. In the novel, Kundera understands her metaphor as a "terrible prophecy."

A prophecy of what? Of a betrayal of himself? A betrayal of his conscience, his own identity? At the end of *Slowness*, when leaving the hotel with his wife, Mr. Kundera carries "a little valise,"[61] the notorious *suitcase* that has become his life premonition. Thus far, it was his fictional characters that have dragged it along; now it is he, the author himself, who leaves the château with it, indicating that his creative journey would never be the same. He is "dead" as a Czech novelist for himself and his compatriots. He would not allow his French novels to be translated into Czech and published in his native country because his intention is to distance himself from his country, its people, and from his origin (and his sin). There are wolves there, waiting for him, and he knows that too well.

The triptych of *Slowness* bears a resemblance to Kundera's three-stage creative period. In the novel, the château is a central meeting of the characters: a) real Mr. and Mrs. Kundera are spending a night in what is now a hotel; b) the imaginary encounter of Vivant Denon's lovers from *Point de lendemain*, which itself is drawn in a three-stage lovemaking that presumably could have taken place in this former château; c) the meeting site of an Entomological scientists congress, which is orchestrated by the author's three-level sardonic view of the acting personae, each resembling a *zanni* in the *Comédie Française* with its roots in the Italian *commedia dell'arte*: Vincent and Julie, Inamorata pursuing Berck, and Mr. Cechoripsky, a Czech scientist, researching a housefly *Musca pragensis*.[62]

Like a tangible triptych, a set of three carved or painted hinged panels, two of which can be folded in toward the central one, Kundera's creative period folds into three-panel-periods; two of which are less significant and less appealing than the central, major one. His desire to keep the left panel of his poetic period permanently folded is apparent but, alas, the hinges allow the panel to fold inside only, overlapping and interfering with, and partly covering, the beauty of the central panel (i.e., his period of productivity [novelistic, playwriting, journalistic, scholarly, and critical], dating from the mid-1960s till the end of the twentieth century). The Velvet Revolution of 1989 stirred a private revolution in every Czech citizen, and Mr. Kundera was no exception. Everything that he endowed as a writer of the post-Velvet Revolution period is in the third panel of his creative triptych. And like in its physical form, this panel located on the right side of human vision, is the least noticeable, especially when slightly folded in toward the center. Kundera's French creative period will remain slightly folded, for it doesn't emanate the sunny glow through a cloudy sky as the central panel of his previous creative period does.

It is not only a bit of awkward *Frenchness* that has replaced his laughable *Czechness*, it is the impersonality of his characters that borders on caricature. In *Slowness*, he calls them exhibitionists, *dancers*—a concept familiar to a small group of friends of Pontevin, a researcher-historian who works in the National Library but feels bored stiff, and invents ideas for his own pleasure. As a character, he is a sketch like his buddies; they leave the reader emotionless and detached as soon as he puts the novel aside. These show-off dancers share common ground with politicians, except for their diverging goal—it's not power but glory they are after. They like to be the center of attention, or "taking over the stage" and for that reason, they need to fight and use "moral judo," as Pontevin points out.

Kundera interweaves his voice throughout the novel, reminding the reader that he is one of the dancers: the one standing aside and orchestrating the performance. He doesn't hate mankind, he conveys indirectly via Pontevin but he has no desire to be in "too close a contact" with the public. Vincent adores Pontevin for his cleverness, and for his self-assuredness about women. Pontevin brags about his girlfriend who wants him to "get rough with her,"[63] and Vincent finds it amusing, along with his other cronies, Machu and the erudite Goujard, and with guests in Café Gascon, which is their usual place of meetings. Whereas the talk and humor of the four friends in the café is rather haphazard, aimed to evoke laughter, it creates merely the laughter printed on pages of *Slowness*. An idea of small, insignificant betrayals creeps in, surrounding the friends' polemics about a politician Duberques and an intellectual Berck, both exhibitionists craving a camera shot of their good deeds immortalized in the French news and around the globe. Connected to contemporaries, who find fame to be an annoyance rather than enjoyment, the author delves into his philosophical musing on the "axiom of existential mathematics," (i.e., a possibility of every single person running into fame). If fame becomes real, it "transforms everything about existence."[64] Inevitably, Kundera speaks from his own experience; his uncanny fame has "transformed everything about his own existence," and like his Pontevin, he refutes the idea of being a center of attention of the public.

The multileveled plot of the novel, with its critical message of today's fast pace in life and lovemaking affairs, is contextualized by a mathematical equation, rather than by underdeveloped characters: "the degree of slowness is directly proportional to the intensity of memory; the degree of speed is directly proportional to the intensity of forgetting."[65] The idea is contrasted with the lovemaking of two couples from two divergent times. Madame de T. leads her Chevalier through the night "shaped like a triptych in three stages": the park, pavilion, and secret chamber of the château. Vincent leads Julie onto the imaginative "theater-stage" by the outside hotel pool. He becomes fascinated so obsessively by the moon in the night sky—its round glowing glory—that it evokes his desire not for Julie's body but for her asshole. However, their three-stage escapade is quite unromantic. It culminates in Vincent's inability to perform, and moreover, is interrupted by a loud-mouthed couple, a filmmaker Immaculata in her beautiful white dress, followed by her cameraman, dressed in pajamas, whom she abhors in her anger and despair. They are joined by a tall, strong, and oddly misshapen Czech scientist. Immaculata attempts to commit suicide by drowning, for she feels betrayed by Berck, a pursuer of hers in her adolescent years. Juvenile Immaculata rejected Berck; she ignored him, laughed at him, and betrayed him by disclosing his love letters that he used to send her, calling her "the nightingale of his dreams." But now that he has attained fame, she is determined to pursue him, chasing after her rejected love. Berck betrays her, showering her with a crudely vulgar rhetoric. Before her cameraman is able to save her from drowning, the Czech researcher on *Musca pragensis*, Mr. Cechoripsky, jumps into the water to assist Immaculata.

He is a genuinely laughable zanni; he feels misunderstood and betrayed by everyone and everything that surrounds him at the Congress. Instead of delivering his carefully prepared paper on a rare fly, he gets melted in emotions over his own fate: twenty years working as a construction laborer instead of pursuing his research on flies. He delivers a speech about his sad country that just stepped out of the dark ages of Communism, forgetting to read his very own paper. Not able to grasp cultural differences, the Czech scientist feels not only alienated from his French colleagues but also finds them blatantly ignorant. They don't know how to pronounce and spell his surname *Čechořipský*, adorned with the Czech diacritical markings; they don't have a clue where Prague is located, who Jan Hus was, or that Mickiewicz was not a Czech but a Polish poet. The last blow strikes when the cameraman attacks Mr. Čechořipský for his good will to try to save the drowning woman in the pool. During the fight, the scientist's tooth cracks, and Mr. Čechořipský realizes that it was his tooth-bridge that held his capped teeth together; now he would need to wear a denture, an idea that revolts him. As ridiculous as Mr. Čechořipský is depicted, he represents a marvelous caricature of the author. Mr. Kundera becomes a *concertatore* of his *commedia dell'arte* show, orchestrating it by means of linguistic, musical, and poetic devices to address his point.

While in the novel, the scientist's name is spelled *Cechoripsky*, linguistically it is a hybrid of *Čech*, a noun denoting a Czech national, as well as the legendary father *Čech*, who has chosen the hill *Říp* (hence *řipský*) by the Vltava River to settle his Czech tribe, a legend popularized by Alois Jirásek, the late nineteenth- and early twentieth-century writer of historical novels. The musicality in *Slowness* is parodied by Julie's voice, "awful, grating, croaking, like an old crow," and Vincent's "feeble and too piercing" voice, which combined with other voices in the novel, form a vocal symphony.[66] As the narrator explains, the poetic device *asshole* represents the ninth portal of a woman's body in Guillaume Apollinaire's poems. In 1915, Apollinaire sent the poems to his two mistresses while he was a soldier in WWI. *Le petit trou,* a small hole, first appeared in his pornographic novel of 1900, titled *Mirely, ou le petit trou pas cher*, a work which eventually became lost. The narrator in Kundera's novel acknowledges the *asshole* to be "the supreme portal," because in his words, "it is the most mysterious, the most secret,"[67] a part of woman's body, that has remained taboo even in pornographic magazines and films.

Feeling humiliated and betrayed to the marrow of his bones, Mr. Čechořipský "suffers" in silence, and so does the eighteenth-century Chevalier. Betrayed by Madame de T., who used him for the night as a screen to hide the Marquis (her real lover) from her husband (betrayed twofold by his wife, Madame de T.), he continues his journey, blissful memories on his mind and the scent of lovemaking with Madame de T. on his fingers. Vincent betrayed Julie by ruining the promised night of lovemaking, and she betrayed him by running away from the unsatisfied encounter. He no longer can reach her because he doesn't know her surname or anything else about her. His failure aside, he intends to betray himself by inventing a marvelous orgiastic night at which his "plural cock" represented the sexual performance of his friends as well. He is rushing to forget his erotic failure and to reach his friends to tell them his lies about what a great and pluralistic lover he was. The nostalgic Chevalier, on the contrary, "wants to be alone in the chaise to be carried slowly, dreamily to Paris,"[68] after learning that there will be no repeat of lovemaking with Madame de T., there will be *no tomorrow*. He wants to imprint in his memory the beautiful moments he spent with Madame de T. and retain them as long as possible. The intensity of his precious memory is directly proportional to the degree of slowness, in which the premise of this novel lies.

One could point out three triptych-like themes that appear and reappear throughout the canvas of Kundera's work: *sex–betrayal–denouncing*. They often overlap one with another, occasionally rising on their own. The denouncing in *Slowness* comes in the subtlest possible way—in the rules of the so-called "moral judo"—and is connected to ridiculing the politicization of the plot. In Pontevin's concept, "moral judo" is the battle of a dancer to remain on the stage, to be the key actor of the game. In Mr. Čechořipský's case, it was *cover-up denouncing* that occurred. His position as chairman of the Prague Entomological Institute was directly threatened and then reduced to nothingness by a small group of "moral judokas," demanding the use of a room in the Institute for their anti-regime meetings. Not having enough courage to oppose, he agreed and by agreeing he was denounced to the appropriate organ (the secret police indirectly implied) and thrown out of his position at the Institute. He lost all the perks of a scientist for the betrayal by "moral judokas," ultimately hating himself for his weakness of not being able to say no.

Slowness shows no deviation from the continuous appearance of the *suitcase* in Kundera's novels. The author himself carries it away as a distancing mechanism that he intended to adopt. There is no death of any characters: they all are happily, but mostly unhappily, dancing on the stage of art-comedy that Kundera has created for them. Death, which has dominated Kundera's existential writings, is behind the corner, though (Immaculata's attempt to drown in the pool). It is also mentioned by passing in Mrs. Véra Kundera's generic reference to people dying on the road every fifty minutes due to speeding drivers in France. Ultimately, death has been replaced with ridicule.

As a writer, Milan Kundera went through his own existential crisis. In the two-decade period between 1995 and 2014, he published four novels written in French and wrote five very slim volumes in Czech on his ideas on literature, art, life, friendship, etc., which he later published in French in their enlarged and modified editions, and in English under the titles, *The Curtain* (2006) and *Encounter* (2010). His French novels, each printed in a bigger-than-usual size font and ranging from 115 to 195 pages only, weave together a number of plot lines, ideas, theories, themes, and characters, giving an impression of underdeveloped novels, almost a sketch to a grander composi-tion. Readers who are thoroughly familiar with his novels written in his native language deeply sense his digression from his familiar eloquence, form, and style. In two of his four French novels, his style seems to gain fluidity in passages referring to Czech characters, as if the author regained the comfort zone in creation of characters and situations. *Slowness* came as a disappointing surprise to both Kundera's readers and critics. For instance, Kundera attributes to Vincent ideas from *The Art of the Novel* about "the human condition that we did not choose and against which we should re-volt."[69] Explaining to Julie the human condition, Vincent sounds like Mr. Kundera, lacking the original voice that belongs to novelistic characters. To prevent the sense of the author's recycling of ideas and concepts, Kundera occasionally inserts his own persona next to Vincent. For instance, together with him he watches Vincent's impotence when his member fails to pene-trate Julie's vagina.[70] In addition to this parabatic trick, *Slowness* amasses further ideas from the author's previous novels, often thrown in the text as a brief idea, notion, or comment but recognized as seen before, dismissed by the reader, and viewed as a lack of the author's fresh creative ideas unless they would be approached in Deleuze's sense of repetition.

Kundera's trio-motif *sex–betrayal–denouncing* is conveniently aligned with the metaphysics of tragedy as discussed in Georg Lukács (1885–1971), a Hungarian literary critic, aesthetician, and philosopher. In his novels, Kun-dera espouses the dark side of life with the fictional practice of *sex–betrayal–denouncing,* culminating in death. "Life is an anarchy of light and dark," concedes Lukács in his work on the metaphysics of tragedy of the human life, stating that "nothing is ever completely fulfilled in life" because everything is in flux, ever-changing, merging into something else. Lukács sees this mixture to be "uncontrolled and impure"—everything being de-stroyed or smashed, and "nothing ever flowers into real life."[71] He recog-nizes "a gleam, illuminating a path of empirical life," assuring us that good things in human life bring enrichment but also confusion and that man is unable to bear "such heights of his own life and its possibilities." He calls the uncertainty of life a "monotonous, reassuring lullaby," and Søren Kierke-gaard (1813–1855), the Danish philosopher, reminds us that *the only certain-ty in the uncertainty* of human life is death. Death is nothingness, a complete and perpetual destruction of man's life, an annihilation of creation and a reduction to commonness.

Some ideas of Milan Kundera on pleasure and how to approach the aesthetics of life, sensorial experiences such as music, drama, and love could be traced to Kierkegaard's work in *Either/Or*. Its fictitious author under the pseudonym "A," who praises Mozart's opera *Don Giovanni*, is the eternal seducer and a great lover of women that Kundera ridicules in the age when Don Juan is dead. Kierkegaard's "A" is placed vis-à-vis "B," the author of a letter on moral ethics written to "A," who eventually fuses with the Judge as if the letter is written by the Judge rather than "B," judging the behavior of "A."[72] This idea of aesthetic versus ethical in *Either/Or* would offer a fascinating polemic with Kundera's Don Juan characters, and even their representation in Milos Forman's films, *Amadeus* and *Valmont*. While Kundera and Forman don't dwell on ethical issues of *don juanism*, their moral message comes out univocally, with death being an inevitable punishment. Their characters like Kierkegaard's "A," are in favor of aesthetic enjoyment, but ultimately they are at the mercy of destiny, which robs them of pleasures and results in death. One could summarize Kierkegaard's concept, which applies to Kundera's and Forman's philosophy, this way: man is a passive player for he is not asked if and when he wants to come to the world, and if and when he wants to depart. The only thing that he is sure of is that "no one returns from the dead."

Kundera relegates this idea to a state of non-being. He describes the double aspect of non-being and "the terrifyingly material being of a corpse."[73] In Part Six, "The Angels" of *The Book of Laughter and Forgetting*, he rejects portrayals in Thomas Mann's story of a young man dying from an illness, to whom death comes in an image of a beautiful naked woman when he reaches an unknown destination on a train. Nor is he attuned to Novalis's sweetness of death colored in blue and associated with the dahlia. Kundera portrays death closer to Kierkegaard's vision of non-return, the brutal insult to man of becoming a corpse, an "unbearable insult and terrible drudgery."[74] In "The Angels" he lines up Tamina's death with the death of his own father, whose dying was hard work, his body incapacitated with fever and bedridden in exhaustion. The images and descriptions of death that Kundera presents in his novels could be, in their existential aspect, viewed as a *betrayal of life* that every single man has to accept.

NOTES

1. T. Shackelford and D. Buss, "Betrayal in Mateships, Friendships, and Coalitions," *Personality and Social Psychology Bulletin*, no. 22 (1996): 1151–64.

2. Kundera, *Life Is Elsewhere*, 225.

3. Kundera, *Life Is Elsewhere*, 169.

4. Kundera, *Life Is Elsewhere*, 217.

5. Herbert Eagle, "Genre and Paradigm in Milan Kundera's *The Book of Laughter and Forgetting*," in *Critical Essays on Milan Kundera*, ed. Peter Petro (New York: G.K. Hall & Co., 1999), 157.

6. Kundera, *Life Is Elsewhere*, 3.

7. Kundera, *Life Is Elsewhere*, 253.

8. Kundera, *Life Is Elsewhere*, 255.

9. Kundera, *Life Is Elsewhere*, 256.

10. Kundera, *Life Is Elsewhere*, 256.

11. Kundera, *Life Is Elsewhere*, 259.

12. Kundera, *Life Is Elsewhere*, 259.

13. Kundera, *Life Is Elsewhere*, 259.

14. Adam Drda, "Český dav, Ohlédnutí za "kauzou Kundera," *Revolver Revue*, XXX, no. 100 (Fall 2015): 61.

15. Paul Ricoeur, "Narrative Identity," *Philosophy Today,* no. 35, (Spring 1991): 77.

16. Kundera, *Life Is Elsewhere*, 266.

17. Daniel Konrad, his review of *Life Is Elsewhere*: V Česku poprvé vychází *Život je jinde*. Román Milana Kundery líčí mladickou nerozvážnost básníků, *Hospodářské Noviny*, (June 22, 2016), www.ihned.cz

18. Milan Kundera, *The Curtain: An Essay in Seven Parts*, trans. from the French by Linda Asher (New York: HarperCollins), 78.

19. Kundera, *The Curtain: An Essay*, 100.

20. Kundera, *Life Is Elsewhere*, 270.

21. Kundera, *Life Is Elsewhere*, 270.

22. Adam Drda, Český dav, Ohlédnutí za "kauzou Kundera," *Revolver Revue*, XXX, no. 100 (Fall 2015): 62. Zdeněk Pešat cites Kundera: "Kundera mi dnes volal a říkal mi, že nyní už není nikdo ochotný chápat tehdejší dobu. Tehdy se děly události jako z detektivky a já na to nebyl zvyklý. Byl jsem přece obyčejný študent. A to přesto, že jsem byl pár měsíců ve fakultním výboru—to už ale bylo po těch všech prověrkách studentů."

23. Michael McCullough, *Beyond Revenge: The Evolution of the Forgiveness Instinct* (San Francisco: Jossey-Bass, 2008), 153.

24. Kundera, *Life Is Elsewhere*, 277.

25. Jason M. Wirth, *Commiserating with Devastated Things: Milan Kundera and the Entitlements of Thinking* (New York: A Fordham University Press, 2016), 30.

26. Milan Kundera, *The Festival of Insignificance*, trans. from the French Linda Asher (New York: Faber & Faber, 2015), 23.

27. Kundera, *The Festival of Insignificance*, 23.

28. Kundera, *The Festival of Insignificance*, 36.

29. Thomas J. Slater, *Milos Forman: A Bio-Bibliography* (New York: Greenwood Press, 1987), 66–73.

30. Kundera, *The Festival of Insignificance*, 36.

31. Kundera, *The Festival of Insignificance*, 43–44.

32. Kundera, *The Festival of Insignificance*, 43.

33. Kundera, *The Festival of Insignificance*, 44.

34. Calvin O. Schrag, "Heidegger on Repetition and Historical Understanding," *Philosophy East and West* 20, no. 3 (1970): 287.

35. Schrag, "Heidegger on Repetition," 289.

36. Schrag, "Heidegger on Repetition," 289–90.

37. Kundera, *Art of Novel*, 26.

38. Kundera, *Slowness*, 101–2.

39. Kundera, *Insignificance*, 102–3.

40. Erik H. Erikson, *Childhood and Society* (New York-London: W.W. Norton & Company, 1963), 42.

41. Ladislav Jehlička, "Lehká jsou jen hovna," *Literární stránka*, http://www.deml.cz/literatura/ladislav-jehlicka

42. A thorough analysis of Deleuze's philosophy is to be found in James Williams, *Gilles Deleuze's Difference and Repetition: A Critical Introduction and Guide* (Edinburgh: Edinburgh

University Press, 2013). It is beyond the scope and intentions of this work to delve into further details; the idea is to indicate that Milan Kundera's repetitions of motifs and situations in his novels are purposeful and often misleading to his readers.

43. Kundera, *Laughter and Forgetting*, 166. Also see more in Karen von Kunes, *Beyond the Imaginable: 240 Ways of Looking at Czech* (Praha: Práh Publishers, 1999), 238–39.
44. In Jason M. Wirth, *Commiserating with Devastated Things,* in the part Tamina and the Border, p. 3. Kundera's *Novel The Unbearable Lightness of Being* begins with a reflection on Nietzsche's idea of Eternal Return, and the novel explores the concept of lightness vs. weight. This theme in Kundera's novel has attracted numerous scholars; however, this book touches it marginally, only when it was judged as necessary.
45. Kundera, *Laughter and Forgetting*, 82–83.
46. Jehlička, "Lehká jsou jen hovna," http://www.deml.cz/literatura/ladislav-jehlicka
47. Kundera, *Insignificance*, 90–91.
48. Kundera, *Insignificance*, 91.
49. Karen von Kunes, "The Art of Buffoonery: The Czech Joke a la Commedia dell'arte Style in Kundera's French Novel *Slowness,*" in *Critical Essays on Milan Kundera*, ed. Peter Petro (New York: G.K. Hall & Co., 1999), 258.
50. Kundera, *Insignificance*, 22.
51. Kundera, *Insignificance*, 76.
52. This situation is partly described in Karen von Kunes's article "The National Paradox: Czech Literature and the Gentle Revolution," *World Literature Today* 65, no. 2 (Spring, 1991): 237–40.
53. Kundera, *Immortality*, 31.
54. Kundera, *Immortality*, 31–32.
55. Kundera, *Slowness*, 7.
56. In addition to Milos Forman's *Valmont* (1989), and Stephen Frears's *Dangerous Liaisons* (1988), there have been the following film interpretations: Roger Vadim's version *Les liaisons dangereuses* (1959), and a more recent one, *Cruel Intentions* (1999) by Roger Kumble with its additional sequels.
57. Kundera, *Slowness*, 2.
58. Kundera, *Slowness*, 3.
59. Kundera, *Slowness*, 91.
60. Kundera, *Slowness*, 91
61. Kundera, *Slowness*, 146.
62. More details in Karen von Kunes, "The Art of Bufoonery," in *Critical Essays on Milan Kundera*, 255–63.
63. Kundera, *Slowness*, 25.
64. Kundera, *Slowness*, 41.
65. Kundera, *Slowness*, 39.
66. von Kunes, "The Art of Bufoonery," 255–63.
67. Kundera, *Slowness*, 96.
68. Kundera, *Slowness*, 153.
69. Kundera, *Slowness*, 101.
70. Kundera, *Slowness*, 120.
71. Georg Lukács, "The Metaphysics of Tragedy: Excerpts," http://www.autodidact project.org/quote/lukacs_tragedy.html
72. Ideas taken from Søren Kierkegaard, *Either/Or* (New York: Penguin, 2004), and John W. Elrod, *Being and Existence in Kierkegaard's Pseudonymous Works* (Princeton: Princeton University Press, 1975).
73. Kundera, *Laughter and Forgetting*, 235.
74. Kundera, *Laughter and Forgetting*, 237.

Chapter Six

Kundera's Sexual Politics?

THE REALITY OF CZECH WOMEN

Milan Kundera has often been accused of misogyny by post-modernist feminists. In his critical work *Milan Kundera & Feminism, Dangerous Intersections*, John O'Brien reveals feminists' perspectives of both "complicity with and critique of the misrepresentation of women"[1] in Kundera's fiction. In what sense is Kundera *misrepresenting* women? O'Brien argues, "the problem with reading Kundera from a feminist perspective is the collective *weight of* mis-representation."[2] It is not just one female character typified as a sex object or one male character with a stereotypical view about women, but it is the repetition of these representations. Further, O'Brien quotes the well-known 1987 interview with Jordan Elgrably, in which Kundera defends his position by saying: "I don't know how to tell you why the women in my novels are the way they are. Neither would I venture to explain why it is that the act of lovemaking plays such a great role in my work. Here is the realm of the unconscious, of the irrational, a realm quite intimate to me."[3]

As intimate to Kundera, it might have been a similarly "intimate" and familiar sphere to men and women living in Czechoslovakia in Kundera's time. Like they, Kundera has been molded into a "product" of Communist society since 1948, a society whose social elements were collective but distinctly divided into two classes: intellectual and blue-collar. Under the Constitution, there was no gender division: both men and women were equal, had guaranteed work, and all were required to have a job outside of their homes. Women were expected to contribute to the labor force, provide goods and services for their families, take care of their children and the household, and at the same time to be feminine, attractive, and desirable for men. They were expected to get married young and produce offspring by the age of twenty-

143

five. Typically, they lived with their husbands and children in small flats, together with their in-laws or their own parents, since a housing shortage, especially in Prague, was eminent. True, they received generous incentives for maternity leave; however, fighting for women's rights was not on their agenda. Under Communism, the life of Czech women was hard and daunting enough that the idea of feminism had not gained much popularity. Noted sociologists researching feminism in the Czech Republic, such as Alena Králíková, Jiřina Šmejkalová, and Amanda Sloat, openly claim that even today feminism is perceived as a negative concept, "viewed as anti-family, anti-child, anti-men, and anti-feminine."[4] Unlike in the United States, where feminism has been associated with activism and the advancement of women's political and social rights, such as equal pay for equal work, in the Czech Republic feminism is perceived by the general population, both men and women, as a hatred for men.

ANTI-FEMINIST KUNDERA?

To a large extent, this view has been embodied in Kundera's authorship and his characters. In "The Angels" in *The Book of Laughter and Forgetting*, he scoffs at the famed French feminist and philosopher, Annie Leclerc, whose *Parole de femme*, a 1974 controversial bestseller in France, came out as a sort of manifesto of feminist consciousness of that period. In it, Leclerc attacks masculinity of the macho type as portrayed by André Malraux or Orson Welles, and opposes male sexual desire as a brief joy—fleeting moments of erection—to female *jouissance,* a continuous pleasure of the senses, the joy of a woman's bodily functions from touching to menstruating and defecating. For forty-six-year-old Mr. Kundera, stepping out of the collectively and hermetically enclosed society of former Czechoslovakia—where women loved their men for virility, sexual dominance, and aggressiveness—to a French society, where men have been sneered at for the same attributes, must have been a shocking experience.

Prior to *The Book of Laughter and Forgetting*, Kundera treated his female characters with distance, at times even with mockery, emphasizing their weakness and eager desire for men. It suffices to mention Helena in *The Joke*; Maman in *Life Is Elsewhere*; and Ruzena in *Farewell Waltz*. His female characters lacked the author's compassion. Kundera did not see women as a threat; his depiction of them and his authorial approach toward them must have felt genuine to him (as he says: "the realm of the unconscious . . . quite intimate to me."). Their way of thinking and acting was the way that he used to perceive women in real life, especially in the 1950s and 1960s. In spite of attributing theatrical, surreal, and metaphorical aspects to his fictional women, they appeared quite natural to him and, to a large extent, behaved the way their society expected them to behave. Contrary to Kundera's own claim in his interview with Elgrably for *Salmagundi*, his fictional female characters most likely were more conscious than unconscious creations, more rational than irrational, and more familiar than intimate.

To put it simply, the poetic and literary streaks of Kundera's twenty-year literary period in Czechoslovakia were loosely contained within the borders of socialist realism as prescribed by government authorities. Artistic directives and censorship required celebrating the working class and its admiration for fulfilling economic plans, and enjoyment of working on collective farms and in factories. An ordinary citizen was transformed into a celebrated hero, a young working class woman in particular. There was no emphasis on higher education: attending university was reserved for a few selected young people (typically children of the Party members) who showed intellectual promise and future commitment to the Party doctrine. The country lacked sufficient institutions at the college and university levels to absorb the large number of young people of the postwar generation; thus, basic education ended with the eighth grade (at the age of fourteen), which was extended in the 1960s to the ninth grade. The majority of young people went to trade schools (similar to community colleges) to acquire practical skills. The American concept of graduating from high school was absent: in order to continue study at the level of *střední škola* (an equivalent of high school), students were admitted selectively based on a series of exams and tests and the Party affiliation of their parents. This trend was reflected in the arts in general and in film in particular. This is one of the sociohistorical reasons why less sophisticated and less educated female characters commonly enter the stage of Kundera's novels and plays.

A SIMPLE HEROINE OF THE POSTWAR TIME

Jan Kadár's independent Slovak feature (1950), a comedy called *Katka* (Katya) became a milestone representative of this social tendency in postwar Communist Czechoslovakia. An inexperienced but ambitious young heroine wants to escape the monotony of a Slovak village, and despite her parents' opposition, she moves to a city. She finds a job in a factory producing socks and stockings.[5] This stereotyped heroine appears in the films of Forman's Czech creative period; notably in his artistically celebrated, *Loves of a Blond* (1965), a film of the New Wave, which brought Forman international fame. While Kadar's Katka acted as a free-willed woman, she soon became caught up in the competitive spirit of collective factory ambitions. Forman's Andula seeks an escape from her small factory town heavily populated by women by searching for a man who would whisk her away from the daily drudgery and offer her a pleasant life. These female characters of the 1950s and early

1960s period are quite traditional and real, reflecting the structure of Communist society: lower, middle, and upper classes blending into two clearly distinctive groups, the intellectual and working classes, closely supervised by Communist Party representatives. They appear in Kundera's Lucie, in Krystyna, a butcher's wife, in *The Book of Laughter and Forgetting*, and in other, usually minor, female characters.

By his careful choice of details, Forman emphasizes the social contrasts between the two classes; in this respect, he imprints a more poignant statement than Kundera. For instance, the pianist Míla has no difficulty luring Andula to the bedroom by telling her naïvely silly lies, such as that he could be seriously harmed and die after she kicks him in the groin. At that instant, Forman cleverly shifts the power structure from Míla onto Andula, and Míla easily wins her trust. After their intercourse, he compares her voluptuous figure to Picasso's guitar but she, not knowing Picasso, asks *what* it is. In his novels completed in Czechoslovakia, Kundera's female characters might be more perceptive and cunning than Forman's heroines; however, both prototypes are fitting, representing the aesthetic influence of that period. Women are less educated than men, and even if equally educated, they are often ridiculously naïve or cunningly vicious. The main difference between their portrayal by Forman and Kundera is in the directorial and authorial attitudes. Forman shows compassion for his Andula, and while her situation results in her vulnerability, ignorance, and social isolation, he is able to build sympathy for his heroine in the eyes of the viewers. The audience is moved from laughter to tears, accompanied by the power of Franz Schubert's sorrowful melody of *Ave Maria*. Unlike Forman, Kundera maintains the readers' distance from his female characters, provoking detached laughter, pity, and occasionally even disgust.

INTELLIGENT VERSUS HIGHLY EDUCATED

Concerning the 1987 interview, it is unclear whether Elgrably had posed the wrong questions to Kundera, or whether Kundera provided the wrong answers. Elgrably sees Sabina in *The Unbearable Lightness of Being* as intelligent but not intellectual. Kundera defended Sabina by clarifying that whether or not intellectual, she thinks *the most lucid, the coldest and most cruel* way. He argues that several fictional female characters, in fact, are intellectual, such as Olga in *Farewell Waltz*, or the female doctor in *Laughable Loves*.[6] There are two representations of female doctors, one unnamed with clear and sharp logical thinking, and the other, Františka. Older Františka has a playful sexual encounter with a young editor (who came to the spa town to interview Dr. Havel), and whom she jokingly confuses with her son of the same age.

Maternal and erotic feelings blend into one emotion, which leaves the young editor frustrated.

Attaching a label of education to female characters would not change their way of thinking and acting because Kundera mostly explores feelings *per se* rather than feelings as a result of intellectual background. His "heroines" are smart and self-confident (Sabina, Olga), weak and dependent (Tereza, Tamina, Kamila), sophisticated and astute (the filmmaker, and the student in *Life Is Elsewhere;* Eva in *The Book of Laughter and Forgetting*), or shrewd and envious (Ruzena, Helena). They represent human characteristics, positive and negative, as people in any society would have. In his defense, Kundera does not entirely disagree with Elgrably's assessment of how readers might see his female characters. Rather he ponders his portrayal of them. Lucie in *The Joke*, he admits openly, was not "taken from real life; in Kundera's revelation, she represents a type of woman that he has not encountered in his life." He asserts: "Never, in reality, have I known a truly simple woman."[7] This part of the interview is crucial for it reveals, knowingly or unknowingly to Kundera, his psyche and the sociopolitical background that he belonged to in Czechoslovakia. Intellectually and politically, he identifies himself with the elite societal stratum. In the interview, he continues saying that he "had known a number of women who were mediocre, women like Helena in *The Joke*."[8] One could only speculate to what extent his fictional women are based on the real women. He indirectly implies that his fictional female characters are mediocre because "he had known a number of them," and referring to Helena, he adds a parenthetical comment in the printed interview: "her I knew by heart."[9] Inevitably, the image of Iva Militká comes to one's mind.[10]

KUNDERA'S FIRST WIFE'S BACKGROUND

It is not publicly known whether any female character is based on his first wife, Olga. In his late twenties, Kundera was married; a well-known fact among his friends, but hidden for years from the public. Czech *Wikipedie* summarizes this information in one sentence: "His first wife was Olga Haas, the daughter of music composer Pavel Haas."[11] All this leads to Olga Haasová-Smrčková, an actress and opera singer at the National Theater in Brno, born in 1937 to a Russian mother, Sofia Nikolaevna Feldmann. Mrs. Feldmann divorced the famed linguist Roman Jakobson in 1935, just four months before marrying Olga's father, Pavel Haas. Mr. Haas was a talented student of Leoš Janáček; but in 1941 was taken to Terezín, and three years later perished in the Auschwitz concentration camp. His father—Olga's grandfather—Zikmund Haas, perished the same year in Terezín (1944); however, his brother, Hugo Haas succeeded in escaping with his wife Bibi to Paris before Hitler reached Prague.

It is not publicly known how close Milan Kundera was to his first wife's family; one can find occasional echoes of her relatives in his novels. For instance, on the second page of *The Unbearable Lightness of Being,* Kundera crudely mentions that while leafing through a book on Hitler, he was touched by some of his portraits because they evoke in him a sensation of his own lost childhood. As insensitive as some readers may find this reference, the author immediately neutralizes this statement by presenting a binary opposition: asserting that *several of his family relatives* perished in Hitler's concentration camps. He evaluates the weight of their death against the weight of his own memories of a past that would never return.

If Kundera portrays female doctors, it is possibly under the influence of the medical environment he was acquainted with through his mother-in-law, who studied medicine in Prague and became a doctor-practitioner. In 1940, she divorced Olga's father, most likely in anticipation of the Nazi's raids against the Jewish population. Olga's family was well known and respected in Brno and Prague. Her uncle, Hugo Haas, was a famous film director and actor, who made his name not only in Czech film but also in Hollywood. Her aunt Marie Bibikoff Haasová, born in Bern, was a daughter of the last Czarist Ambassador, Baron Michail Bibikoff. Her Czech mother had connections with Jan Masaryk, the son of the first Czechoslovak President, and with other prominent politicians of the time. Olga's aunt was nicknamed Bibi by her husband. It is an unusual sounding name in Czech for its deviation from the morphological system. In *The Book of Laughter and Forgetting*, Kundera named one of his characters Bibi: a young, ignorant, self-centered woman with a one-year-old child in a small Western European town. Kundera's Bibi is an antipode of the fictional Tamina, and especially of the real Bibi—Olga's sophisticated, generous and highly educated aunt of aristocratic origin. Through the fictional character Bibi, Kundera criticizes people's yearning to write autobiographies and books for an impersonal audience because no friends and family are willing to listen to them. Tamina is a good listener, but Bibi is an obnoxious, quite simplistic young woman, who searches for a way out of her family, in which she feels trapped, by aspiring to be a writer. Yet she has no idea how to write creatively or what to write about. While Kundera might not have any such negative associations with a relative of his former wife, it is quite striking that he would choose such an uncommon name for a character that he deprecates. Naturally, he might have done it unconsciously, or was unaware that the information about his first wife's aunt would ever come to light in public. He wrote this novel long before the widespread online access to information that allowed these dots to be connected.

A SIMPLE HERO IN HRABAL, KUNDERA, HAVEL

Kundera is not the only Czech writer whose work has continued to incorporate the aesthetics of socialist realism by depicting ordinary, simple women of a lower socioeconomic background, a trend that bore elements of surrealism and avant-garde art. In particular, this phenomenon has been exemplified by the works of Bohumil Hrabal. Hrabal earned a law degree but also worked in a variety of nontraditional jobs. His characters—both men and women—are out of the norm, on the outskirts of society, living at the bottom of the societal ladder; they are drunkards, thieves, prostitutes, gypsies, waiters, and manual workers. Concurrent with his linguistic neologism *pábitel* (*palaverer* in English), Hrabal created an exuberant non-heroic hero, an uncouth antihero without a specific aim in life—a dreamer who loves the discovery of the poetic in the mundaneness of everyday life. Among the contemporary writers, Hrabal has been considered the best Czech writer by both Czech readers and critics despite his novels occasionally causing uproar for being too subversive and erotically explicit. Descriptions detailing the sexual, such as the following goings-on in whorehouses, are not infrequent in his novels: "Jaruška quietly slipped off my trousers, pulled down my underpants, and kissed the inside of my thighs, and suddenly I was so distracted by the thought of what went on in Paradise's that I began to tremble and I curled up into a ball and I said, Jaruška, what are you doing?"[12]

Even Kundera admires Hrabal's writing easiness, grotesque style of collages, whimsical anecdotes, simplicity of vernacular, which by its definition implies complexity. However, there is a significant difference between Kundera's elegant and reasoning style and Hrabal's colloquial approach, which includes Moravian dialect and rich description of characters, images, and adventures. Unlike Hrabal, Kundera has shown little affection for his characters, both men and particularly for women: he approaches them with detachment and often with absurdity, while Hrabal approached them with love and admiration despite their baseness and absurdity.

Along with his predecessor Jaroslav Hašek, Václav Havel completes the line of writers who have depicted an ordinary hero. Havel's is the recurring character "Vaněk" from his earlier plays (*The Garden Party*)—often a dissident intellectual, who like Havel loves a stein of beer in the pub and a chat with ordinary folks; a dissident working in a brewery (in *Vernisáž*), or two Sidneys from a local paper mill (in *Largo Desolato*). Like Havel himself, this "hero" was demoted from his former position and forced to earn his living among blue-collar people. Sarcasm and absurdity in the life of this everyman, the so-called *Vaněk*, was an indirect and relatively inoffensive way of laughing at the inefficiency of Czech government.

In *Critical Essays on Vaclav Havel*, Robert Skloot quotes Kundera, who asserted that Czech writers "were suffocating under art conceived as educational, moral or political,"[13] and for that reason, once introduced into Czech theater in the 1960s, Ionesco produced a strong, liberating force.[14] The so-called *Theatre of the Absurd* became the leading artistic trend of this period and had an omnipresent influence on the whole Czech cultural scene. Havel sees it as "the most significant theatrical phenomenon of the 20th century, for it depicts a modern society in state of crisis."[15] This effect, embodied in works of Czech artists, might explain Kundera's detachment from and laughing at (and occasional derision of) his characters. Unfortunately, Kundera has chosen a woman more often than a man to ridicule, and hence has attracted the displeasure of Western critics and feminists.

FORMAN'S AND KUNDERA'S LAUGHING AT COMMON PEOPLE?

Milos Forman has been less criticized than Milan Kundera for portraying weak, uneducated, and dependent women, partly because the general, non-Czech audience, may not be familiar with his very first films, particularly *Konkurs (Audition),* a semi-documentary of the Semafor Theater fake audition (1963). In his memoir, *Turnaround,* Forman states his reason for filming the mock audition. It was the "power of microphone" that made these "homely young women to vamp shamelessly, tone-deaf singers to wail away at the top of their voices, shy neurotics to put themselves through the torture of public scrutiny." He saw in them "something so skewed and self-loving that you wanted to look away."[16] Czech film critics, especially Vratislav Effenberger, picked up the elements of cruelty, viciousness, and abrasiveness in his films, but they did not focus on women alone. These critics evaluated his pictures within the frame of the whole society, a progression of which Forman has shown in *Loves of a Blonde* and *Fireman's Ball. Loves of a Blond* was a highly successful film in Czechoslovakia and at foreign film festivals. At home, it earned him the State Prize of Klement Gottwald (named for the first Communist president), and in Hollywood the 1966 Oscar nomination for Best Foreign Language Film. It also brought Carlo Ponti, the Italian producer and Sophia Loren's husband, into Forman's creative life. Ponti financed Forman's *Fireman's Ball,* but found the film shocking in its mockery of the common man, and indeed of Czech society as a whole, including its totalitarian bureaucracy. The picture of ordinary Czechs under the microscopic scrutiny of Forman's absurdist lens displeased and repelled not only Ponti but many Western, Russian, and Czech film critics. Ponti broke the contract and Forman had to refund him for the expenses spent on the film.

Yet, as the *de facto* representative of the New Wave in Czech cinema, Forman struck an emotional cord with his classic *Loves of a Blonde.* He used a balance of actors and non-actors to capture spontaneity of picture since he believed that "every moment in a film, every word and every reaction should carry a psychological truth."[17] The plot of *Loves of a Blonde* carries a triple "psychological truth." The kernel of the film screenplay was lifted straight from real life, and on the flipside, the life story of one of the non-actresses became the story taken straight out of the film. The girl Andula—dependent, confused, poorly educated, and lonely—is a mirror image of Ruzena, Tamina, the redhead, and other of Kundera's female protagonists. In reference to Kundera's female characters, Ladislav Jehlička named this simple woman "Anča," using a domestic version of Andula, representing the archetypical village girl: earnest, of good heart and intentions, but defenseless and naïve, her naivety bordering on plain ignorance. Kundera endows his "Anča" with intriguing aspirations, such as Tamina's desire to recover her lost letters, Ruzena's desire to get pregnant by a famous trumpeter, or the redhead pursuing a young and up-and-coming Communist poet.

In contrast, Forman's "Anča" is an unpretentious, real-life Andula. In his screenplay, written with his colleagues, Ivan Passer and Jaroslav Papoušek, he retells a story of a village girl that he met in person and accompanied through Prague in search of her boyfriend's house. The girl's boyfriend gave her a nonexistent address, and Forman took the girl to the train station so she could return home. In the film, she finds the boyfriend's home but he refuses to recognize her. His parents, especially his mother, are judgmental, disapproving of her uninvited appearance in their home, and criticize her actions with cruel words behind her back. As if this were not enough, real life played another cruel joke on "Anča," one of the prettiest factory girls in the non-actress role in *Loves of a Blonde* who fell in love with a technician on the filming set. Just like in the movie, the technician, working on Forman's set, promised to bring her to Prague once he had prepared their "nest." After long weeks of waiting, she became a laughingstock of other non-actress factory girls. The envious girls called her sarcastically "a movie star, a Hollywood actress," until she could bear it no longer. Just like Andula in the film, she decides to leave for Prague to join her boyfriend. Alas, there she finds out that her technician is married with a child. He never intended to have her in his life, except for the brief love affair during the film shooting. Unlike in the movie, where Andula returns to her factory town and invents lies about what happened in Prague, the real girl was too ashamed to return home and admit she had been taken advantage of. Due to her lack of education and practical skills, she ended up working as a prostitute in a Prague hotel, alternating between her illegal activity and jail time.[18]

Of course, French and Western feminists might suggest a number of viable solutions for the Czech "Anča" (both real and fictional), but Kundera and Forman know well that the totalitarian regime deprived many of them of such opportunities. Thus, accusing Kundera (Forman, Hrabal, or any other Czech writer) of being a misogynist or attaching a negative label to his name for choosing a young but ordinary and mediocre woman (rather than intellectual) is misleading. It simply might be the perception of Western critics who evaluate Kundera's fictional women from the subjective angle, placing them under the conditions of their free societies with abundance of opportunities. Portraying intellectual women next to intellectual men in the Czech society of the 1960s would certainly ring false, an art detached from the reality of the time, as well as from the cultural directives dictated by Communist censorship.

THE AUTHOR'S DISCOVERY

In reference to his interview with Elgrably, Kundera further explains that what drew him to female characters like Lucie was his desire to discover precisely the kind of woman he had never known. And what did he discover? He clarifies: "Lucie is so simple that I did not understand her."[19] Writers Hašek, Hrabal, Havel (whose first wife Olga was a down-to-earth working class woman), and even Kafka (who was known for visiting Prague brothels, and whose female characters served Josef K. as a means to an end in *The Trial*) mingled with ordinary Czech men and Czech women. But unlike them, Kundera emphasizes his intellectual and elitist superiority and his lack of identification with—or understanding of—the working class of his time. As a profoundly minded Communist until his exclusion from the Party in the early 1970s, he lived in the "Party's Ivory Tower" with all the perks and benefits it offered, yet with a clear detachment from the real-life masses of ordinary blue-collar Czechs. At the same time, however, he needed to acknowledge them because the Party was promoting the working class as the true backbone of Communist society. For a similar reason, he attempted to rewrite his autobiography once living in France and gaining fame, and in particular when being approached by an inquisitive press.

As previously quoted in his 1984 interview with the British writer Ian McEwan, Kundera said: "We constantly re-write our own biographies and continually give matters new meanings. To re-write history in this sense— indeed, in an Orwellian sense—is not at all inhuman. On the contrary, it is very human."[20] Having nurtured this perspective since his sojourn in France, Kundera "humanizes" his life to fit the demands of the Western media. For instance, in his 1980 interview with Philip Roth, he said that after being expelled from the university, he lived among the workers and played the trumpet in a jazz band in small-town cabarets.[21] Additionally, in an interview in *The Village Voice,* Kundera told Philip Roth that intimate life should be understood as "one's personal secret, as something that is valuable, inviolable, the basis of one's originality."

Milan Jungmann, the leading Czech literary critic, called Kundera's distortions of reality *kitsch*: "Those who knew Milan Kundera in the 1950s and

1960s could hardly recognize him. But even if these selected *insignificant* facts were truthful, Kundera's self-portrait has been changed to the extent that his real personality has vanished."[22] However, Robert Solomon, a proponent of the moral sentiments theory propounded by Hume and Shaftesbury, has defended the sentiments that *kitsch* evokes. He typifies Kundera's investigation to a moral aversion to propaganda.[23] Kundera's evasion of interviews and tendency to seclude himself in a bubble of privacy is evident from some of his statements in previously published interviews. Occasionally he contradicts himself, and the easiest way to get out of the confusion is to ignore everyone who could cause harm to his reputation. For instance, he told Elgrably that once you've written a novel, everyone in France assumes that it is a biography. Specifically, he mentions his wife, Věra, who has been approached with a question, "You were a photographer?" Obviously, this is a reference to Tereza in *The Unbearable Lightness of Being*, and while Kundera left the question hanging in the air, it would not damage his reputation to disclose that his wife, Věra, was a TV reporter in Prague in the 1960s. It is understandable that he doesn't want the public associating his fictional character with his wife; at the same time, ignoring the press and cloaking himself in the mantle of pretentions and distortions of reality does not help his credibility. Milos Forman, Václav Havel, Arnošt Lustig, and many other writers revealed details of their private lives with sincerity, and for that reason, readers are able to separate the fictional from the authentic, all the while showing more respect for their honesty than they do for Kundera's dissembling. Readers can access their creative aspect without having to ponder a puzzle of often blurred and contradicting information.

KUNDERA'S LOVE FOR HIS CZECH WOMEN

As we know now, Milan Kundera has found himself in a very precarious position as a person and writer of moral bearing due to the "Kauza Kundera." As suggested, he might have felt all those years that knowing Dlask and Militká was his bad omen. A pact of silence created between him and Dlask is reminiscent of a pact created between Jaromil and his friend, the janitor's son, after Jaromil denounced the redhead and her brother in *Life Is Elsewhere*. Jaromil was envious of his friend's position as a man in power, a secret service policeman, who in addition was married, had a child, and kept secrets away from his wife. "Listen, my friend, there are some things I can't even tell my wife about."[24] Dlask and Militká married shortly after Dvořáček's arrest and had a child as well. Dlask kept the secret of telling Kundera about Dvořáček away from his wife for forty years. Kundera's denial in 2008 of ever having known Militká despite the evidence from his 1953 book dedication to her and her husband indicates that he intended to erase her existence from his life in "an Orwellian sense," considering it "very human."

It is plausible that a number of descriptions of his female characters might have initially departed from his perception of Militká; no doubt, he has imposed some negativity upon his female protagonists. Once he had left Czechoslovakia, his authorial treatment of Czech female characters became more sympathetic. The barbed wire dividing France and his home country gave him a sense of security and a desire to erase his past, to start anew. To some degree, his outlook on women has changed, and the isolation from his homeland allowed him to invent female protagonists to his liking. He started relying on historical figures (Bettina in *Immortality*, linking her to his fictional Laura), surreal situations in which women exhibit unusual behavior (Tamina in *The Book of Laughter and Forgetting*, Chantal in *Identity*), professionally unfulfilled European women (Agnes and Laura in *Immortality*), or independent and free-spirited women (Sabina in *The Unbearable Lightness of Being*; Alain's mother in *The Festival of Insignificance*).

Through Sabina, Kundera points out cultural differences. Sabina could hardly comprehend Franz's respect for Marie-Claude and herself, solely by dint of being women. In her *Czech outlook*, Sabina had no reason to take pride or shame in being a woman; it was her natural state of being. This reference in "A Short Dictionary of Misunderstood Words," emphasizes cultural differences on life, relationships, music, history, and politics (May Day parades, the Soviet invasion of Czechoslovakia), underlined by betrayal. For the first time, readers feel the narrator's strong emotional attachment to Sabina, and even his love for Tereza. Beginning with Tamina, Kundera elevates Czech female characters spiritually above their male and female counterparts of Western Europe (French, Swiss, etc.).

Dismissing Kundera as a mere misogynist would be a simplistic conclusion. Tamina is depicted with affection and more strength of character than Hugo, who feels threatened by her beauty and the pride with which she bears her life experiences. He betrays her by not going to Prague to retrieve her letters as he promised because she is emotionally unresponsive to his sexual advances. Her pride that she carries like an aureole humiliates him. In almost every interaction with Franz, Sabina exhibits superiority over him. Despite his high level of education, societal position of a university professor, and his strong muscles, he reminds her of a baby; suggestively, their physical relationship lasted nine months. Seeing him either as a "gigantic puppy or an infant sucking milk from her breasts" during their intercourse, Sabina finds this image repulsive and decides to leave him for good. And even Tereza carries her femininity proudly. She tells a Swiss woman-photographer that she prefers being a housewife rather than photographing cactuses: "My husband is my life, not cactuses."[25] It is not education that makes Kundera's heroines strong; it is their self-possession, self-awareness, their generosity of spirit, and their perceptiveness of the world that surrounds them. They make their own decisions about what is fulfilling to them whether it is their profession, their hobby, or devotion to their man. Inevitably, a question arises: Is French/Swiss Agnes in *Immortality* any stronger or superior to Sabina because she is better educated—excelled in mathematics but has chosen the wrong profession of being a housewife and mother?

WHERE DO FEMALE CHARACTERS STAND?

In his monograph, John O'Brien gives an excellent detailed overview of Kundera's female characters. His approach is multifaceted, based on Kundera's comments published in *The Review of Contemporary Fiction* in 1989: "Because of Kundera's refusal to endorse any single approach to his work, interpretation is even more strongly dependent on the critic's particular perspective."[26] However, O'Brien challenges Kundera's claim that "all great novels express both a feminine and a masculine vision of the world,"[27] because he sees Kundera's representation of women from a male-focused perspective only. The male-focused perspective dominated Kundera's earlier novels, all written while he still lived in Prague. His polyphonic novel, *The Joke,* has three male narrators and one female. Helena, a female member of the Party, along with Pavel, her husband, is the most educated character in the novel, holding the highest positions (she is a journalist, and he is a professor), but she is also the most confused. In need of love, affection, and social status, she is deeply dependent on being loved by a man and the Party. Her sincere voice is full of self-justifying thoughts but also of revulsion and hate toward those who in her view have harmed her. She is one of the most vivid and yet most repulsive characters among Kundera's fictional women: a woman-opportunist who would act the same way under any political system.

Women in *The Joke* are a function of the political system that had subjected them to its ideology. Marketa blindly believes in the Party doctrine, yet life-wise is quite ignorant. Helena entrusts her private and public life into the care of the Party, yet discovers betrayal and disappointment. Vlasta, Jaroslav's wife, reflecting the values of a farming village community, is an adjuster to the system with its "modernity." Miss Broz is phlegmatic to past crime revelations of the Party and selfishly adores herself, mindlessly taking advantage of the political restructuring. She and her peers admire Pavel, a political chameleon, who under the *détente* switched his expertise from Marxism-Leninism to philosophy. The other spectrum of women in *The Joke* reflects the larger stratum of Communist society: the working class. Lucie is poorly educated and has no knowledge of or interest in politics. Tied to nature, she is above politics. Her life is affected by the breaking of her family (and not necessarily by the regime) and she is pushed toward the edge of society. Prostitutes that Ludvik and his detained-in-mines companions once encountered and received sexual favor from belong to the lowest social stratum. As bleakly as Kundera depicts women in *The Joke*, his view is based on a post-war society that has undergone dramatic socioeconomic and political changes; a society that was reduced to two classes, both largely dominated by men, in which women accepted their roles as dictated by the regime led by men. On the surface, women were celebrated (March 8, the International Day of Women), but underneath they were subjugated to men and the system at large. There were hardly any situations in which women lived on their own and could act entirely independently. Women were either living with their parents, in dorms, with their husbands, or, in the case of older women, with their children and/or grandchildren. The system did not provide the luxury or refuge for women to own or rent an apartment on their own and to exercise their free will.

O'Brien emphasizes binary oppositions: Madonna/Whore; Beauty/Ugliness; Male Friendship/Female Antagonism; Strength/Weakness; Free Will/Fate. He addresses the issue of Kundera's rejection of criticisms that he is bound to a male-focused stereotype, insisting rather that he is merely influenced by his sub-consciousness. O'Brien quotes a feminist, Vivian Gornick, who argues that Kundera refuses to fulfill "the novelist's obligation to make people out of his characters."[28] She sees his characters as lacking sufficient depth to become true portraits of the human condition, remaining rather "cartoon figures." Her statement in *The Village Voice* 1982 article, "Everything to Regret, Everything to Suspect," does not necessarily fit *The Joke* but is applicable to some of Kundera's fiction and particularly to the four French novels written in the past two decades. O'Brien seems to be concerned with a small number of critical studies on Kundera's representation and *mis*representation of women. He partly quotes premises by Peter Hruby and Robert Porter, but criticizes both on grounds of their stereotypical approaches that are reduced to yet additional stereotypical dimensions. Hruby links Kundera's male characters' actions to the author's personal experiences (with an occasional anecdotal analysis of non-scholarly approach), while Porter's focus on the erotic, tragic, and absurd leads to the stereotypical view, too.[29]

Denuding Kundera's female characters of their nudity by stripping them of the clothes of their surroundings of the political, the historical, and the philosophical would lead to what Jehlička suggested: Kundera's readers might not be aware that the idea of woman's place in "Kirche, Küche, Bett" (Church, Kitchen, Bed), as presented in unworthy fiction for a certain type of readership (mostly female), was attacked long before Kundera, but unfortunately in Kundera's works only *bed* remains. A woman's function is only to spread her legs ("Žena je tu jen k tomu, aby roztahovala nohy"). Jehlička also agrees with an opinion of a female writer (whose name is not mentioned) who warned him: Each subsequent Kundera novel is worse than the previous one.[30] This quite schematic and simplistic opinion bears a certain amount of truth, especially beginning with Kundera's "French creative period," after he had abandoned the Czech language, politics, and characters.

John O'Brien points out the stereotypical representations of women to be "agonizingly recognizable."[31] One could concur that the problem lies in the fact that *most of his fiction* is "agonizingly recognizable" due to the repetitions *without progression*. Kundera repeats himself in a variety of approaches, be they philosophical (either Nietzsche or Heidegger), linguistic (either *lítost* or *nostalgia*), political (either Gottwald or Stalin), historic (either Russia or Bohemia), poetic (either real famous poets or questionable fictional poets), erotic (either breasts and vagina, or anus), bodily secretions (either feces or urine), or structural (either seven parts or fifty-plus short chapters), etc. The narrator in "The Hitchhiking Game," asks what kind of role the girl was playing, and he answers: "It was a role out of trashy literature."[32] At times, this statement could be taken as a metaphor for Kundera's depicting women and sex.

Writing *Laughable Loves* at the time of history when Czech literature was in crisis, Kundera replaced the emphasis on factory workers and their fulfilling economic norms with problematic interactions of intimate nature between men and women, focusing on women's problems as seen and evaluated from a man's perspective. His stories, written between 1963 and 1969, later collected under the title *Laughable Loves,* worked like a miracle. Czechs read them for their ease, novelty, fun, and daring approach. They could have been a reminder of the novels in a Red Library series "Červená knihovna," which were based on the dichotomy (poor girl/rich man, docile girl/wicked mother-in-law, Madonna/ Whore, etc.) and written with a purpose of relaxation and enjoyment. However, Kundera's stories were written with a style, in beautiful literary Czech, and contained a slight criticism of the system albeit enrobed in sarcasm. In the 1960s, Czech standard language still lacked comfortable words for sex, having either medical terms or a heap of vulgarisms, used mainly by men among themselves. Women used a variety of euphemisms of plain verbs, such as *dělat* (to do), *rozdat si* (give to another), and *spát s* (sleep with), intermingling them with the verb *milovat se* (to love) where the particle *se* implies mutuality; thus, *milovat se* means both "to love one another" and/or "to make love (to one another)." Kundera managed to render the erotic descriptions in standard, attractive, and familial language and approach, though occasionally bordering on kitsch. And contextually interwoven with philosophical and thoughtful ideas, his descriptions were accepted as a norm. Occasionally, however, they felt as *clichés,* as if devoid of purely logical sense, such as his frequent mirroring of reversed ideas: "He felt responsible for his destiny, but his destiny did not feel responsible for him."[33] In addition, as a representative of the Party, he was showing the literary community the way literature should go, what problems Czech society should deal with, how men and women should or should not interact, and what the possible implications of such interactions were. He was the first one to come with this original approach, and his success was instantly guaranteed.

For instance, Mirek in "Lost Letters" in *The Book of Laughter and Forgetting* remembers intercourse with his ugly partner, Zdena, the following way: "He moved on her with feigned fierceness, emitting a lengthy growl like a dog struggling with his master's slipper, at the same time observing (with mild astonishment) the very calm, silent, and nearly impassive woman stretched out under him."[34] Similarly, Hugo gets aroused by the "fleeting sight of Tamina's rump (of the open eye of that mature and beautiful rump, of the eye that stared at him pitilessly),"[35] and the eye of her rump leads him to orgasm: "pleasure ran through him like lightning."[36] To make his erotic descriptions acceptable to censorship, Kundera used items of everyday life, such as comparisons, metaphors and similes, which reduced its erotically charged text to causal daily events.

SEXUAL EXPLORATION

Milan Kundera was thrilled by his success, and Czech readers were thrilled by his openness about the problems that existed between the two sexes throughout human history, and that no one had dared to discuss them in a literary context as evocatively as he. Under such circumstances, it wasn't a priority to be concerned about how male-female relationships were depicted and from whose perspective. Kundera learned that mild eroticism, wrapped in a beauty of thoughtful ideas and colorful metaphors worked splendidly. He found his vocation.

He has remained faithful to his approach in depicting women from the male angle; after all, Czech women liked to hear how they were seen, portrayed, discussed, and approached by their men; all done in decent rather than lewd and vulgar language and mannerism. Some recognized themselves in passive roles, and it gave them a topic for discussion or provided them with the realization of their lot and how to better handle men. In the 1970s, the enemies of Kundera's fictional women were Western critics, and particularly feminists, but mostly their criticism did not reach him and his Czech readers because it could not penetrate the iron curtain of Communist Czechoslovakia. In his country, Kundera was celebrated and appreciated for what he wrote. Binary oppositions based on tensions between men and women were seen as a natural state of *private affairs*. The woman's role being depicted traditionally by a male narrator did not provide grounds for accusations of misogyny.

It is not the lack of education but rather lack of self-confidence and reliability, decisions, or IQ that Kundera emphasizes in women. However, in some relationships, his male characters are dependent on women, be it for their status (Dr. Havel for the beauty of his wife), friendship (Tomas on Sabina), inner strength (Franz on Sabina), income (Jean-Marc on Chantal in *Identity*), vitality (Gustaf on Irena's mother in *Ignorance*), or inner peace (Josef on his Danish wife in *Ignorance*). Thus, it would be erroneous to claim that women are depicted only as weak and sex objects. In certain situations, men become sexual "objects" of women. In a sense, one might say that Kundera's fictional men appreciate women for their own goals, purposes, and benefits. They typically value female beauty for the effect it has on them rather than for the beauty itself. In this respect, Steven Pinker offers an interesting analogy: "Could it be that men learn to want sexual variety? Perhaps it is a means to an end, the end being status in our society. The Don Juan is revered as a dashing stud; the pretty woman on his arm is a trophy. Certainly anything that is desirable and rare can become a status symbol. But that does not mean that all desirable things are pursued because they are status symbols. I suspect that if men were given the hypothetical choice between clandestine sex with many attractive women and a reputation for sex with many attractive women, but without the sex, they would go for the sex. Not only because sex is incentive enough, but because a reputation for having sex is a disincentive. Don Juans do not inspire admiration, especially in women, though they may inspire envy in men, a different and not always welcome reaction."[37]

Kundera's references to masturbation are occasional. The reader finds them in the author's alter ego Jaromil in *Life Is Elsewhere*, or in his sarcastic naming *Masturbov* for Andrei Zdanov (Stalin's designated successor, who ironically died before him) in *The Book of Laughter and Forgetting*. In several instances this novel bears references to orgies; the story "Mama," explores the erotic relationship of a triangle, husband Karel and his wife Marketa and their mutual lover Eva. In "The Border" Pascal is lured by naked Barbara and two naked women to get aroused but is thrown out for his inability to get an erection within one minute. Another example is in *Identity* where Chantal finds herself in a blurred orgiastic situation. Traces of homosexuality are hardly seen in Kundera's fiction; however, a suggestion to lesbian attraction is noted between Sabina and Tereza. The lack of homosexuality may be possibly explained by the taboo that it carried in Czech society in Kundera's time.

Passages of humiliation and brief references to fetishism—male characters' obsession with certain parts of women's body—could be detectable in the novels as well. It usually points to women, if only for the reason that women are mostly depicted through men's eyes. The relationships among women are often marked by resentment, jealousy, envy, spite, hostility, and ignorance rather than by mutual understanding, collective appreciation, or sympathy. O'Brien points out sympathy among Kundera's male-male characters; however, it cannot be taken for a general rule. Pavel's betrayal of

Ludvik in *The Joke;* F.'s betrayal of Jean-Marc in *Identity;* or some degree of animosity among the four friends in *The Festival of Insignificance* are just a few examples, proving that this premise could not be fully validated.

Czech informal culture thrives on referring to people by the names of domestic animals and pets, often to women or to parts of their bodies. Most of these names bear negative connotations but not all. Grammatically, this type of noun belongs to the feminine gender, but if the noun's gender is neuter, they refer to both men and women. If the noun's gender is masculine, it typically denotes men, occasionally also women, such as *vůl* (ox). For instance, calling a teenage girl *žába* (frog) is rather a common, and in certain situations, endearing metaphor, while *koza* (goat), *husa* (goose), *slepice* (hen) are somewhat pejorative, but *kráva* (cow) is a derogatory designation. *Kočka* (cat) denotes an attractive and/or sexy woman and its use can be perceived either positively or negatively. Thus, Kundera's use of metaphors and similes, such as "lamp-post" for the prostitute in *The Joke*, or a woman looking like a "giraffe and a stork" in *The Unbearable Lightness of Being*, and additional similes, describing their faces, bodies, or personal characters, such as "homely girl, skinny girl, muscular girl, chattering woman," are fully justified in Kundera's contextual writing.

John O'Brien discerns a common motif in Kundera's heroines: the weak woman attracts the man and then traps him.[38] He provides a brief but thorough analysis, beginning with Jaroslav's relationship with his wife, Vlasta, in *The Joke*. When finding out that Vlasta lied to him about their son being a part of the folkloric procession, he got furious and violently started breaking the plates. "Why hadn't she started crying ten minutes ago? I could have let myself be taken in by the old self-delusion and seen her again as the poor servant girl."[39] Just as Jaroslav had married Vlasta because he saw in her a helpless "poor servant girl," Franz married his wife because he saw in her a weak woman who needed his protection. When Marie-Claude threatened to commit suicide, he agreed to marry her. But for twenty years Franz ignored the similarities between his own mother and Marie-Claude. Tomas married Tereza for a similar reason: she was brought to him defenseless in a biblical bulrush basket, and had remained in "the camp of the weak" throughout the novel. In *Immortality* Laura used her sexual seduction as a weapon to win back her younger lover, Bernard, when she feared she was losing him. In addition, she used a similar approach to get closer to Paul, her sister Agnes's husband, even while Agnes was still alive. After her sister's death, Laura married Paul.

SUICIDAL WOMEN

It appears that Kundera, the author, has a weakness, or a fetish for weakness, in women. In every single one of his novels a woman intends to commit suicide. This facet could hardly be traced to his cultural background. From today's viewpoint, his fictional women might be looked down upon, being humiliated by men (which could justify their tendency to commit suicide) but Czech culture did propagate divorce or separation for women humiliated, misused, or abandoned by their husbands or partners. Looking closely at female characters with suicidal tendencies in Kundera's fiction, one might call this phenomenon the author's observing women through *his own fictional suicidal lens.*

One by one, each novel includes a female character thinking about committing suicide, or attempting to commit suicide, or pretending to attempt suicide. Following the publication order of Kundera's novels, the first example of this appears in *Laughable Loves*, with Alzhbeta's fake attempt to take her life when she falls asleep while gas is leaking from the stove. Then Helena in *The Joke* attempts to commit suicide by consuming pills after Ludvik tells her that he never loved her. By a silly error she consumes laxatives and is discovered—in the most humiliating pose sitting outside on the latrine—by Ludvik whom she now hates, and by her young TV technician who has been in love with her. In *Life Is Elsewhere*, it is Xavier's "snowmaiden" who lets herself die in the snow while watching Xavier through the window of a restaurant where he interacts with an older woman. In *Farewell Waltz,* Ruzena mentions several times that she would take her life rather than have a baby with her boyfriend. In *The Book of Laughter and Forgetting,* Tamina swam all night to get away from the erotic touches by the children on the island, the next day wishing "to die somewhere midwater, far from all contact, alone with nothing but the fish."[40] In *The Unbearable Lightness of Being*, it is Tereza who has been contemplating suicide, an expression of her weakness, and Marie-Claude who threatened with suicide if Franz left her. In *Immortality*, Laura's attempt to take her life in her boyfriend's villa in Martinique is dramatically described in a phone conversation between her sister, Agnes, and brother-in-law, Paul, both at that time in Paris. Ultimately, it is the suicidal girl who causes Agnes's death. In *Slowness*, it is Immaculata, dressed in symbolic white, who jumps into the hotel pool, hoping to find her death after Berck has banished her with brutal profanity. In *Identity* it is Chantal who leaves Jean-Marc in some nebulous attempt to disappear (though it might be only in a dream) after she discovers that he rummaged in her underwear drawer to see if she had kept his love letters, which she had taken to be letters from an unknown admirer. Heat rising through her body, she finds herself naked, in a strange place with a nondescript septuagenarian who asks her where she wants to go, just like

Raphael asked Tamina when taking her to the island occupied by children. In *Ignorance*, it is Milada who, as a teenage girl, intends to die in the frosty cold in the mountains during a school trip by consuming sleeping pills. A reminder of Xavier's trip to the mountains and the "snowmaiden," Milada is ready to take her young life because her boyfriend, Josef, intends to ditch her if she undertakes the school trip instead of staying with him. Just as in Marketa's case in *The Joke*, this is a clear reminiscence of a young man's rejection of a girl when he intends to seduce her at the time she is ordered by an authority to participate in a school activity. Milada survives with one ear removed, but Josef remains incognizant of the consequences of his selfish insistence.

And finally *The Festival of Insignificance* portrays one of the most uncomfortable suicide attempts—that of a young pregnant woman, Alain's mother. Because of "her hatred" of being pregnant, she jumps over the bridge into the river, but does not die instantly. A good swimmer, she attempts to resist her swimming instinct by getting the cold water into her lungs. But there is a young man, a teenager, who comes to her rescue, yelling at her: "Stop, stop." When he pulls toward her, she grabs him and pulls him down into the water. The author gives gruesome details of his death: she "stretches the whole length of her body along the boy's back to keep his head underwater. He fights back, he thrashes, he has already taken in water, he tries to strike the woman, but she stays lying firmly on him; he can no longer lift his head to get air, and after several long, very long seconds, he ceases to move."[41] She returns to her car and drives away as if nothing happened, and no one finds that she was a murderer. She is never punished for the young man's death, like most of the culprits in Kundera's novels. They commit crimes by denouncing innocent people or by being complicit in the misfortunes of their companions for their own sheer satisfaction and selfishness. The scene of attempted suicide by Alain's mother can be linked with the suicidal girl in *Immortality*, who sits on a road, hoping that a car would run her over. She couldn't care less that her selfish act could (and in fact does) cause the deaths of other people. Kundera defends her act by citing her invisibility in life: "That's how I imagine her, and I am sure that she sees herself that way, too: as a woman walking through a valley among people who do not hear her."[42] He gives additional allusions to her loneliness and depersonalization, some of them bordering on the surreal: for example, a man in a doctor's office doesn't notice her and sits on top of her.

In his critical study, John O'Brien concentrates on many additional examples of men's violence and women's submissiveness; once presented in a detailed summary of a scholarly analysis, Kundera's novels become not only collectively repetitive but also propelled by a bullet of *viciousness and aggressiveness* toward women, sometimes toward men as well, and toward the world that surrounds the author. For instance, the author's voice reprimands the teenage boy who tries to save Alain's mother from drowning, for hoping to become famous by having "his picture in the papers."[43] Since the narrator does not provide any other details of this boy's past or present, of his true intentions, or of his family's reaction to his cruel death, the reader can only agree or disagree with Kundera's cynical views of the boy's craving for fame rather than for trying to save a human life as a result of his good deed and altruism.

Kundera's fictional characters are saturated with bitterness and anger, with a feeling of vengeance and unhappiness of life. Whether fictionally or figuratively real, rape is present, often depicted as the rapist's enjoyment, with the voluntary participation of the victim. When describing the woman looking like a giraffe, the narrator says about Tomas: "Now that he was standing over her, he grabbed her under the knees and lifted her slightly parted legs in the air, so that they suddenly looked like the raised arms of a soldier surrendering to a gun pointed at him."[44] And Kundera concludes: "Clumsiness combined with ardor, ardor with clumsiness—they excited Tomas utterly."[45]

Sexual imagination and performance of Kundera's fictional characters can be defined as quiet enjoyment, uniqueness, or masochistic domination with occasional overtones of fetishism. Often a blunt revelation strikes the reader: the characters do not question their evil act nor seem to carry conscious guilt or be punished. Everything about Kundera's childhood and his mother is deeply sealed and his two marriages reveal very little, if anything. His current wife mentioned in *Slowness*, is profoundly devoted to him, handling his administrative affairs. Like a number of his married female characters, she is younger than her husband but their union (at least seen from outside) looks a happy one. If Kundera retains anger against women, it may go back to his unfortunate incident initiated by Iva Militká because, after all, denying knowing her, he has denied an existence of an evidenced reality from the past. Unfortunately it does leave a dark stain on his career as a writer and contributor to human consciousness.

NOTES

1. John O'Brien, *Milan Kundera & Feminism, Dangerous Intersections* (New York: St. Martin's Press, 1995), XII.
2. O'Brien, *Milan Kundera & Feminism*, 3.
3. Jordan Elgrably, "Conversations with Milan Kundera," *Salmagundi Magazine,* no. 73 (Winter 1987): 3–24.
4. Kirstie Ratzer-Farley, "Feminism Movement in Czech Republic," Kent State University, http://kentinprague.com/wp-content/uploads/2013/09/The-Czech-Feminist-Movement.pdf
5. The feature *Katka* by Ján Kadár was labeled negatively for encouraging young people to leave villages and move to cities. However, Ján Kadár is best known for his Oscar winning foreign language film, *The Shop on Main Street*, which he made together with Elmar Klos in 1965. It depicts a process of Aryanization and the deportation of Jews in a small Slovak town during WWII. Its war theme has a larger implication: opportunism, ignorance, and apathy that have permeated both the Nazi and Communist societies.
6. Elgrably, "Conversations with Milan Kundera," 3–24.
7. Elgrably, "Conversations with Milan Kundera," 3–24.

8. Elgrably, "Conversations with Milan Kundera," 3–24.

9. Elgrably, "Conversations with Milan Kundera," 3–24.

10. This does not imply that he knew Militká closely and intimately, although she called him a friend. It only indicates that in the years and decades following the March 14, 1950 episode, Kundera disliked her more and more, realizing the implications into which he was dragged by information she had confessed to Dlask and Dlask confessed to him. In 2008, their mutual animosity erupted: she blaming him for denouncing Dvořáček, he—from his viewpoint—denying her existence (not knowing her at all). Could the Biblical Scripture, 1 Corinthians 15:33 "Bad company corrupts good character" be applied in this case?

11. Jeho první ženou byla Olga Haasová, dcera skladatele Pavla Haase. https://cs.wikipedia.org/wiki/Milan_Kundera

12. Bohumil Hrabal, *I Served the King of England*, trans. Paul Wilson (New York: New Directions Books, 1989), 9.

13. Robert Skloot, "Vaclav Havel: The Once and Future Playwright," in *Critical Essays on Vaclav Havel*, ed. Marketa Goetz-Stankiewicz and Phyllis Carey (New York: G.K. Hall & Co., 1999), 200–208.

14. This idea is Kundera's, quoted in Robert Skloot's "Vaclav Havel: The Once and Future Playwright." See Note 13.

15. Vaclav Havel, *Disturbing the Peace*, trans. Paul Wilson (New York: Vintage Books, 1991), 53.

16. Milos Forman (and Jan Novak), *Turnaround* (New York: Villard Books, 1994), 134.

17. Forman and Novak, *Turnaround*, 188.

18. Forman and Novak, *Turnaround*, 148–53.

19. Elgrably, "Conversations with Milan Kundera," 3–24.

20. Ian McEwan, "An Interview with Milan Kundera," *Granta*, no. 11 (1984): 34–35.

21. Jan Čulík, "Byla éra stalinismu dobou 'naivní bezstarostnosti'?" *Britské listy* (October 25, 2002), http://blisty.cz/art/11931.html

22. Milan Jungmann, "Kunderovské paradoxy," in *Cesty a rozcestí* (London: Rozmluvy, 1988), 228–29.

23. Jason M. Wirth, *Commiserating with Devastated Things: Milan Kundera and the Entitlements of Thinking* (New York: Fordham University Press, 2016), 201.

24. Kundera, *Life Is Elsewhere*, 218.

25. Kundera, *Unbearable Lightness*, 71.

26. O'Brien, *Milan Kundera & Feminism*, XIII.

27. O'Brien, *Milan Kundera & Feminism*, 3.

28. O'Brien, *Milan Kundera & Feminism*, 2.

29. Ladislav Jehlička, "Lehká jsou jen hovna," *Literární stránka*, http://www.deml.cz/literatura/ladislav-jehlicka, 3.

30. Jehlička, "Lehká jsou jen hovna," 11.

31. O'Brien, *Milan Kundera & Feminism*, 5.

32. Kundera, *Laughable Loves*, 72.

33. Kundera, *Book of Laughter and Forgetting*, 14.

34. Kundera, *Book of Laughter and Forgetting*, 17.

35. Kundera, *Book of Laughter and Forgetting*, 153.

36. Kundera, *Book of Laughter and Forgetting*, 154.

37. Steven Pinker, *How Does Mind Work* (New York: W.W. Norton & Company, 1999), 475.

38. O'Brien, *Milan Kundera & Feminism*, 42.

39. Kundera, *The Joke*, 307.

40. Kundera, *Book of Laughter and Forgetting*, 261.

41. Kundera, *The Festival of Insignificance*, 39.

42. Kundera, *Immortality*, 252.

43. Kundera, *The Festival of Insignificance*, 39.

44. Kundera, *Unbearable Lightness of Being*, 205–6.

45. Kundera, *Unbearable Lightness of Being*, 206.

Chapter Seven

An Example of Interdisciplinary Analysis

KANT'S UNIVERSALIZABILITY PROJECTED
INTO KUNDERA'S NOVELS

As perplexing and often misleading—if not contradictory—as Kundera's novels are, they offer many perspectives to analysis. His unflagging preponderance for vacillation between intriguing existentialism, enigmatic ambiguity, and stylish finesse—his ideas often distilled into a single pithy phrase of forceful and meaningful expression—can be analyzed from a variety of comparative angles: philosophical, historical, scientific, or cultural. In addition, they can be discussed against the background of almost any literary work and artwork. This final chapter attempts to present two angles of prospective analysis. One concerns the rebellion of the human spirit over the imposition of conformity analyzed against Immanuel Kant's philosophy. The other involves selected behavioral scientists' views applicable to Kundera's fictional characters' behavior. While the kernels of analysis are Kundera's novels, the discussion overlaps with the selected passages from the works of Milos Forman, Bohumil Hrabal, Franz Kafka, Wang Xiaobo, and Goh Poh Seng.

Kant's *theory of universalizability* implies subjective rules that guide human actions. Kant termed these rules *maxims* and viewed them as self-imposed subjective laws that are morally good, and therefore can be universalized. If everyone can practice maxims, they must be morally acceptable; therefore, *good* means *universalized.* But stepping out of philosophical concepts presented in Kant's *Groundwork of the Metaphysics of Morals*, one might view the paradoxical nature of his philosophy as seen in literature.

In *The Art of the Novel*, Milan Kundera writes: "Man desires a world where good and evil can be clearly distinguished, for he has an innate and

165

irrepressible desire to judge before he understands."[1] Kundera argues that
when interpreting a novel the reader seeks a moral position, influenced by his
own cultural and religious values or ideologies, and requires that characters
be right or wrong. He gives examples from Kafka's *The Trial* and Tolstoy's
Anna Karenina. Is it Josef K. who is an innocent victim of the unjust Court,
or is it the Court that represents justice in finding Josef K. guilty? And who is
at fault in *Anna Karenina*? Is it she, the immoral wife-adulteress, or is it he,
Anna's older husband, a dry, unattractive, and narrow-minded bureaucrat?

As is known, Kundera views the novel as "an inquiry into human existence"; thus it cannot represent one "single and absolute truth." He calls this
inability *wisdom of uncertainty.* It governs his approach to novel writing and
interpreting. If Kant's idea of *good will* presupposes that a human being
would "do the right thing," which according to Kant constitutes morality,
then Kundera's idea of *good will* in the novel would correspond to *knowledge*—knowledge that he considers to be "the novel's only morality."[2] In
other words, knowledge is discovery and that's the only reason for the novel
to exist: "A novel that does not discover a hitherto unknown segment of
existence is immoral."[3]

For Kant, reasoning is the *categorical imperative* that guides a human
being; that is, a rational being by reason alone is led to *good will;* hence,
universalizability of morality. However, the disparity between reason and
action has been explored in a number of artistic works, and this concept
could be easily applied to Kundera's novels, as well as Forman's films. Both
Kundera and Forman have achieved a significant degree of critical and commercial success primarily because they focus on portrayals of the paradoxical
and tormented nature of man; that is, the disparity between reason and action
or, in Kundera's terms, *quest for the self.* It is through actions that the man
becomes an individual by distinguishing himself from others.[4]

In Forman's film, based on Ken Kesey's novel, *One Flew Over the Cuckoo's Nest*, it might be a boisterous, free-spirited convict, Randle McMurphy
(played by Jack Nicholson). He arrives in a mental hospital energetic, playful, and hopeful. He believes that by pretending insanity, he will escape from
a prison of the work-farm to a place of relative freedom. Led by reasoning,
he ignores his actions, and instead he sets forth toward his death. It is the
disparity between McMurphy's own image and his act that leads to discovery
of the human-inhuman dichotomy for both McMurphy's character and the
audience.

As pointed out, Kundera sees his fictional characters as *his unrealized
possibilities*, and the novel as *an investigation of human life in the trap the
world has become.*[5] The mental hospital in *One Flew Over the Cuckoo's
Nest* becomes "the trap the world has become" not only for the patients,
McMurhpy including, but also for its staff, particularly the chief nurse,
Ratched (acted by Louise Fletcher). She turns out to be an evil person

through the ways she treats the patients; but her reasoning and the internal motivations behind her actions are decent and morally acceptable. She wants to help, but her desire to help and to be good pushes her to be excessively controlling to the point of becoming dictatorial. She gradually breaks down the spirit and self-confidence of individual patients and manipulates them into fighting with one another. She deprives them of self-control and the sense of self-being, turning them into puppets of her own desire. Through his actions of mocking the hospital authorities and encouraging patients to reason and speak for themselves, McMurphy gradually becomes the leader in the mental ward. As a result, he enters into a power-ego war between nurse Ratched and himself.

In his *Generalization in Ethics,*[6] Marcus Singer summarized Kant's *universalizability* into three statements: a) *the goal* one intends to achieve; b) *the action* one uses to achieve the goal; c) *circumstances* under which acting that particular way helps to achieve the goal. Applying these statements to Kundera's or Forman's characters, one would only prove how perfect and, by the same token, how imperfect this generalization could be. The title alone of *The Book of Laughter and Forgetting* suggests Kundera's anomalous approach to the serious, (i.e., *forgetting,* by placing it into the circumstances of the *laughable*). The stories—united by the theme of the *paradox of life* show man's actions aimed at a goal he intends to achieve; however, he is thrown into circumstances, which often take him onto a contradictory path of his intended goal—resulting in the laughable. Within Kant's notion of *universalizability*, such a deviation is the paradox of man's reasoning and actions.

Tamina's character in Kundera's novel serves as a connecting device to the theme of sorrowfulness, which surfaces in each of the seven parts of the novel. When her goal to obtain a packet in Prague—which contains her husband's love letters written to her—fails with Bibi, her goal shifts onto Hugo. Infatuated with Tamina, Hugo is willing to travel to Prague to fetch her packet, believing it holds secret political documents. Tamina lets Hugo make love to her but her emotions and body are detached. Her only motivation for the intimate encounter is her goal of obtaining the letters. The action she uses to achieve her goal mingles with circumstances in the wrong way: "Tamina stares at Hugo, and suddenly he can no longer endure that stare and loses the thread of what he is saying. He wants to imprison her in the universe of his blood and thoughts, but she is utterly enclosed in her own world."[7] The Kant *universalizability* statement c), circumstances under which acting that particular way helps to achieve the goal, here escalates into a paradox that deprives Tamina of reaching her intended goal: the link that documents and connects her past with the present. She falls into the *forgetting of being,* and in the end Kundera lets her disappear in the murky water of a remote island. And yet, the circumstances that lead to her death have been simple and evident. After their lovemaking, Hugo hates Tamina, realizing that she has never loved him, and he convinces himself that she is exploiting her fate of a widow and *émigré*.

In a parabatic passage, Kundera comments that he is unable to explain why Tamina is taken to die on a surreal island governed by erotically provocative children. But he depicts Tamina as someone whose human spirit rebels against the conformity of a society—she steps out to reach *beyond the border*. In the story itself, Kundera writes that Tamina's misfortune "is not that the children are bad but that she is beyond their world's border."[8] He makes an allusion to men who kill animals without remorse because the animal species is outside of human law, just as Tamina is "outside of the children's law." If we apply Kant's *categorical imperative* of the rational being, which implies that the rational being of *good will* is supposed to evaluate his actions, we can conclude that both, the children's erotic desire and Tamina's desire for obtaining her letters, are the attributes for personal enjoyment: for the pleasure of the children and Tamina's own satisfaction. However, these attributes become inferior motives that deviate from the *good will* of a rational being, and thus, *the punishment* follows.

MAN'S IRRATIONAL NATURE

Kant's premise is the following: a rational being with good will's maxims acts within the *categorical imperative*—that is, *always rightly and in accordance with duty*. But in his essence, man is *an irrational being*; he desires happiness, pleasure, goodness, attention, etc. His self-interest alone affirms the irrationality of his nature. Man's rational nature is supreme for it becomes *an end in itself*. Most things for man have value only as a means to an end of greater value, such as the above mentioned satisfaction, pleasure, and happiness. Nurse Ratched attempts to act in accordance with the *categorical imperative* of the mental hospital, *her duty*. In Kesey's novel, she is portrayed as a monstrous power of a huge organization that forces people into passiveness by intimidation. But in the film, she is more human. Thomas Slater, in his study on Forman's films, affirms that "because she is more human, she is ironically a greater source of evil in the film than in the novel."[9] He goes further, saying: "Her statements seem logical and reasonable, not openly vindictive as in the novel."[10] Forman's choice of Louise Fletcher to personalize the character of nurse Ratched is of importance. She is an attractive woman of pleasant and mild features with a nice and modest smile. The more she appears physically pleasing and docile in her lukewarm mannerism, the more horrifying she is in conducting *her duty* of *good will*.

The duality of her rationality and irrationality goes hand-in-hand with Kundera's character of Jaromil, a young poet of desire and imagination but also of dogma. It is his dogmatic nature that makes him a *monster*, leading an idiosyncratic life, balancing his light and dark sides. As mentioned in Chapter Two, Kundera sees potential monstrosity in all human beings. Out of anger and humiliation for not being popular and accepted among his peers, Jaromil becomes a pro-Communist poet. His anti-Communist relatives regard him as a clumsy youth, mocking him for his lack of experiences with women. The feelings of inadequacy and jealousy lead Jaromil to becoming an instrument of the Communist Party and a police informant. It is his personal revolt against his own lot and against his liberally inclined relatives. It is a rebellion of his *human spirit over the imposition of conformity* under the circumstances created for him by his peers and his relatives, and by his dominant mother and absentee father.

During lovemaking with his redhead girlfriend, Jaromil forces her to declare that she loves him above everything else and that she couldn't live without him. Their dialogue continues in the same emotional vein and progresses with intensity. The narrator lets the two fictional characters act in *good will* up to the moment when Jaromil realizes that he has become a victim of complete misunderstanding. His girlfriend's love for him is not the Romeo and Juliet type. If he dies, she only would be sad and feel lonely. The switch ensues at the moment when Jaromil's ulterior motives are revealed. He stops acting rationally: his rational nature stops being *an end in itself,* and his ulterior motives take over his irrational nature. The incongruity of this situation is implied in Jaromil's feelings that it is *his duty* to denounce his girlfriend's brother to the secret police, without rationalizing over potential consequences. Inevitably, his denouncement is contradictory; it leads to several arrests, including his girlfriend's. Within the Kant theory of *universalizability,* this paradox might be termed a *hypothetical imperative,* a command that is intended to attain a particular outcome. But what is the outcome of Jaromil's action? In fact, it is not his girlfriend's brother's arrest and her own jail sentence but the paradox of the girlfriend's invented story about her brother in order to conceal from Jaromil the fact that she was with another lover. In Kant's term, here the reason the girl lied to Jaromil functions as a *hypothetical imperative,* which sets a chain of paradoxical events and lifelong misfortunes for Jaromil's girlfriend and her family, and inevitably for Jaromil himself.

These *hypothetical imperatives*, idiosyncratic in their nature and occasionally pathetically laughable, are abundant in Kundera's novels. They appear in Forman's films, too, because they both drew from the cultural and political heritage of their homeland that often appeared unsettled or contradictory. Black humor and sorrowful laughter have been their specific way to show the rebellion of human spirit over the imposition of strict Communist conformity. Both artists carry on the tradition specific in Czech literature and culture, which goes back to Jaroslav Hašek's *idiotic* character Švejk: a Czech soldier, who pretends to be defending the interests of Franz Josef, the Austro-

Hungarian Emperor, and culminates in Bohumil Hrabal's idle characters. His characters, the so-called "Czech laughing beasts" are wonderfully portrayed in Jiří Menzel's film based on Hrabal's novel, *Closely Watched Trains*. The spirit of rebellion has been continued in Kundera's and Forman's works created within and beyond the boundaries of their country. It is these *human- ly inhuman paradoxes* that distinguish their works from others, and place them on the top of any scale of artistic ranking.

To escape conformity of the mental hospital and nurse Ratched's iron fist, McMurphy revolts. He steals a bus to take his fellow patients on a fishing trip, organizes a basketball game in the hospital yard, sneaks prostitutes into the ward for a farewell party once he is determined to escape with Chief Bromden. To rebel his own way over the sterility of the mental hospital, Bromden, a Native American, has been cleverly playing deaf and dumb for years. Within Kant's terminology, his quiet and unobtrusive rebellion em- powers him with *rational good will*. In the end, his pretending to not know what goes on around him makes him the winner. On the other hand, Dale Harding, a homosexual, acts as the leader of the ward until McMurphy's arrival. He obeys and assists nurse Ratched. He agrees with her to gain attributes and benefits for his personal enjoyment. In Kant's terminology, he embodies *imposition of conformity,* not rebellion. He is free to leave the mental ward but prefers to stay to exercise *his duty* of conformity side-by- side with Ratched. For Harding, life outside of mental ward would be too confusing and challenging.

Whether Forman's characters subject themselves to conformity or wheth- er they attempt to escape it, they all seem to be thirsting for power. In the film based on Kasey's novel, they intend to impose their vision and will by pressuring mental patients into their own mode of conformity. It is here that Kant's *categorical yet paradoxical imperative* takes place. As a result, McMurhpy dies, because he intends to assert power over the ward's patients and personnel. As a punishment for his rebellion, he receives a treatment of lobotomy and remains in unconscious vegetative state until Chief Bromden strangles him to save him from suffering.

Every one of Forman's films contains examples of a contradiction that paradoxically deviates from its intended conception. This *performative contradiction* is seen in Andula in *Loves of a Blond,* in *Firemen's Ball*, and also in his films made in America. The inefficiency of firemen of a small town—symbolic representatives of the Czech government and its nation— causes a house to burn down, and uncovers the corruption raging through the whole society. Just like McMurphy and Andula are punished for their ignor- ance, so the whole town is punished for not understanding and for ignoring the reality that surrounds them. Be it Andula, McMurphy, the firemen, or Larry Flynt, they all overstep the laws of reality. In their way of rebellion against the conformity to their environment, they are doomed unless they learn the *wisdom of uncertainty*. And true, in the last shot of *Loves of a Blonde*, for instance, Forman's camera focuses on Andula's bed, showing a ray of morning light coming through a window, a glimmer of hope, and an allusion to Andula's awaking from a dream-like scene, suggesting her lot might change. In *One Flew Over the Cuckoo's Nest*, it is Chief Bromden whose *wisdom of uncertainty* leads him to escape to freedom.

PERFORMATIVE CONTRADICTION IN LITERARY CHARACTERS

Kant's notion of *performative contradiction* can be traced in a number of characters in Kundera's novels. For instance, in *The Book of Laughter and Forgetting* it is often a blatant situation of paradoxical sexual motion. Jan who defines his border at "the maximum acceptable dose of repetitions,"[11] tells his friend: "Talk about world revolution! We are living in the historic epoch when the sexual act is being definitively transformed into ridiculous motions."[12] After meeting a young woman whose ultimate goal is to reach an orgasm ("a religion to her, a goal, the highest requirement of hygiene, a symbol of health . . . a source of pride"),[13] Jan attempts to escape the conformity of the erotic life into his illusory border of meaning. In this respect, Milan Kundera's approach is close to Wang Xiaobo's, the Chinese author of *Wang in Love and Bondage*. Wang uses a satiric genre *zawen*, which easily provokes social and political arguments. If viewed from an emotional platform, sex in Kundera's and Wang's writings is easily perceived as a detached motion of repetition, cruel lack of sentiment and morality. However, the erotic approach of both authors is often a rebellion against political and social conformity—an absurd comedy aimed to flatten the cruel, and to provoke laughter while preserving their characters' individuality and creativity, and above all, sanity in politically oppressive situations.

In Wang Xiaobo's award-winning novella "The Golden Age" a young female doctor, Chen Quinyang has been sent to a countryside camp for peasants' reeducation during the Mao Zedong revolution. Her husband imprisoned, she is haunted by a rumor of being promiscuous or, as Wang calls it, *damaged goods*. Her situation is not far from Josef K.'s plight in Kafka's *The Trial*. To avoid a punishment of being put under the surveillance of proletarian masses, Chen attempts to prove her innocence, just like Josef K. attempts to prove that he is not guilty. She contacts Wang Er in hope that he will help her prove the rumors are false, but instead he suggests proving the rumors to be true, and to show the revolutionary masses that she is, indeed, *damaged goods*. When Josef K. seeks advice from the court painter, the painter admits that the law allows "an innocent person to be acquitted."[14] However, throughout his experience with the court, the painter does not know of *any actual acquittals*, not a single one. In other words, Josef K. and Chen Quinyang are doomed to live up to their fictitious crimes. In these fictional cases, a societal pressure forces the protagonists to give up their hopes, subjecting them to their requirements, no matter how cruel or illogical they might be. As a result, these situations are dealt with by means of the characters' erotic desires and their underlining forces, culminating in sexual rebellion. For instance, Josef K. relies on erotic interactions with women to help him to get out of his accusation trap of guilt. His inquiry into whether or not he is guilty, rather than into what he is guilty of, is a continuation of Gregor's metamorphosis from a human being to a vermin, which he hardly notices. Gregor's struggle begins with his difficulty going to work and continuing to help his family rather than questioning his unusual state of becoming a non-human.

As discussed previously, in Kundera's story "Edward and God," Edward pretends to be religious in order to have a sexual encounter with Alice, a believer, who has been refusing him in the name of God. In terms of Kant's *universalizability,* Edward has a goal that he intends to achieve. He takes an action—starts going to church—to reach his goal. And while these particular circumstances help him achieve it, they paradoxically lead to his oppression by an unattractive, hairy old directress who attempts to seduce him rather than to politically educate him. Edward forces the naked directress onto her knees, ordering her to repeat prayer after him, and only at that moment of intoxication, his body awakens from the passive resistance, and he gets excited. This paradoxical sexual scene has several levels of oppression: the kneeling of a naked directress humiliated by her subordinate; a naked Communist humiliated by prayer; a woman humiliated by her nakedness; and above all, humiliated Edward by being forced to have sex with his supervisor in spite of his emotional and physical desire.[15] In this case, *malgré lui*, Edward gains two mistresses, the directress and Alice.

APPLYING PINKER'S UNDERSTANDING OF MORALIZATION

The idea of submission and conformity to societal norms is connected with morality, and is tied to one's perception and purpose based on a complex, multileveled, and subjective premise. A societal norm can be defined as a way of accepted feelings, thinking, and behaving as emphasized by a particular community and social group. In his provocative interview with Lane Greene, entitled "Steven Pinker: Less morality for a better society," Pinker argues that "Understanding, recruiting, and indeed minimizing human moralization is a great way to leverage greater understanding of human nature to make the world a better place."[16]

Undoubtedly, this idea is reflected in the works of Kundera, Kafka, Forman, Wang, Goh Poh Seng, and of many other authors. For instance, in *I Served the King of England*, Hrabal's naïve protagonist, a busboy and later a waiter, admires everything around him. For the most part, his surrounding world is nothing but congruent with his vision and wishes. But his perceptions and actions are as absurd as they are surreal. However, when he, the young Czech man, named Dítě, falls for a German woman with a Czech name, Lisa Papánek, and his name is Germanized into Ditie, he finds himself in a situation in which the minimizing of Nazi moralization leads to his understanding of human nature. Trying to conceive the future New Man, *the founder of the New Europe* at the insistence of his newlywed SS wife, he is unable to perform. The erotic is reduced to nothingness as an expression of rebellion against the imposing authority. He says: "When I heard all this, I felt everything that makes a man drain out of me, and I just lay there staring at the ceiling, dreaming about a lost paradise, about how wonderful everything had been before we were married, about how I slept with all women . . . whereas now I had a job to do."[17] Hrabal's tall-tale, picaresque storytelling, sprinkled with colloquialisms, resembles more closely Wang Xiaobo's *zawen* than Kundera's polished literary style. Like in Kundera and Wang, the sexual performance in Hrabal's novel acquires a significant function. It is a rebellious act, often hilarious, that undercuts its function and leads to an unexpected discovery in human nature. For instance, when Ditie masturbates to produce his sperm to be scrutinized by an SS doctor in order to determine whether he, a Czech national, is eligible under the Nuremberg Laws to impregnate his German wife,[18] his conscience is finally awakened, and he arrives to the understanding that Czechs are being deported and killed by the Nazis' societal machine.

THE THEORY OF GROUP SELECTION

In his essay "The False Allure of Group Selection,"[19] Pinker challenges *the theory of group selection* of two leading scientists, evolutionary biologist E.O. Wilson, and social psychologist Jonathan Haidt. They see the human condition tied to a morality that "can be explained as adaptation to *group-against-group* competition."[20] Behavioral sciences distinguish group theories into biological and cultural evolutions, and Pinker additionally clarifies misconceptions between biologically endowed self-interested, self-oriented, *selfish* behavior in humans, and culturally inherited *moral* behavior. Both Wilson and Haidt contrast the biological evolution of *group selection* of genetic composition to moral virtues—*products of group selection*, such as honor, loyalty to community, conformity to social norms, and obedience to authority.

From the time when Chen Qingyang admits publicly that she is *damaged goods* and Wang Er is her lover, she violates the conformity to social norms *of group selection* in the reeducation camp, so that camp villagers turn their backs on her. Wang Er says: "People were so afraid of this kind of damaged-good behavior in broad daylight that they didn't even dare talk about it."[21] By Pinker's definition of *culturally inherited moral behavior,* this leads to Wang Er's revolt by disappearing into the mountains. Living in a little hut, Wang remains in touch with nature in a poetic way, "listening to the leaves rustling all over the mountain, finally reaching a state where object and subject were both forgotten."[22] When Chen Qingyang follows him, he is preoccupied with his penis that he calls Buddha, personifying it through various metaphorical descriptions, such as, "My little Buddha pointed to the sky like an arrow, bigger than ever,"[23] and using his genital organ as the proof of his existence in the non-existential world in the mountains. His daily preoccupation of his sexual escapades with Chen Qingyang qualifies for *culturally inherited moral behavior.*

In his study *The Selfish Gene*, the evolutionary biologist, Richard Dawkins, further supports the theory that human beings contribute to society as a result of rewards and fear of punishment. He writes: "We are survival machines—robot vehicles blindly programmed to preserve the selfish molecules known as genes . . . a predominant quality to be expected in a successful gene is ruthless selfishness. This gene selfishness will usually give rise to selfishness in individual behavior. . . . Anything that has evolved by natural selection should be selfish."[24]

As observed in Kundera's *The Joke*, Helena, the unhappy spouse of a Stalinist opportunist, Pavel, exhibits *group selection* behavior by her emotional attachment to the Communist Party. In her monologue chapter, she convincingly claims, "the Party is almost like a living being, I can tell it all my most intimate thoughts now that I have nothing to say to Pavel."[25] Like Pavel, she chooses to join the Party under the influence of mass brainwashing, misguided by the idea of *cultural group selection* that Pinker discusses so effectively. Her falling in love with Ludvik is an existential rebellion against the oppressive Communist authority through sexuality. However, selfishness is prominent in Ludvik's behavior, too. As an individualist, a lone wolf, in *group-against-group* competition, he fights against the societal injustice that he feels was imposed on him, but he cannot win. Toward the end of his journey, he arrives at the conclusion that avenging Pavel by abusing his wife leads to further frustration, and he accepts his lot as redemption.

E.O. Wilson holds an applicable theory that: "In a group, selfish individuals beat altruistic individuals. But, groups of altruistic individuals beat groups of selfish individuals."[26] A group that fosters cohesion by sharing social, political and religious values overcomes individualistic selfishness by promoting these values in the community and eliminating selfish individuals.

The behavior of *eliminating selfish individuals* is prominently described in Wang's novel. Once Chen Qingyang is summoned to the stage to confess, the people treat her with brutality: screaming, yelling and tying her up, submitting her to public shame and insults. Similarly, when Helena in *The Joke* cheats on her husband, she is accused of being a hypocrite at a public meeting. Her actions harm the community by breaking up marriages, her own and others, the committee members say. In Wilson's interpretation, she was destroying the altruism of Communist society. After being disapproved of by her group for communitarian disloyalty, Helena is "terrified of that awful transformation" and desperately keeps looking for love. She sees it as "a love I can embrace just as I am, with all my old dreams and ideals, because I don't want my life to split down the middle, I want it to remain whole from beginning to end, that's why I was so fascinated when I met you, Ludvik, oh Ludvik."[27] However, Helena's selfishness leads her to personal destruction.

Pinker clarifies the notion of *group selection* by claiming that it has "a superficial appeal because humans are indisputably adapted to group living and because some groups are indisputably larger, longer-lived, and more influential than others. This makes it easy to conclude that properties of human groups, or properties of the human mind, have been shaped by a process that is akin to *natural selection* acting on genes."[28] He further concedes that as alluring as the theory of *group selection* sounds, it plays no useful or purposeful role in psychology or the social sciences because it is too vague and refers to too many things, "most of which are not alternatives to the theory of gene-level selection but loose allusions to the importance of groups in human evolution."[29]

Richard Dawkins remains skeptical about building a society "in which individuals cooperate generously and unselfishly towards a common good." He states that "you can expect little help from biological nature. Let us try to teach generosity and altruism, because we are born selfish."[30] His idea is reflected in Ludvik, Helena's love object. While she fantasizes about him, Ludvik is setting a vengeful trap for her that he calls "a beautiful demolition." In his college days in Prague, like other citizens around him, Ludvik tried to contribute toward "the common good" of a Communist society—an oppressive group that stripped an individual of individualistic tendencies. However, highly individualistic himself, Ludvik sends a postcard to his girlfriend, Marketa, to a Party Training location where she is exposed to the essentials of Communist doctrine. Out of jealousy and anger by Marketa's rejection of his sexual advances, Ludvik has attempted to confuse and shock her. In that effect, he writes on the postcard: "Optimism is the opium of the people! A healthy atmosphere stinks of stupidity! Long live Trotsky!"[31]

In this instance, Ludvik's behavior is perceived as *indirect reciprocity,* a concept introduced by Richard Alexander in his book *The Biology of Moral Systems.* Alexander explains that human beings approach others by *constant-*

ly evaluating them for possible future benefits and gainful interactions, and reject those who in their eyes violate these norms of reciprocity. What Ludvik calls "a beautiful demolition" is, in fact, a selfish sexual act. Ludvik intends to destroy Pavel's marriage as brutally as Pavel destroyed Ludvik's private and professional life. His interaction with Helena is meant to be gainful to bring him "possible future benefits"—that is, the satisfaction of revenge for his exclusion from the university and for spending time in a Communist labor camp. It was Ludvik's infamous postcard with Trotsky's name on it that led to the succession of his downfall. And it was Pavel, his university friend, who raised his hand at the youth communist meeting in favor of Ludvik's expulsion from the college and the Party. Pavel's betrayal of Ludvik has its roots in selfishness and his eager conformity to societal norms. His act reaffirms Pinker's conviction that human beings conform to societal norms out of fear of losing their good reputation. Pavel needs to receive applause, and at any opportunity he joins the groups of individuals who are ready to applaud him.

Ludvik's attempt to seek revenge against Pavel by abusing his wife Helena both emotionally and sexually is purely an evil act that exposes his selfish inborn nature, as scientist-selectionists would call it, *by gene selection.* But ultimately, life plays a joke on Ludvik. After his "beautiful demolition" is over, Helena confides in him that she has been estranged from her husband for years. With sheer horror, Ludvik realizes that, on the contrary, he performed a great service to Pavel, who would happily welcome a divorce from Helena. Ludvik's insult to injury escalates when he learns that Pavel dates a beautiful young woman, a kind of women that Ludvik was deprived of dating when forced into labor camps due to Pavel's psychosis of *group conformity* at the time of severe political persecutions.

Pavel goes with the flow, and like a chameleon adapts to new leadership, ideologies, political structures, people, and ideas. By doing so, he avoids punishment, even at the expense of his own morality. His morality remains that of self-admiration and of being admired by others in his *selected group* of individuals. *In a group, selfish individuals beat altruistic individuals,* E.O. Wilson reminds us, and Pavel is an excellent example in the novel of such an individual. He is a "fabulous speaker," and is able to cut any opponent to pieces in a debate,[32] Pavel's girlfriend tells Ludvik during an embarrassing meeting of the two old opponents at a folkloristic celebration in a small Moravian town where Ludvik grew up.

SOCIAL CONQUEST IN HUMAN BEHAVIOR

Scientists see the evolutionary success of the human species as reflected in "the social conquest" of all other species on Earth. For instance, in his work *The*

Social Conquest of Earth, E.O. Wilson writes: "An unavoidable and perpetual war exists between honor, virtue, and duty, the *products of group selection*, on one side, and selfishness, cowardice, and hypocrisy, the *products of individual selection*, on the other side."[33] It is inevitable that the aspirations of an individual would not necessarily coincide with the goals of a large entity. A literary example can be found in Goh Poh Seng's celebrated Singaporean novel *If We Dream Too Long*. In this work, the so-called *products of group selection* are seen and reinforced by a government that encourages its people to perform their duty: to work hard and make sacrifices for the common good of Singapore as a successful nation. These values, as honorable as they may be, are in sharp contrast with those of the protagonist of the novel, Kwang Meng. He has difficulty transitioning from youth to adulthood; he finds the adult world too stereotyped, discriminatory, divided by races and wealth. His friends follow the traditional path of exemplary societal virtues by pursuing successful professional careers. Kwang Meng's friend Portia, who adopted his nickname from the play *Merchant of Venice*, chooses to study law in England as expected by his family, traditional upper class Indians. Likewise, another school friend, Hock Lai, who became an insurance agent, marries a girl from a wealthy family. But Kwang Meng struggles to accept these values and the ultimate *product* of his *individual selection* is only his dreaming about the better, adventurous, and happier world, ironically perhaps even the same world, which his friends have embraced.

Like Kundera's Ludvik, Kwang Meng feels alienated by society. While in the labor camp, Ludvik experiences the *penumbra of depersonalization*, a mental state that "his life was taken out of his hands and it lost its continuity." Kwang Meng goes through a similar state of alienation, a sort of internal exile because he is unable to identify with the immediate *products of his group selection*. When he puts a tie around his neck for a social occasion, it feels to him "like a noose." In Pinker's view, one should promote individual flourishing and personal expansion to its maximum rather than blindly encourage deference to authority. On its part, it would positively influence the predominant side of inborn human nature—selfishness—that selectionists believe is due to the *selfish, evil gene*.

Kwang Meng attempts his transformation under the influence of his uncle Cheong. But the uncle's moralizing leads to Kwang Meng's feeling ashamed not only for his own failures but also for his father's failures throughout life. Furthermore, it leads to Kwang Meng's realization that his father has neglected his parental duties; he did not teach his son in childhood what uncle Cheong tries to instill in him in adulthood. Ultimately, the uncle's preaching and moralizing about Kwang Meng's poor prospects in life and his need to get out of his state of depression prove to be ineffective; we see Kwang Meng drinking and being depressed more than ever before.

As shown above, an attempt to mold fictional characters into "good human beings" by deference to conformity could prove erroneous; the results are depression, stagnancy, anger, despair and revenge. Pinker's theory of minimizing restrictions that might lead to maximizing human flourishing and thus satisfaction is, in fact, largely seen through analyzing Ludvik's and Kwang Meng's behaviors and actions. In the end each character grows and shows redemption. Ludvik achieves his growing by realizing that Helena's attempt to commit suicide (because of how he treated her) played yet another ugly joke on him. As he admits, consuming laxative tablets by mistake (instead of poisonous pills) saved Helena's life "but at the price of her immense humiliation; I knew that, and I also knew that it was a humiliation without purpose, a humiliation without meaning, utterly unjust."[34]

Kwang Meng is transformed by his self-education: by reading novels by Graham Greene, Hemingway, and Dostoyevsky. It was his neighbor, a teacher, who motivated him in this intellectual pursuit. And finally, when his father falls ill, Kwang Meng is ready to make sacrifices for the welfare of his family. When he stands on the balcony, looking at the full moon, his father tells him what Kwang Meng missed hearing from him as a child: "Don't allow what has happened to me spoil your life entirely."[35] Thus, Kwang Meng's journey takes him from dreaming and longing for freedom in the selfish sense to a gradual growing desire to embrace the reality of belonging to the middle class and assuming responsibility for his family and especially for himself—for his own life.

Using E.O. Wilson's classification in Kwang Meng's case, the *products of group selection* "honor, virtue and duty" would be the ones that he attains after he wins his own battle over the *products of his individual selection*, that is, self-centeredness, confusion, and denial. Likewise, Ludvik comes to the realization that his journey has reached its peak when he joins the folk music group of his school friends. He attains redemption not only through music but also through the realization that "one's destiny is often complete long before death."[36] His close friend suffers from a stroke and Ludvik realizes that instead of striking his hated enemy, he was holding his "stricken friend in his arms." He confesses, "Yes, at that moment I saw myself . . . holding him and carrying him, big and heavy, as if I were carrying my own obscure guilt."[37]

SEXUALITY AS AN EXPRESSION OF REBELLION

One might conclude that sexuality as an expression of rebellion against oppressive authority is embedded in a number of works of European and Eurasian writers, and most likely it will remain a catchy topic for existentialists. This proves that human nature is and will continue to be in flux: it is exposed not only to psychological influences but, largely to biological and genetic coding, and for that reason alone, some degree of oppression among humans will be indefinite. As for Kant's theory of *universalizability*, when tested in fictional characters, it can be argued that it proves that man is trapped in the world of confusion, uncertainty, and insecurity, and that his societal conformity to some degree is inevitable, no matter whether and how it dehumanizes him.

However, hope derived from these works is visible and tangible: it is an inquiry into man's nature that helps him better understand the global world in which he lives and struggles till his death, leaving behind the legacy of creation and art. Literature will continue examining human behavior and sexuality from the existential viewpoint for as long as it exists. Milan Kundera's fiction is a perfect candidate for the continuation of such an examination, and the "Kauza Kundera" supports that premise. After all, his works will always remain heavy, as "if he was carrying his own obscure guilt."[38]

NOTES

1. Kundera, *Art of the Novel*, 5–6.
2. Kundera, *Art of the Novel*, 6.
3. Kundera, *Art of the Novel*, 5–6.
4. Kundera, *Art of the Novel*, 23.
5. Kundera, *Unbearable Lightness*, 221.
6. Marcus Singer, *Generalization in Ethics* (New York: Alfred Knopf, 1961), Chapters VIII and IX.
7. Kundera, *Laughter and Forgetting*, 156–57.
8. Kundera, *Laughter and Forgetting*, 255.
9. Thomas J. Slater, *Milos Forman. A Bio-Bibliography* (New York: Greenwood Press, 1987), 54.
10. Slater, *Milos Forman. A Bio-Bibliography*, 54.
11. Kundera, *Laughter and Forgetting*, 295.
12. Kundera, *Laughter and Forgetting*, 295.
13. Kundera, *Laughter and Forgetting*, 278.
14. Franz Kafka, *The Trial* (New York: Schocken Books, 1998), 153.
15. Kundera, *Laughable Loves*, 232–33.
16. Taken from the online interview with Lane Greene "Steven Pinker: Less morality for a better society?" that took place at the 2013 Festival of *The Economist's World*.
17. Bohumil Hrabal, *I Served the King of England* (New York, New Directions Books, 1989), 146.
18. Hrabal, *I Served the King*, 139.
19. Published in *Edge*, March 29, 2015: http://edge.org/conversation/the-false-allure-of-group-selection
20. Published in *Edge*, March 29, 2015.
21. "The Golden Age," in *Wang in Love and Bondage* (New York: State University of New York Press), 77.
22. "The Golden Age," 78.
23. "The Golden Age," 65.
24. Richard Dawkins, *The Selfish Gene* (Oxford: Oxford University Press, 2006), 19.
25. Kundera, *The Joke*, 20.
26. Published in *Edge*, March 29, 2015.
27. Kundera, *The Joke*, 22.
28. Published in *Edge*, March 29, 2015.
29. Published in *Edge*, March 29, 2015.

30. Published in *Edge*, March 29, 2015.

31. Kundera, *The Joke*, 22.

32. Kundera, *The Joke*, 271.

33. Edward O. Wilson, *The Social Conquest of Earth* (New York: Liveright Publishing Corporation, 2012), 56.

34. Kundera, *The Joke*, 302–3.

35. Goh Poh Seng, *If We Dream Too Long* (Singapore: Island Press, 1972), 175.

36. Kundera, *The Joke*, 317.

37. Kundera, *The Joke*, 317.

38. The paraphrasing of Kundera's statement in the previous note, (No. 37).

Bibliography

WORKS CITED, AND SELECTED SOURCES CONSULTED

Adams, Vicki. "The Search for Self in a Post-Modern World." *Imagination, Emblems and Expressions: Essays on Latin American, Caribbean, and Continental Culture and Identity.* Bowling Green: Popular, 1993.

Aji, Aron, ed. *Milan Kundera and the Art of Fiction: Critical Essays.* New York: Garland Press, 1992.

Alexander, Richard D. *The Biology of Moral Systems.* New Brunswick: Aldine Teamsaction, 2009.

Aragon, Luis. "Ce roman que je tiens pour une oeuvre majeure." Preface to *La plaisanterie.* Paris: Gallimard/Folio, 1968.

Arnim, Achim von. *The Columbia Electronic Encyclopedia*, 6th edition. http://www.infoplease.com/encyclopedia/people/arnim-achim-von.html

Barańczak, Stanislaw. "The Incredible Lightness." *The New Republic.* September 9, 1996.

Barthes, Roland. "The Death of the Author." In translation by Richard Howard. *UbuWeb Paper*, 1967.

Barthes, Roland. "The Structural Activity." In *Critical Essays.* Translated by Richard Howard. Evanston: Northwestern University Press, 1972, 213–20.

Bittner, Jochen. "Günter Grass's Germany, and Mine." *The New York Times*, The Opinion Pages. April 14, 2015.

Blahynka, Milan. "Čekání Milana Kundery." *Světová literature živě.* April 3, 2009. www.literarni.cz

Bloom, Harold, ed., and Aaron Tillman. *Milan Kundera*, Bloom's Modern Critical Views. New York: Chelsea House Publications, 2003.

Bolton, Jonathan. Interviewed by Karel Hvížďala, "O úskalích překladu i „kauze Kundera" s bohemistou z Harvardu." *iDnes.* September 19, 2009. https://zpravy.idnes.cz/o-uskalich-prekladu-i-kauze-kundera-s-bohemistou-z-harvardu-p4o / zpr_archiv.aspx?c=A090918_165220_kavarna_bos

Carlisle, Olga. "A Talk with Milan Kundera." An interview with Milan Kundera, (1985): http://www.kundera.de/english/Info-Point/Interview_Carlisle/interview_carlisle.html

Češka, Jakub. *Království motivů. Motivická analýza románů Milana Kundery.* Praha: Togga, 2005.

Češka, Jakub. "The Process which Turned Milan Kundera into an Informer." *Britské listy.* June 8, 2009. https://legacy.blisty.cz/art/47276.html

Chvatík, Květoslav. *Svět románů Milana Kundery*. Brno: Atlantis, 2008 (dotisk 2014).
Čulík, Jan. *Britské listy*, 2000. http://blisty.cz/video/Slavonic/Kundera.htm, and http://blisty.cz/art/11931.html
Čulík, Jan. "Byla éra stalinismu dobou 'naivní bezstarostnosti'?" *Britské listy*. October 25, 2002. http://blisty.cz/art/11931.html
Čulík, Jan. "Man, a Wide Garden: Milan Kundera as a Young Stalinist." *Blok, miedzynarodowe pismo poswiecone kulturze stalinowskiej i poststalinowskiej*. http://eprints.gla.ac.uk/3806/1/Milan_Kundera.pdf
Dawkins, Richard. *The Selfish Gene*. Oxford: Oxford University Press, 2006.
de Laclos, Choderlos. *Dangerous Liaisons*. Translated by Helen Constantine. London: Penguin Books Ltd., 2007.
Derrida, Jacques. *Margins of Philosophyi*. Translated by Alan Bass. Chicago: University of Chicago Press, 1982.
Doctorow, E.L. "Four Characters under Two Tyrannies: *The Unbearable Lightness of Being*." In *Critical Essays on Milan Kundera*. Edited by Peter Petro. New York: G.K. Hall & Co., 1999.
Drda, Adam. "Český dav. Ohlédnutí za 'kauzou Kundera,'" *Revolver Revue* XXX, no. 100, Fall 2015.
Drda, Adam. "Problém udavače aneb Komu je Kundera podobný?" *Hospodářské Noviny*. October 16, 2008.
Eagle, Herbert. "Genre and Paradigm in Milan Kundera's *The Book of Laughter and Forgetting*." In *Critical Essays on Milan Kundera*. Edited by Peter Petro. New York: G.K. Hall & Co., 1999.
Eagleton, Terry. "Estrangement and Irony." In *Bloom's Modern Critical Views: Milan Kundera*. Edited by Harold Bloom. Langhorne: Chelsea House Publishers, 2003, 47–54.
Eagleton, Terry. *Literary Theory*. London: Blackwell Publishers, 1996.
Edge. March 29, 2015. http://edge.org/conversation/the-false-allure-of-group-selection
Elgrably, Jordan. "Conversations with Milan Kundera." *Salmagundi Magazine,* no. 73, (Winter 1987): 3–24. Reprinted in *Critical Essays on Milan Kundera*. Edited by Peter Petro. New York: G.K. Hall & Co., 1999, 53–68.
Elrod, John W. *Being and Existence in Kierkegaard's Pseudonymous Works*. Princeton: Princeton University Press, 1975.
Forman, Milos (and Jan Novak). *Turnaround*. New York: Villard Books, 1994.
Foucault, Michel. "What is an Author?" Originally presented at the Société française de philosphie. February 22, 1969 (modified translation by Josué V. Harari).
Freud, Sigmund. *On Dreams*. The James Strachey Translation. New York: W.W. Norton & Company, 1952.
Goetz-Stankiewicz, Marketa, and Phyllis Carey. *Critical Essays on Vaclav Havel*. New York: G.K. Hall & Co., 1999.
Goh Poh, Seng. *If We Dream Too Long*. Singapore: Island Press, 1972.
Greene, Lane. "Steven Pinker: Less Morality for a Better Society?" *The Economist's World* (in the section Festival of 2013).
Haman, Aleš, and Vladimír Novotný, eds. *Hommage à Milan Kundera, Pocta Milanu Kunderovi*. České Budějovice: Artes Liberales, 2009.
Havel, Václav. "Český úděl?" *Tvář* 4, no. 2 (February 1969): 30–33.
Havel, Václav. "Czech Destiny?" in translation by Tim West. https://www.academia.edu/2503514/Czech_Destiny_Václav_Havel_
Havel, Vaclav. *Disturbing the Peace*. Translated from the Czech by Paul Wilson. New York: Vintage Books, 1991.
Havel, Vaclav. "Words on Words." Translated by A.G. Brain. *The New York Review of Books*. January 18, 1990.
Higgins, Bernie, and David Vaughan. "Czech Books: Milan Kundera's *Ignorance*, a Novel that Offers Insight into Exile and Memory." *Czech Radio 7, Radio Prague* 2004. http://www.radio.cz/en/article/55813

Hospodářské Noviny. 3.9.2015, www.ihned.cz, Milan Kundera: Ptákovina. 3. Výstup, já vím, nemusí to být všechno pravda, ale ono není šprochu, aby na něm nebylo pravdy trochu. http://art.ihned.cz/c1–64545560-milan-kundera-ptakovina-ukazka

Hrabal, Bohumil. *I Served the King of England*. Translated from the Czech by Paul Wilson. New York: New Directions Books, 1989.

Hradilek, Adam. "Udání Milana Kundery,"*Respekt,* no. 42 (December 10, 2008): 40–45.

Hradilek, Adam, and Martin Tichý. "Osudová mise Moravcova kurýra." *Paměť a dějiny*, no. 1 (2009).

Jehlička, Ladislav. "Lehká jsou jen hovna." *Literární stránka*. 1998, 1–17. http://www.deml.cz/literatura/ladislav-jehlicka

Jones, Tim. "Milan Kundera's Slowness: Making it Slow." *Review of European Studies* 1, no. 2 (2009): 64–75.

Jungmann, Milan. "Kunderovské paradoxy." *Cesty a rozcestí*. London: Rozmluvy, 1988.

Kafka, Franz. *The Metamorphosis*. Translated and edited by Stanley Corngold. New York: Bantam Classic, 1972.

Kafka, Franz. *The Trial*. Translated from the German by Willa and Edwin Muir. New York: Schocken Books, 1998.

Kalous, Jan. "K obsahu jedné přednášky. Jaroslav Jerman o Dvořáčkově případu, Studie a články." *Paměť a dějiny*. Praha: Ústav pro studium totalitních režimů, 4, 2009. http://www.ustrcr.cz/data/pdf/pamet-dejiny/pad0904/048-051.pdf

Kant, Immanuel. *Groundwork of the Metaphysics of Morals*. Translated by Thomas Kingsmill Abbott. Radford: Wilder Publications, 2008.

"Kauza Kundera: Přes 50 let žiji s pocitem viny." An interview with Iva Militká conducted by Eliška Bártová a Ludvík Hradilek for *Aktuálně*, October 18, 2008. www.aktualne.cz

Kierkegaard, Søren. *Either/Or. A Fragment of Life*. Translated from the Danish by Alastair Hannay. New York: Penguin Classics, 1992.

Konrad, Daniel. "V Česku poprvé vychází *Život je jinde*. Román Milana Kundery líčí mladickou nerozvážnost básníků." *Hospodářské Noviny*. June 22, 2016. www.ihned.cz

Kovačević, Nataša. "History on Speed: Media and the Politics of Forgetting in Milan Kundera's Slowness." *Modern Fiction Studies* 52, no. 3 (Autumn 2006): 634–55.

Kubíček, Tomáš. *Středoevropan Milan Kundera*. Olomouc: Periplum, 2012.

Kubíček, Tomáš. *Vyprávět příběh: Naratologické kapitoly k románům Milana Kundery*. Brno: Host, 2001.

Kundera, Milan. "Český úděl," *Listy*, nos. 7–8 (December 1968): 1–5.

Kundera, Milan. "Czech Destiny," in translation by Tim West. https://www.academia.edu/2503513/Czech_Destiny_Milan_Kundera_

Kundera, Milan. *Encounter*. Translated from the French by Linda Asher. New York: Harper-Collins Publishers, 2010.

Kundera, Milan. *Farewell Waltz*. Translated from the French by Aaron Asher. New York: HarperPerennial, 1998.

Kundera, Milan. *Identity*. Translated from the French by Linda Asher. New York: HarperFlamingo, 1998.

Kundera, Milan. *Ignorance*. Translated from the French by Linda Asher. New York: Harper-Collins Publishers, 2002.

Kundera, Milan. *Immortality*. Translated from the Czech by Peter Kussi. New York: HarperPerennial, 1992.

Kundera, Milan. *Jacques and His Master*. A Homage to Diderot in Three Acts. Translated from the French by Michael Henry Heim. New York: HarperPerennial, 1985.

Kundera, Milan. *Kastrující stín svatého Garty*. Brno: Atlantis, 2006.

Kundera, Milan. *Laughable Loves*. Translated from the Czech by Suzanne Rappaport. New York: Penguin Books, 1975.

Kundera, Milan. *Life Is Elsewhere*. Translated from the Czech by Peter Kussi. New York: Penguin Books, 1986.

Kundera, Milan. *Můj Janáček*. Brno: Atlantis, 2004.

Kundera, Milan. *Nechovejte se tu jako doma, příteli*. Brno: Atlantis, 2006.

Kundera, Milan. *Nesmrtelnost*. Brno: Atlantis, 1990.

Kundera, Milan. *O hudbě a románu.* Brno: Atlantis, 2014.
Kundera, Milan. *Ptákovina. Divadelní hra z roku 1968.* Brno: Atlantis, 2015.
Kundera, Milan. "Ptákovina." *Literární noviny* (in Literatura). September 10, 2015.
Kundera, Milan. "Ptákovinu jsem měl vždy moc rád." Reviewed by Ivan Matějka. *Literární noviny.* September 4, 2015. http://www.literarky.cz/literatura/recenze/20540-milan-kundera-ptakovinu-jsem-ml-vdy-moc-rad
Kundera, Milan. *Slova, pojmy, situace.* Brno: Atlantis, 2014.
Kundera, Milan. *Slowness.* Translated from the French by Linda Asher. New York: HarperCollins Publishers, 1995.
Kundera, Milan. *Testament Betrayed.* Translated from the French by Linda Asher. New York: HarperPerennial, 1995.
Kundera, Milan. *The Art of the Novel.* Translated from the French by Linda Asher. New York: Harper & Row Publishers, 1988.
Kundera, Milan. *The Book of Laughter and Forgetting.* Translated from the French by Aaron Asher. New York: HarperPerennial, 1996.
Kundera, Milan. *The Curtain: An Essay in Seven Parts.* Translated from the French by Linda Asher. New York: HarperCollins Publishers, 2006.
Kundera, Milan. *The Farewell Party.* Translated from the Czech by Peter Kussi. New York: Penguin Books, 1977.
Kundera, Milan. *The Festival of Insignificance.* Translated from the French by Linda Asher. New York: Faber & Faber, 2015.
Kundera, Milan. *The Joke.* Definitive version fully revised by the author. New York: HarperPerennial, 1993.
Kundera, Milan. *The Unbearable Lightness of Being.* Translated from the Czech by Michael Henry Heim. New York: HarperPerennial, 1985.
Kundera, Milan. *Valčík na rozloučenou.* Brno: Atlantis, 1997.
Kundera, Milan. *Zahradou těch, které mám rád.* Brno: Atlantis, 2014.
Kundera, Milan. *Zneuznávané dědictví Cervantesovo.* Brno: Atlantis, 2005.
Lacan, Jacques. "The Mirror Stage as Formative of the I Function as Revealed in Psychoanalytic Experience." *Ecrits.* Translated by Bruce Fink. London: W. W. Norton and Company, 2002, 75–81.
Le Grand, Eva. *Kundera or The Memory of Desire.* Translated by Lin Burman. Waterloo: Wilfrid Laurier University Press, 1999.
Lidové noviny, editions 2008.
Lodge, David. "Idea of the Author." *Critical Quarterly* 26, nos. 1–2 (March 1984): 105–21. Reprinted in *Critical Essays on Milan Kundera.* Edited by Peter Petro. New York: G.K. Hall and Co., 1999, 137–50.
Lodge, David. *The Modes of Modern Writing: Metaphor, Metonymy, and the Typology of Modern Literature.* London: Arnold, 1977.
Lukács, Georg. "The Metaphysics of Tragedy: Excerpts." http://www.autodidactproject.org/quote/lukacs_tragedy.html
Lustig, Arnošt, Milan Kundera, and Josef Škvorecký. *Velká trojka.* Praha: Edice Galaxie, 1991.
McAdams, Dan P. *The Art and Science of Personality Development.* New York: The Guilford Press, 2015.
McCullough, Michael E. *Beyond Revenge: The Evolution of the Forgiveness Instinct.* San Francisco: Jossey-Bass, 2008.
McEwan, Ian. "An Interview with Milan Kundera." *Granta*, no. 11 (1984): 34–35.
Merrill, Trevor Cribben. *The Book of Imitation and Desire: Reading Milan Kundera with René Girard.* London: Bloomsbury, 2014.
"Milan Kundera." https://cs.wikipedia.org/wiki/Milan_Kundera
Miller, Nancy K. "Libertinage and Feminism." *Yale French Studies*, no. 94 (1998): 17–28.
Misurella, Fred. *Understanding Milan Kundera: Public Events, Private Affairs.* Columbia, SC: University of South Carolina Press, 1993.
Němcová-Banerjee, Maria. *The Terminal Paradox, The Novels of Milan Kundera.* New York: Grove Weidenfeld, 1990.

O'Brien, John. *Milan Kundera & Feminism: Dangerous Intersections*. New York: St. Martin's Press, 1995.

Petro, Peter, ed. *Critical Essays on Milan Kundera*. New York: G.K. Hall & Co., 1999.

Pešat, Zdeněk. "V Kunderově kauze udával student Dlask, tvrdí pamětník." *Novinky.cz*. October 15, 2008. https://www.novinky.cz/domaci/152041-v-kunderove-kauze-udaval-student-dlask-tvrdi-pametnik.html

Píchová, Hana. *The Art of Memory in Exile: Vladimir Nabokov and Milan Kundera*. Carbondale: Southern Illinois University Press, 2002.

Pinker, Steven. *How the Mind Works*. New York: W.W. Norton & Company, 1999.

Pinker, Steven. "Thinking Does Not Imply Subjugating." *Edge*.org. (2015).

Prikryl, Jana. "How Did Milan Kundera's Antipathy toward the Media Become as Curdled as the Czechs' Allergy to His Success?" *The Nation*. May 20, 2009. https://www.thenation.com/article/kundera-conundrum-kundera-respekt-and-contempt/

Ráčková, Patricia. "Dangerous Liasions of Film and Literature: Two Film Versions of Choderlos de Laclos's Epistolary Novel." *Theory and Practice in English Studies* 4 (2005). Proceedings from the Eighth Conference of British, American and Canadian Studies. Brno: Masarykova univerzita, 223–27.

Ratzer-Farley, Kirstie. "Feminism Movement in Czech Republic." Kent State University. http://kentinprague.com/wp-content/uploads/2013/09/The-Czech-Feminist-Movement.pdf

Reslová, Marie. "Policejní záznam jako divadelní scéna." *Hospodářské noviny* (October 16, 2008): 11.

Ricard, François. *Le dernier après-midi d'Agnès: essai sur l'oeuvre de Milan Kundera*. Collection Arcades 74. Paris: Gallimard, 2003.

Richterová, Sylvie. "Totožnost člověka ve světě znaků." In *Slova a ticho*. Praha: Arkýř, Československý spisovatel, 1991.

Ricoeur, Paul. "Narrative Identity." *Philosophy Today*, no. 35 (Spring 1991): 73–80.

Roth, Philip. "An Interview with Philip Roth." *New York Times Book Review*. November 30, 1980: 7 and 78–80.

Roth, Philip. "The Most Original Book of the Season." Philip Roth interviews Milan Kundera. *The Village Voice*. November 30, 1980.

Rozen, Jonathan. "Does Milan Kundera Still Matter?" *The Atlantic*. July/August, 2015.

"Rozhovor: Že v tom měl Kundera prsty, vím už 15 let," an interview with Iva Militká in *Aktualne.cz*. October 15, 2008. https://nazory.aktualne.cz/rozhovory/rozhovor-ze-v-tom-mel-kundera-prsty-vim-uz-15-let/

Sabatos, Charles. "Criticism and Destiny: Kundera and Havel on the Legacy of 1968." In *Dramatic Milestones in Czech and Slovak History*. Edited by Laura Cashman. Routledge Europe-Asia Studies Series. London: Routledge, 2010, 183–201.

Sbírka rozhovorů. Rozhovor s Ivou Militkou-Dlaskovou. Praha, ÚSTR, 26. 5. 2008.

Schrag, Calvin O. "Heidegger on Repetition and Historical Understanding." *Philosophy East and West*. 20, no. 3 (1970): 287–95.

Shackelford, T., and D. Buss. "Betrayal in Mateships, Friendships, and Coalitions." *Personality and Social Psychology Bulletin* 22 (1996): 1151–64.

Singer, Marcus. *Generalization in Ethics*. New York: Alfred Knopf, 1961.

Skloot, Robert. "Vaclav Havel: The Once and Future Playwright." In *Critical Essays on Vaclav Havel*. Edited by Marketa Goetz-Stankiewicz and Phyllis Carey. New York: G.K. Hall & Co., 1999.

Slater, Thomas J. *Milos Forman. A Bio-Bibliography*. New York: Greenwood Press, 1987.

Sloat, Amanda. "The Rebirth of Civil Society: The Growth of Women's NGO's in Central and Eastern Europe." *European Journal of Women's Studies* 12 (2005): 437–52.

Solzhenitsyn, Alexander. *Cancer Ward*. Translated from the Russian by Nicholas Bethell and David Burg. New York: Farrar, Straus and Giroux, 1974.

Solzhenitsyn, Alexander. *The First Circle*. Translated from the Russian by Thomas P. Whitney. New York: Bantam Books, 1976.

Šťastný, Jiří. "Kauzu Kundera začaly vzpomínky pro vnuky." *idnes.cz*. October 30, 2008. http://zpravy.idnes.cz/kauzu-kundera-zacaly-vzpominky-pro-vnuky-fi1-/doma-ci.aspx?c=A081030_083148_domaci_jte

Steinby, Liisa. *Kundera and Modernity*. West Lafayette, IN: Purdue University Press, 2013.

The Columbia Electronic Encyclopedia, 6th edition. New York: Columbia University Press, 2007, eBook.

Trensky, Paul I. *The Fiction of Josed Škvorecký*. London: MacMillan Academic and Professional Ltd., 1991.

Volková, Bronislava. "The Unbearable Heaviness of Being, Or Is It Lightness? Kundera's Values." *Kosmas, Czechoslovak and Central European Journal* 12, no. 2 (1997).

von Kunes, Karen. "The Art of Buffoonery: The Czech Joke a la Commedia dell'arte Style in Kundera's French Novel *Slowness*." In *Critical Essays on Milan Kundera*. Edited by Peter Petro. New York: G.K. Hall & Co., 1999.

von Kunes, Karen. "The National Paradox: Czech Literature and the Gentle Revolution." *World Literature Today*. Spring 1991.

von Kunes, Karen. *Beyond the Imaginable: 240 Ways of Looking at Czech*. Praha: Práh Publishers, 1999.

Vorel, Ladislav. "Co mi kdysi o Milanu Kunderovi vyprávěl spisovatel Petr Chudožilov." *idnes*. January 29, 2009. http://zpravy.idnes.cz

Wang, Xiaobo. *Wang in Love and Bondage*. Translated by Hongling Zhang and Jason Sommer. New York: State University of New York Press, 2007.

Ward, Brian. "A Big Piece of Nonsense for His Own Pleasure: The Identity of Milan Kundera." *Limina* (2002): 144–55. http://www.archive.limina.arts.uwa.edu.au/__data/page/186574/8Ward2.pdf

Williams, James. *Gilles Deleuze's Difference and Repetition: A Critical Introduction and Guide*. Edinburgh: Edinburgh University Press, 2013.

Wilson, E.O. *The Social Conquest of Earth*. New York: Liveright Publishing Corporation, 2012.

Wirth, Jason M. *Commiserating with Devastated Things: Milan Kundera and the Entitlements of Thinking*. New York: Fordham University Press, 2016.

Wood, James. "Laughter and Forgetting." *The New Republic* (December 23, 2002): 33–38.

Woods, Michelle. *Topics in Translation: Translating Milan Kundera*. Toronto: Multilingual Matters Ltd., 2006.

Index

absurd, 60, 76, 97, 125, 130, 171, 173;
  absurdism, 99; absurdist play, 64, 68;
  absurdity, 2, 23, 64, 149; *Theatre of the*
  Absurd, 150
accidental: death, 54, 79; details, 59;
  hatred, 56; meetings, 54; role, 59; ties,
  55
actors, 26, 31, 35, 36, 96, 117, 150
adventure, 46, 55, 149
adversity, 6, 84
aesthetic: approach, 13; beauty, 126;
  enjoyment, 139; expression, 66;
  function, 124; ideal, 89; influence, 146;
  treatment, 19; value, 54
aesthetics, 13, 19, 20, 22, 31; fake, 124; of
  The Joke, 86; of repetition, 125; of
  socialist realism, 149
Aji, Aaron, 3
Aktuálně.cz, 32, 33
alienation, 177
allusions, 32, 162, 175
altruism, 163, 175
altruistic individuals, 174, 176
Amadeus, 119, 139; fame, 119; identity,
  119; jealousy, 119
ambiguous, 13, 28, 53; feelings, 8; words,
  102n14
American Intelligence Service, 23, 33
American professors, 6
"The Angels," 64, 127, 139, 144
Anna Karenina, 9, 166

anthropologic laboratory, 19
anti-Communist, 122, 124, 169
anti-feminist, 144–145
anti-regime, 34, 123, 128, 137
Apollinaire, Guillaume, 136
appeals, 14, 175
April 1, 1929, 24
Aquinas, Thomas, 69
Aragon, Louis, 87
archaic, 24
archives, 38, 103n48; Prague Security
  Services, 2
Aristotle, 69
army, 28–30, 31, 61; deserter, 1, 25, 30,
  37, 76, 99; French, 131; Major, 73;
  Red, 64. *See also* Dvořáček, Miroslav
Arnim, Achim von, 181
arrest, 24, 27, 35, 57, 58, 76, 78, 80. *See*
  also Dvořáček, Miroslav
The Art of the Novel, 14; complexity vs.
  simplicity, 9, 38, 149; definition of the
  novel, 9; "Sixty-three Words" meaning,
  13
Asher, Aaron, 183
Asher, Linda, 16n3
assassination of an author, 26
The Atlantic, 185
audience, 7, 68; Czech, 66; impersonal,
  148; intellectual, 8; McMurphy's, 166;
  non-Czech, 150; Salieri's, 119
Auschwitz, 147

About the Author

Karen von Kunes is a literary scholar who has contributed to Czech studies. She holds a PhD in Slavic languages and literatures from McGill University and was a visiting student at Oxford and Georgetown. For a decade, Dr. von Kunes taught at Harvard where she reinvigorated Czech studies. Currently, she teaches at Yale University and is the director of Yale Summer Session in Prague. Dr. von Kunes has received many academic awards including recognition in The Princeton Review of *The Best 300 Professors*, published by Random House in 2012. She is a contributor to *Critical Essays on Milan Kundera* and to *Between Texts, Languages and Cultures*. In addition, she is the author of the Hippocrene *Czech-English/English-Czech Practical Dictionary* and of *Beyond the Imaginable: 240 Ways of Looking at Czech*, as well as the coauthor of *Barron's Travel Wise Czech*. A former freelance journalist, Dr. von Kunes wrote a weekly column on Czech language and culture for *The Prague Post*. As a fiction writer, she has recently published a well-received novel, *Among the Sinners*, and wrote a screenplay, *Leaving Far Behind*, that was highly commended by the late film director Milos Forman. Dr. von Kunes is currently working on a critical manuscript, *Milos Forman's Vision, Mission and Execution*, and on an innovative textbook, *Czech Crystal Clear*.

www.ingramcontent.com/pod-product-compliance
Lightning Source LLC
Chambersburg PA
CBHW022312280326
41932CB00010B/1074